Research Design
in Social Research

Research Design in Social Research

David A. de Vaus

Los Angeles | London | New Delhi
Singapore | Washington DC

First published 2001

Reprinted 2013

SAGE Publications Ltd
1 Oliver's Yard
55 City Road
London EC1Y 1SP

SAGE Publications Inc.
2455 Teller Road
Thousand Oaks, California 91320

SAGE Publications India Pvt Ltd
B 1/I 1 Mohan Cooperative Industrial Area
Mathura Road
New Delhi 110 044

SAGE Publications Asia-Pacific Pte Ltd
3 Church Street
#10-04 Samsung Hub
Singapore 049483

British Library Cataloguing in Publication data

A catalogue record for this book is available
from the British Library

ISBN 978-0-7619-5346-3
ISBN 978-0-7619-5347-0 (pbk)

Library of Congress catalog record available

Typeset by Mayhew Typesetting, Rhayader, Powys
Printed and bound by CPI Group (UK) Ltd, Croydon, CRO 4YY
Printed on paper from sustainable resources

CONTENTS

LIST OF FIGURES

LIST OF TABLES

PREFACE

In 1963 Campbell and Stanley quoted McCall's 1923 statement that 'There are excellent books and courses of instruction dealing with the statistical manipulation of experimental data, but there is little help to be found on the methods of securing adequate and proper data on which to apply statistical procedure.' There are now excellent books on some of the technical aspects of collecting quality data (e.g. sampling, question design, observational techniques). However, it remains true that there is a lack of attention given to 'securing adequate and proper data' in the sense of the *logic* of the type of data that are collected and the capacity to make useful and convincing comparisons between groups. This may be less so in psychology, and to some extent in educational research, but in the other social sciences it remains true that students are typically poorly prepared to think about this most basic of research issues. Computers and sophisticated statistical analysis programs have helped in some of the analysis questions, but analysis without first designing the structure of the data collection will be flawed and limited. These flaws are all too often evident in a considerable amount of postgraduate research and in the work of too many established researchers.

Many texts and overview courses teach different data collection strategies such as interviews, questionnaires and observation. This book is designed around the belief that these are subsidiary issues and that the focus on data collection strategy and methods of statistical analysis neglects the core issues, namely the structure and design of the research. The focus on data collection techniques leads to the neglect of appropriate comparison groups and pays too little attention to the notion of evaluating alternative explanations of a phenomenon.

The need to attend to issues of research design – the structure of the research – applies equally to 'qualitative' researchers as to 'quantitative' researchers. It applies regardless of the particular methods that are used to collect data.

The book is designed to show social science students the importance of attending to design issues when undertaking social research. One of the fundamental flaws of a great deal of social science research is that its design and structure are inappropriate for the uses to which it is being put and often do not support the conclusions that are frequently drawn from it.

Technology has assisted greatly in the conduct of social research. But some of the basic thinking about the *logic of research* is still missing in research, and no amount of technology will replace the need for a clear-sighted understanding of the principles of research design.

The aims of the book are:

1 to provide social science students with a clear understanding of the importance of research design and its place in the research process
2 to describe the main types of research designs in social research
3 to discuss these designs in terms of their logic so that students and researchers will be able to evaluate particular design strategies and to select strategies appropriate to the problem at hand
4 to provide students and researchers with the principles of design such that they will be able to adapt designs effectively to meet the contingencies of real world research situations
5 to provide students and researchers with the tools by which they can evaluate the strengths and weaknesses of various design strategies
6 to highlight the main techniques for analysing data collected using the various design strategies and to provide an understanding of how to select the most appropriate method of analysis.

The book is divided into five parts. Part I considers types of research, research concepts, research questions, causality and some of the concepts that are basic to understanding research design. Each of the other four parts focuses on a broad type of research design: experimental, longitudinal, cross-sectional and case study. Within each part the book:

• describes the basic design and its variants and provides examples of studies using these designs
• identifies the strengths and weaknesses of the design and ways of maximizing the strengths and minimizing the weaknesses, centred around the three core areas of methodological, practical and ethical considerations
• outlines the main ways of analysing the type of data that are collected using the particular design.

In preparing a book such as this there are many people to whom one owes thanks. I want to acknowledge my special appreciation to Chris Rojek, Ken Dempsey, Ian Winter and June de Vaus for their encouragement, advice and time.

PART I

WHAT IS RESEARCH DESIGN?

1

THE CONTEXT OF DESIGN

Before examining types of research designs it is important to be clear about the role and purpose of research design. We need to understand what research design is and what it is not. We need to know where design fits into the whole research process from framing a question to finally analysing and reporting data. This is the purpose of this chapter.

Description and explanation

Social researchers ask two fundamental types of research questions:

1   *What* is going on (descriptive research)?
2   *Why* is it going on (explanatory research)?

Descriptive research

Although some people dismiss descriptive research as 'mere description', good description is fundamental to the research enterprise and it has added immeasurably to our knowledge of the shape and nature of our society. Descriptive research encompasses much government sponsored research including the population census, the collection of a wide range of social indicators and economic information such as household expenditure patterns, time use studies, employment and crime statistics and the like.

Descriptions can be concrete or abstract. A relatively concrete description might describe the ethnic mix of a community, the changing age profile of a population or the gender mix of a workplace. Alternatively the description might ask more abstract questions such as 'Is the level of social inequality increasing or declining?', 'How secular is society?' or 'How much poverty is there in this community?'

Accurate descriptions of the level of unemployment or poverty have historically played a key role in social policy reforms (Marsh, 1982). By demonstrating the existence of social problems, competent description can challenge accepted assumptions about the way things are and can provoke action.

Good description provokes the 'why' questions of explanatory research. If we detect greater social polarization over the last 20 years (i.e. the rich are getting richer and the poor are getting poorer) we are forced to ask 'Why is this happening?' But before asking 'why?' we must be sure about the fact and dimensions of the phenomenon of increasing polarization. It is all very well to develop elaborate theories as to why society might be more polarized now than in the recent past, but if the basic premise is wrong (i.e. society is not becoming more polarized) then attempts to explain a non-existent phenomenon are silly.

Of course description can degenerate to mindless fact gathering or what C.W. Mills (1959) called 'abstracted empiricism'. There are plenty of examples of unfocused surveys and case studies that report trivial information and fail to provoke any 'why' questions or provide any basis for generalization. However, this is a function of inconsequential descriptions rather than an indictment of descriptive research itself.

Explanatory research

Explanatory research focuses on *why* questions. For example, it is one thing to describe the crime rate in a country, to examine trends over time or to compare the rates in different countries. It is quite a different thing to develop explanations about why the crime rate is as high as it is, why some types of crime are increasing or why the rate is higher in some countries than in others.

The way in which researchers develop research designs is fundamentally affected by whether the research question is descriptive or explanatory. It affects what information is collected. For example, if we want to explain why some people are more likely to be apprehended and convicted of crimes we need to have hunches about why this is so. We may have many possibly incompatible hunches and will need to collect information that enables us to see which hunches work best empirically.

Answering the 'why' questions involves developing *causal* explanations. Causal explanations argue that phenomenon Y (e.g. income level) is affected by factor X (e.g. gender). Some causal explanations will be simple while others will be more complex. For example, we might argue that there is a *direct* effect of gender on income (i.e. simple gender discrimination) (Figure 1.1a). We might argue for a causal chain, such as that gender affects choice of field of training which in turn affects

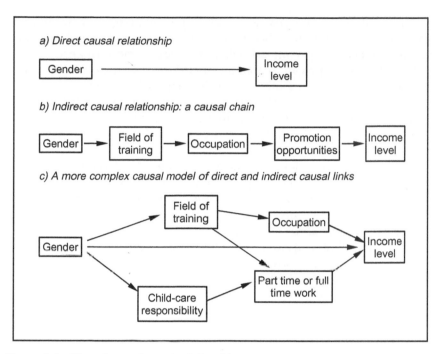

Figure 1.1 *Three types of causal relationships*

occupational options, which are linked to opportunities for promotion, which in turn affect income level (Figure 1.1b). Or we could posit a more complex model involving a number of interrelated causal chains (Figure 1.1c).

PREDICTION, CORRELATION AND CAUSATION

People often confuse correlation with causation. Simply because one event follows another, or two factors co-vary, does not mean that one causes the other. The link between two events may be coincidental rather than causal.

There is a correlation between the number of fire engines at a fire and the amount of damage caused by the fire (the more fire engines the more damage). Is it therefore reasonable to conclude that the number of fire engines causes the amount of damage? Clearly the number of fire engines and the amount of damage will *both* be due to some third factor – such as the seriousness of the fire.

Similarly, as the divorce rate changed over the twentieth century the crime rate increased a few years later. But this does not mean that divorce causes crime. Rather than divorce causing crime, divorce and crime rates might both be due to *other* social processes such as secularization, greater individualism or poverty.

Students at fee paying private schools typically perform better in their final year of schooling than those at government funded schools. But this need not be because private schools *produce* better performance. It may be that attending a private school and better final-year performance are *both* the outcome of some other cause (see later discussion).

Confusing causation with correlation also confuses prediction with causation and prediction with explanation. Where two events or characteristics are correlated we can predict one from the other. Knowing the type of school attended improves our capacity to predict academic achievement. But this does not mean that the school type affects academic achievement. Predicting performance on the basis of school type does not tell us *why* private school students do better. *Good prediction does not depend on causal relationships. Nor does the ability to predict accurately demonstrate anything about causality.*

Recognizing that causation is more than correlation highlights a problem. While we can observe correlation *we cannot observe cause*. We have to *infer* cause. These inferences however are 'necessarily fallible . . . [they] are only indirectly linked to observables' (Cook and Campbell, 1979: 10). Because our inferences are fallible we must minimize the chances of incorrectly saying that a relationship is causal when in fact it is not. *One of the fundamental purposes of research design in explanatory research is to avoid invalid inferences.*

DETERMINISTIC AND PROBABILISTIC CONCEPTS OF CAUSATION

There are two ways of thinking about causes: deterministically and probabilistically. The smoker who denies that tobacco causes cancer because he smokes heavily but has not contracted cancer illustrates deterministic causation. Probabilistic causation is illustrated by health authorities who point to the increased chances of cancer among smokers.

Deterministic causation is where variable X is said to cause Y if, and only if, X *invariably* produces Y. That is, when X is present then Y will 'necessarily, inevitably and infallibly' occur (Cook and Campbell, 1979: 14). This approach seeks to establish causal *laws* such as: whenever water is heated to 100 °C it always boils.

In reality laws are never this simple. They will always specify particular *conditions* under which that law operates. Indeed a great deal of scientific investigation involves specifying the conditions under which particular laws operate. Thus, we might say that *at sea level* heating *pure* water to 100 °C will always cause water to boil.

Alternatively, the law might be stated in the form of 'other things being equal' then X will always produce Y. A deterministic version of the relationship between race and income level would say that other things being equal (age, education, personality, experience etc.) then a white person will [always] earn a higher income than a black person. That is, race (X) causes income level (Y).

Stated like this the notion of deterministic causation in the social sciences sounds odd. It is hard to conceive of a characteristic or event that will invariably result in a given outcome even if a fairly tight set of conditions is specified. The *complexity* of human social behaviour and the *subjective, meaningful and voluntaristic* components of human behaviour mean that it will never be possible to arrive at causal statements of the type 'If *X*, and *A* and *B*, then *Y* will always follow.'

Most causal thinking in the social sciences is *probabilistic* rather than *deterministic* (Suppes, 1970). That is, we work at the level that a given factor increases (or decreases) the probability of a particular outcome, for example: being female increases the probability of working part time; race affects the probability of having a high status job.

We can improve probabilistic explanations by specifying conditions under which *X* is less likely and more likely to affect *Y*. But we will never achieve complete or deterministic explanations. Human behaviour is both *willed* and *caused*: there is a double-sided character to human social behaviour. People *construct* their social world and there are creative aspects to human action but this freedom and agency will always be constrained by the structures within which people live. Because behaviour is not simply determined we cannot achieve deterministic explanations. However, because behaviour is constrained we can achieve probabilistic explanations. We can say that a given factor will increase the likelihood of a given outcome but there will never be certainty about outcomes.

Despite the probabilistic nature of causal statements in the social sciences, much popular, ideological and political discourse translates these into deterministic statements. Findings about the causal effects of class, gender or ethnicity, for example, are often read as if these factors invariably and completely produce particular outcomes. One could be forgiven for thinking that social science has demonstrated that gender completely and invariably determines position in society, roles in families, values and ways of relating to other people.

Theory testing and theory construction

Attempts to answer the 'why' questions in social science are theories. These theories vary in their *complexity* (how many variables and links), *abstraction* and *scope*. To understand the role of theory in empirical research it is useful to distinguish between two different styles of research: theory testing and theory building (Figure 1.2).

Theory building

Theory building is a process in which research begins with observations and uses *inductive* reasoning to derive a theory from these observations.

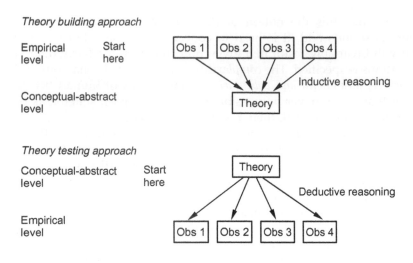

Figure 1.2   *Theory building and theory testing approaches to research*

These theories attempt to make sense of observations. Because the theory is produced *after* observations are made it is often called *post factum* theory (Merton, 1968) or *ex post facto* theorizing.

This form of theory building entails asking whether the observation is *a particular case of a more general factor*, or how the observation *fits into a pattern or a story*. For example, Durkheim observed that the suicide rate was higher among Protestants than Catholics. But is religious affiliation a particular case of something more general? Of what more general phenomenon might it be an indicator? Are there other observations that shed light on this? He also observed that men were more suicidal than women, urban dwellers more than rural dwellers and the socially mobile more than the socially stable. He argued that the common factor behind all these observations was that those groups who were most suicidal were also less well socially integrated and experienced greater ambiguity about how to behave and what is right and wrong. He theorized that one of the explanations for suicidal behaviour was a sense of normlessness – a disconnectedness of individuals from their social world. Of course, there may have been other ways of accounting for these observations but at least Durkheim's explanation was consistent with the facts.

Theory testing

In contrast, a theory testing approach *begins* with a theory and uses theory to guide which observations to make: it moves from the general to the particular. The observations should provide a test of the worth of the theory. Using *deductive* reasoning to derive a set of propositions from the theory does this. We need to develop these propositions so that

	Parents divorced?	
	No	Yes
Low	(a)	(b)
Parental conflict		
High	(c)	(d)

Figure 1.3   *The relationship between divorce and parental conflict*

if the theory is true then certain things should follow in the real world. We then assess whether these predictions are correct. If they are correct the theory is supported. If they do not hold up then the theory needs to be either rejected or modified.

For example, we may wish to test the theory that it is not divorce itself that affects the wellbeing of children but the level of conflict between parents. To test this idea we can make predictions about the wellbeing of children under different family conditions. For the simple theory that it is parental conflict rather than divorce that affects a child's wellbeing there are four basic 'conditions' (see Figure 1.3). For each 'condition' the theory would make different predictions about the level of children's wellbeing that we can examine.

If the theory that it is parental conflict rather than parental divorce is correct the following propositions should be supported:

- *Proposition 1: children in situations (a) and (b) would be equally well off* That is, where parental conflict is low, children with divorced parents will do just as well as those whose parents are married.
- *Proposition 2: children in situations (c) and (d) should be equally poorly off* That is, children in conflictual couple families will do just as badly as children in post-divorce families where parents sustain high conflict.
- *Proposition 3: children in situation (c) will do worse than those in situation (a)* That is, those with married parents in high conflict will do worse than those who have married parents who are not in conflict.
- *Proposition 4: children in situation (d) will do worse than those in situation (b)* That is, those with divorced parents in high conflict will do worse than those who have divorced parents who are not in conflict.
- *Proposition 5: children in situation (b) will do better than those in situation (c)* That is, children with divorced parents who are not in conflict will do better than those with married parents who are in conflict.
- *Proposition 6: children in situation (a) will do better than those in situation (d)* That is, children with married parents who are not in conflict will do better than those with divorced parents who are in conflict.

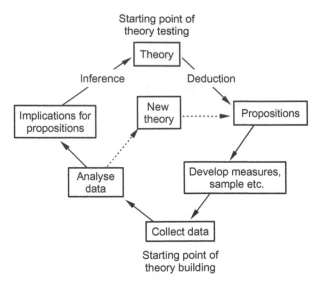

Figure 1.4 *The logic of the research process*

No single proposition would provide a compelling test of the original theory. Indeed, taken on its own proposition 3, for example, would reveal nothing about the impact of divorce. However, taken as a package, the *set* of propositions provides a stronger test of the theory than any single proposition.

Although theory testing and theory building are often presented as alternative modes of research they should be part of one ongoing process (Figure 1.4). Typically, theory building will produce a plausible account or explanation of a set of observations. However, such explanations are frequently just one of a number of possible explanations that fit the data. While plausible they are not necessarily compelling. They require systematic testing where data are collected to specifically evaluate how well the explanation holds when subjected to a range of crucial tests.

What is research design?

How is the term 'research design' to be used in this book? An analogy might help. When constructing a building there is no point ordering materials or setting critical dates for completion of project stages until we know what sort of building is being constructed. The first decision is whether we need a high rise office building, a factory for manufacturing machinery, a school, a residential home or an apartment block. Until this is done we cannot sketch a plan, obtain permits, work out a work schedule or order materials.

Similarly, social research needs a design or a structure before data collection or analysis can commence. A research design is *not* just a work plan. A work plan details what has to be done to complete the project but the work plan will flow from the project's research design. *The function of a research design is to ensure that the evidence obtained enables us to answer the initial question as unambiguously as possible.* Obtaining relevant evidence entails specifying the type of evidence needed to answer the research question, to test a theory, to evaluate a programme or to accurately describe some phenomenon. In other words, when designing research we need to ask: given this research question (or theory), what type of evidence is needed to answer the question (or test the theory) *in a convincing way*?

Research design 'deals with a *logical* problem and not a *logistical* problem' (Yin, 1989: 29). Before a builder or architect can develop a work plan or order materials they must first establish the type of building required, its uses and the needs of the occupants. The work plan flows from this. Similarly, in social research the issues of sampling, method of data collection (e.g. questionnaire, observation, document analysis), design of questions are all subsidiary to the matter of 'What evidence do I need to collect?'

Too often researchers design questionnaires or begin interviewing far too early – before thinking through what information they require to answer their research questions. Without attending to these research design matters at the beginning, the conclusions drawn will normally be weak and unconvincing and fail to answer the research question.

Design versus method

Research design is different from the method by which data are collected. Many research methods texts confuse research designs with methods. It is not uncommon to see research design treated as a mode of data collection rather than as a logical structure of the inquiry. But there is nothing intrinsic about any research design that requires a particular method of data collection. Although cross-sectional surveys are frequently equated with questionnaires and case studies are often equated with participant observation (e.g. Whyte's *Street Corner Society*, 1943), data for any design can be collected with any data collection method (Figure 1.5). How the data are collected is irrelevant to the *logic* of the design.

Failing to distinguish between design and method leads to poor evaluation of designs. Equating cross-sectional designs with questionnaires, or case studies with participant observation, means that the designs are often evaluated against the strengths and weaknesses of the method rather than their ability to draw relatively unambiguous conclusions or to select between rival plausible hypotheses.

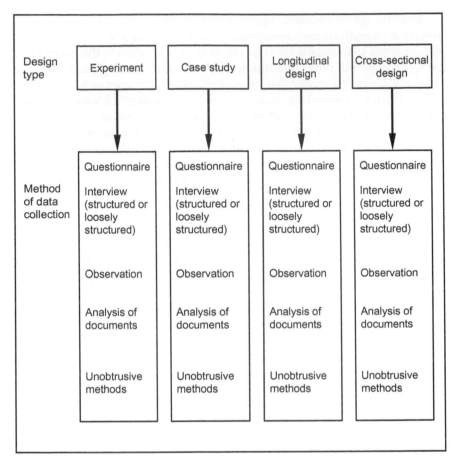

Figure 1.5   *Relationship between research design and particular data collection methods*

QUANTITATIVE AND QUALITATIVE RESEARCH

Similarly, designs are often equated with qualitative and quantitative research methods. Social surveys and experiments are frequently viewed as prime examples of quantitative research and are evaluated against the strengths and weaknesses of statistical, quantitative research methods and analysis. Case studies, on the other hand, are often seen as prime examples of qualitative research – which adopts an interpretive approach to data, studies 'things' within their context and considers the subjective meanings that people bring to their situation.

It is erroneous to equate a particular research design with either quantitative or qualitative methods. Yin (1993), a respected authority on case study design, has stressed the irrelevance of the quantitative/qualitative distinction for case studies. He points out that:

a point of confusion . . . has been the unfortunate linking between the case study method and certain types of data collection – for example those focusing on qualitative methods, ethnography, or participant observation. People have thought that the case study method required them to embrace these data collection methods . . . On the contrary, the method does not imply any particular form of data collection – which can be qualitative or quantitative. (1993: 32)

Similarly, Marsh (1982) argues that quantitative surveys can provide information and explanations that are 'adequate at the level of meaning'. While recognizing that survey research has not always been good at tapping the subjective dimension of behaviour, she argues that:

Making sense of social action . . . is . . . hard and surveys have not traditionally been very good at it. The earliest survey researchers started a tradition . . . of bringing the meaning from outside, either by making use of the researcher's stock of plausible explanations . . . or by bringing it from subsidiary in-depth interviews sprinkling quotes . . . liberally on the raw correlations derived from the survey. Survey research became much more exciting . . . when it began including meaningful dimensions in the study design. [This has been done in] two ways, firstly [by] asking the actor either for her reasons directly, or to supply information about the central values in her life around which we may assume she is orienting her life. [This] involves collecting a sufficiently complete picture of the context in which an actor finds herself that a team of outsiders may read off the meaningful dimensions. (1982: 123–4)

Adopting a sceptical approach to explanations

The need for research design stems from a sceptical approach to research and a view that scientific knowledge must always be provisional. The purpose of research design is to reduce the ambiguity of much research evidence.

We can always find some evidence consistent with almost any theory. However, we should be sceptical of the evidence, and rather than seeking evidence that is *consistent* with our theory we should seek evidence that provides a *compelling* test of the theory.

There are two related strategies for doing this: eliminating rival explanations of the evidence and deliberately seeking evidence that could *disprove* the theory.

PLAUSIBLE RIVAL HYPOTHESES

A fundamental strategy of social research involves evaluating 'plausible rival hypotheses'. We need to examine and evaluate alternative ways of explaining a particular phenomenon. This applies regardless of whether the data are quantitative or qualitative; regardless of the particular research design (experimental, cross-sectional, longitudinal or case

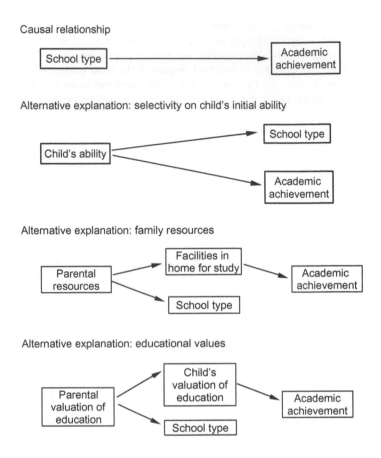

Figure 1.6   *Causal and non-causal explanations of the relationship between school type and academic achievement*

study); and regardless of the method of data collection (e.g. observation, questionnaire). Our mindset needs to anticipate alternative ways of interpreting findings and to regard any interpretation of these findings as provisional – subject to further testing.

The idea of evaluating plausible rival hypotheses can be illustrated using the example of the correlation between type of school attended and academic achievement. Many parents accept the causal proposition that attendance at fee paying private schools improves a child's academic performance (Figure 1.6). Schools themselves promote the same notion by prominently advertising their pass rates and comparing them with those of other schools or with national averages. By implication they propose a causal connection: 'Send your child to our school and they will pass (or get grades to gain entry into prestigious institutions, courses).' The data they provide are consistent with their proposition that these schools produce better results.

But these data are not compelling. There are at least three other ways of accounting for this correlation without accepting the causal link between school type and achievement (Figure 1.6). There is the *selectivity* explanation: the more able students may be sent to fee paying private schools in the first place. There is the *family resources* explanation: parents who can afford to send their children to fee paying private schools can also afford other help (e.g. books, private tutoring, quiet study space, computers). It is this help rather than the type of school that produces the better performance of private school students. Finally, there is the family *values* explanation: parents who value education most are prepared to send their children to fee paying private schools and it is this family emphasis on education, not the schools themselves, that produces the better academic performance. All these explanations are equally consistent with the observation that private school students do better than government school students. Without collecting further evidence we cannot choose between these explanations and therefore must remain open minded about which one makes most empirical sense.

There might also be methodological explanations for the finding that private school students perform better academically. These methodological issues might undermine any argument that a causal connection exists. Are the results due to questionable ways of measuring achievement? From what range and number of schools were the data obtained? On how many cases are the conclusions based? Could the pattern simply be a function of chance? These are all possible alternative explanations for the finding that private school students perform better.

Good research design will anticipate competing explanations *before* collecting data so that relevant information for evaluating the relative merits of these competing explanations is obtained. In this example of schools and academic achievement, thinking about alternative plausible hypotheses beforehand would lead us to find out about the parents' financial resources, the study resources available in the home, the parents' and child's attitudes about education and the child's academic abilities before entering the school.

The fallacy of affirming the consequent Although evidence may be consistent with an initial proposition it might be equally consistent with a range of alternative propositions. Too often people do not even think of the alternative hypotheses and simply conclude that since the evidence is consistent with their theory then the theory is true. This form of reasoning commits the logical *fallacy of affirming the consequent*. This form of reasoning has the following logical structure:

- If A is true then B should follow.
- We observe B.
- Therefore A is true.

If we apply this logic to the type of school and achievement proposition, the logical structure of the school type and achievement argument becomes clearer.

Initial proposition:

• Private schools produce better students than do government schools.

The test:

• *If A then B*   If private schools produce better students (A) then their students should get better final marks than those from government funded schools (B).
• *B is true*   Private school students do achieve better final marks than government school students (observe B).
• *Therefore A is true*   Therefore private schools do produce better students (A is true).

But as I have already argued, the better performance of private school students might also reflect the effect of other factors. The problem here is that any number of explanations may be correct and the evidence does not help rule out many of these. For the social scientist this level of indeterminacy is quite unsatisfactory. In effect we are only in a position to say:

• If A [or C, or D, or E, or F, or . . .] then B.
• We observe B.
• Therefore A [or C, or D, or E, or F, or . . .] is true.

Although explanation (A) is still in the running because it is consistent with the observations, we cannot say that it is the most plausible explanation. We need to test our proposition more thoroughly by evaluating the worth of the alternative propositions.

FALSIFICATION: LOOKING FOR EVIDENCE TO DISPROVE THE THEORY

As well as evaluating and eliminating alternative explanations we should rigorously evaluate our own theories. Rather than asking 'What evidence would constitute support for the theory?', ask 'What evidence would convince me that the theory is *wrong*?' It is not difficult to find evidence consistent with a theory. It is much tougher for a theory to survive the test of people trying to disprove it.

Unfortunately some theories are closed systems in which any evidence can be interpreted as support for the theory. Such theories are said to be non-falsifiable. Many religions or belief systems can become closed systems whereby all evidence can be accommodated by the theory and nothing will change the mind of the true believer. Exchange theory (Homans, 1961; Blau, 1964) is largely non-falsifiable. It assumes that we always maximize our gains and avoid costs. But we can see almost anything as a gain. Great sacrifices to care for a disabled relative can be interpreted as a gain (satisfaction of helping) rather than a loss (income, time for self etc.). We need to frame our propositions and define our terms in such a way that they are capable of being disproven.

THE PROVISIONAL NATURE OF SUPPORT FOR THEORIES

Even where the theory is corroborated and has survived attempts to disprove it, the theory remains provisional:

> falsificationism stresses the ambiguity of confirmation . . . corroboration gives only the comfort that the theory has been tested and survived the test, that even after the most impressive corroborations of predictions it has only achieved the status of 'not yet disconfirmed'. This . . . is far from the status of 'being true'. (Cook and Campbell, 1979: 20)

There always may be an unthought-of explanation. We cannot anticipate or evaluate every possible explanation. The more alternative explanations that have been eliminated and the more we have tried to disprove our theory, the more confidence we will have in it, but we should avoid thinking that it is *proven*.

However we can *disprove* a theory. The logic of this is:

- If theory A is true then B should follow.
- B does *not* follow.
- Therefore A is not true.

So long as B is a valid test of A the absence of B should make us reject or revise the theory. In reality, we would not reject a theory simply because a single fact or observation does not fit. Before rejecting a plausible theory we would require multiple disconfirmations using different measures, different samples and different methods of data collection and analysis.

In summary, we should adopt a sceptical approach to explanations. We should anticipate rival interpretations and collect data to enable the winnowing out of the weaker explanations and the identification of which alternative theories make most empirical sense. We also need to ask what data would challenge the explanation and collect data to evaluate the theory from this more demanding perspective.

Summary

This chapter has outlined the purpose of research design in both descriptive and explanatory research. In explanatory research the purpose is to develop and evaluate causal theories. The probabilistic nature of causation in social sciences, as opposed to deterministic causation, was discussed.

Research design is not related to any particular method of collecting data or any particular type of data. Any research design can, in principle, use any type of data collection method and can use either quantitative or qualitative data. Research design refers to the *structure* of an enquiry: it is a logical matter rather than a logistical one.

It has been argued that the central role of research design is to minimize the chance of drawing incorrect causal inferences from data. Design is a logical task undertaken to ensure that the evidence collected enables us to answer questions or to test theories as unambiguously as possible. When designing research it is essential that we identify the type of evidence required to answer the research question in a convincing way. This means that we must not simply collect evidence that is consistent with a particular theory or explanation. Research needs to be structured in such a way that the evidence also bears on alternative rival explanations and enables us to identify which of the competing explanations is most compelling empirically. It also means that we must not simply look for evidence that supports our favourite theory: we should also look for evidence that has the potential to disprove our preferred explanations.

2

TOOLS FOR RESEARCH DESIGN

To achieve a reasonable research design we need to attend to a number of matters before we arrive at the final design. The first section of this chapter outlines these preliminary steps that precede design. It then expands on the idea of alternative rival hypotheses that was introduced in Chapter 1. The second section introduces a number of concepts that are fundamental to designing good research – internal validity, external validity and measurement error.

Before design

In the same way that an architect needs to know the purpose of the building before designing it (is it an office building, a factory or a home?) social researchers must be clear about their research question before developing a research design.

Focusing and clarifying the research question

The first question to ask is, 'What question am I trying to answer?' Specifying a question is more than identifying a topic. It's not enough to say, 'I'm interested in getting some answers about family breakdown.' What answers to what questions? Do you want to know the extent of family breakdown? Who is most vulnerable to family breakdown? Changing rates of breakdown? Over what period? Where? Or are you really looking at the causes of breakdown? The effects of family breakdown? All the effects or just particular ones?

FOCUSING DESCRIPTIVE RESEARCH QUESTIONS

To narrow the focus of descriptive research we need to specify the scope of what is to be described. The following guidelines, using family breakdown as an example, help narrow down a descriptive research topic into a researchable question.

1 What is the *scope of the core concepts*? What is to be included in the concept *family breakdown*? Do we mean divorce? What about

separation? Are we referring only to the breakdown in marital relationships? Do we mean the *total* breakdown or simply poor relationships? What about relationships between parents and children or between children? Until we specify what we mean by our core concepts it is going to be impossible to begin the description.

2   What is the *time frame* for the description? Is our interest in change over time or just about *contemporary* levels of family breakdown? If it is about change, over what period?

3   What is the *geographical* location for the description? Is the interest in family breakdown in a particular community, in different regions or the whole nation? Is it comparative, looking at breakdown in different types of countries (e.g. highly industrialized versus rapidly industrializing versus impoverished countries)?

4   How *general* is the description to be? Do you want to be able to describe patterns for specific subgroups (e.g. among those who married as teenagers, among those who are in *de facto* relationships, second marriages etc.)?

5   What *aspect* of the topic are you interested in? Is the interest in rates of breakdown? The experience? Laws? Attitudes and beliefs?

6   How *abstract* is your interest? Is your interest in family breakdown or in family breakdown as a reflection of something more abstract (e.g. social fragmentation, social conflict, individualism, the role of the state in the private lives of citizens)?

7   What is the *unit of analysis*? The unit of analysis is the 'thing' about which we collect information and from which we draw conclusions. Often this is a person (e.g divorced person) but it may be 'things' such as organizations (divorce courts), a family as a whole, events (e.g. divorces), periods (divorce in different years), places (communities, countries).

The questions we can answer will depend on the unit of analysis. We could compare divorced individuals with non-divorced individuals (individual as the unit of analysis). We could study a series of divorces and examine what the process of becoming divorced was (event as unit of analysis). We might use year as the unit of analysis and track changes in divorce rates since 1945. Using countries we might examine the different divorce rates in different types of countries with a view to comparing the patterns in different types of countries. Alternatively families might be the units of analysis and we may want to look at the characteristics of divorcing families (e.g. size, family income, family type, nature of relationships in family) compared with those of non-divorcing families.

Thinking beyond individuals as units of analysis broadens the range of research questions we ask and broadens the range and sources of data available. For example, if years were the unit of analysis we would obtain statistics from the relevant national collection agencies regarding divorce for each year. We would also collect other information about each year (e.g. unemployment level, inflation rate, changes to laws) that was relevant to the hypotheses.

FOCUSING EXPLANATORY RESEARCH QUESTIONS

In framing explanatory questions we need to further specify our focus. Explanatory research explores causes and/or consequences of a phenomenon, so the research question must be clear about the style of explanatory research and identify which causes or consequences it will investigate.

Before outlining some different types of explanatory research it is useful to introduce some terms.

- *Dependent variable* This is the variable that is treated as the *effect* in the causal model: it is dependent on the influence of some other factor. The dependent variable is also referred to as the outcome variable and in causal diagrams it is conventionally designated as the Y variable.
- *Independent variable* This is the variable that is the presumed *cause*. It is also called the predictor variable, the experimental variable or the explanatory variable and is designated in causal diagrams as the X variable (as in education $(X) \rightarrow$ income level (Y)).
- *Intervening variables* These variables come between the independent variable and the dependent variable in a causal chain. They are the *means* by which cause X produces effect Y. Intervening variables are represented in causal diagrams by the symbol Z, as illustrated in Figure 2.1.
- *Extraneous variables* Two variables can be correlated without being causally related. The correlation may be due to the two factors being outcomes of a third variable (see Chapter 1). This third variable is called an extraneous variable and is also symbolized as Z in causal diagrams, and the form of this relationship is illustrated in Figure 2.2.

Searching for causes or effects This is the least focused type of explanatory research. It involves identifying the core phenomenon (e.g. changes in divorce rate since World War II) and then searching for causes or consequences of this. Searching for causes would involve identifying possible causal factors (e.g. changing values, decline in religion, changing population mix, economic changes, legal reforms, changes in welfare support for lone parents). We would then design research to evaluate which of these causes helps explain changes in divorce rates. This form of research question is illustrated in Figure 2.3.

Alternatively we might focus on the consequences rather than causes of changes in divorce rate (Figure 2.4).

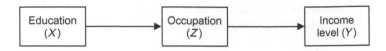

Figure 2.1   *An intervening variable*

Figure 2.2   *An extraneous variable*

Figure 2.3   *Searching for causes*

Figure 2.4   *Searching for effects*

Exploring a simple causal proposition   A more focused research question will specify a *particular* causal proposition to evaluate (Figure 2.5). It might propose an impact of a particular factor or examine a specific consequence. For example, we might propose that changes in government benefits to lone parents have led to an increase in divorce rates since World War II.

More complex causal models   Such propositions are simplistic in that they do not spell out the mechanisms by which the two factors might be related. We might develop more complex models that spell out some of the mechanisms in the causal chain. This fuller model then becomes the focus of the research and provides the framework within which the research design will be framed (Figure 2.6).

When clarifying a research question it is helpful to draw diagrams like those in Figures 2.1–2.5. It is also helpful to ask four key questions:

1   What am I trying to explain (i.e. what is the dependent variable)?
2   What are the possible causes (what are the independent variables)?
3   Which causes will I explore?

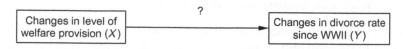

Figure 2.5   *A specific causal proposition*

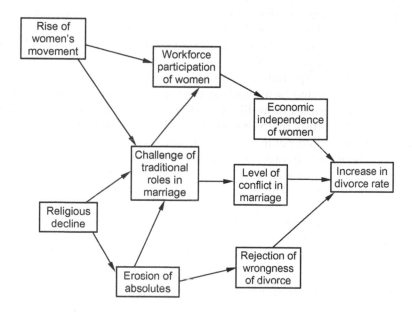

Figure 2.6   *A more complex causal model for increases in divorce*

4   What possible mechanisms connect the presumed causes to the presumed effects (what are the intervening variables)?

Another way of framing research questions is to formulate different ways of understanding a phenomenon and then compare which of these competing approaches best fits the facts. For example, we might compare three different ways of understanding changes in divorce rates: an economic approach, a social values approach and a legislative approach. The economic approach might argue that changes in divorce rates stem from economic factors such as the level of affluence, access of women to work and levels of welfare support for lone parents. The social values explanation might seek to explain the increased divorce rate in terms of increasing levels of individualism and greater social acceptance of divorce. A legislative approach might focus on the impact of legislative changes such as no-fault divorce or new rules regarding property division.

The above examples focus on particular causes and consequences and attempt to provide only a *partial* explanation of changes in divorce rates. These explanations are called *nomothetic* explanations – partial explanations of a class of cases rather than a 'full' explanation of a particular case. They involve an examination of relatively few causal factors and a larger number of cases. In contrast, *idiographic* explanations focus on particular cases and develop as complete an explanation of each case as possible. They involve examining as many factors as possible that contribute to the case including unique factors.

A nomothetic explanation of divorce might focus on the importance of a single contributing factor such as the intergenerational transmission of divorce. Are couples more likely to divorce if one of their parents have divorced? The study might involve comparing people who had divorced with those who had not to see if the divorcees were more likely to have a family history of divorce. In contrast, an idiographic approach might focus on a particular divorced couple and build a full explanation of why *this* couple divorced. The explanation would consider the family history of the couple and examine this along with many other contributing factors. The idiographic explanation would provide us with a good understanding of the *case* while the nomothetic explanation would provide an understanding of the influence of a *factor*.

Identifying plausible rival hypotheses

In Chapter 1 I stressed the importance of identifying plausible rival ways of accounting for the phenomenon being studied. Obviously it makes sense to anticipate these alternatives before carrying out the research. But how do we identify these alternative explanations? There are two main types of rival hypotheses and these suggest ways of anticipating alternative explanations.

There is no magical way of producing a set of alternative substantive or theoretical explanations. In the end the researcher must formulate them. The more familiar the researcher is with the particular substantive topic and with social science models and theories, the more likely they are to anticipate different ways of interpreting a given set of results. The following provide sources of alternative explanations.

The theoretical literature   Broad approaches in a discipline can present different ways of viewing any question. Suppose, for example, that we wanted to understand why some people seem to have happier marriages than other people do. An explanation could concentrate on the *personal attributes* of the couple – their personality, their values and beliefs and their interpersonal skills. It could focus on *economic* factors and interpret marital happiness in terms of the costs and benefits to each partner. Alternatively, the explanation could adopt a *life course perspective* that interprets differences in marital happiness according to where the couple is in the life course (e.g. newly married, before children, young children, adolescent children, empty nest, later life). A feminist approach might try to explain marital happiness in terms of gender roles, division of labour and power within the relationship. A demographer might focus on the birth cohorts (e.g. depression marriages, postwar marriages, 1990s marriages etc.). Other researchers might seek to explain marital happiness in structural terms such as the couple's level of social disadvantage. Social network theorists might concentrate on the extent to which a couple is integrated into the wider family and community and is able to receive support from these networks.

This list is not exhaustive. The point is that different approaches (e.g. psychological, life course, exchange, structural, feminist) will have a particular 'angle' which alerts us to different ways of looking at an issue. When thinking about a problem, ask yourself questions such as 'How might a feminist account for this?', 'How might a Freudian psychologist explain this?', 'How would an exchange theorist account for this?', 'What might a conflict theorist say?'

Other researchers   Previous research on the topic can be a rich source of competing explanations. Read the literature in journals and search electronic databases. Review articles and introductory overviews can be extremely helpful.

Practitioners, key informants, policy makers, advocates   'Insiders' with practical knowledge of a field can be invaluable. In a study on divorce, marriage counsellors, married couples, divorced people and advocacy groups can provide valuable insights. Literature such as novels and plays can also provide keen ideas that can be tested systematically (e.g. Tolstoy's novel *Anna Karenina* provides one way of interpreting marital unhappiness).

Own experience, hunches, and intuitions   Do not ignore your own experience, your own intuitions and hunches. In the end all explanations start with hunches that spring from individuals who have ideas and observe things around them. Use these insights, experiences and observations and test them systematically.

There is no right way of developing ideas. Do not limit yourself to formal social science research or to research on the very specific topic you are working on. Use diverse sources of ideas. Brainstorm with a group and debate the topic. Think laterally: if your topic is marriage breakdown, look beyond the marriage and divorce literature.

TECHNICAL/METHODOLOGICAL RIVALS

If findings are likely to be due to poor measurement (see below) then any theoretical interpretation of these results will be unconvincing. Throughout this book I will identify many technical and methodological factors that can undermine the conclusions we draw from our research. Good research design will minimize the threat from these sources.

I will not at this point go into these methodological issues in detail. However, it will be helpful to highlight the types of methodological rivals that will be examined. These are outlined in Goldenberg (1992).

1 *Demand characteristics of the situation.*
2 *Transient personal characteristics* such as the respondent's mood, attention span, health etc.
3 *Situational factors* such as anonymity, people present when data were being collected, gender, age and class of investigator and respondent.
4 *Sampling of items* Are the concepts well measured?
5 *Nature of the sample* Can we generalize from the sample?
6 *Lack of clarity of the instrument* Are the questions clear and unambiguous?
7 *Format of data collection* Are the results an artifact of the data collection method? Would different patterns be found if a different method was used (e.g. observation rather than questionnaire)?
8 *Variation in the administration of the instrument* in studies tracking change over time.
9 *Processing/analysis errors.*

Operationalization

Most social science research involves making observations that we presume tap concepts. If we were conducting a study on the effect of marital breakdown on the wellbeing of children we would need first to work out what is meant by marriage breakdown, wellbeing and children. This involves defining these concepts, which in turn requires developing a *nominal definition* and an *operational definition* of each concept.

Concepts are, by their nature, not directly observable. We cannot see social class, marital happiness, intelligence etc. To use concepts in research we need to translate concepts into something observable – something we can measure. This involves defining and clarifying abstract concepts and developing indicators of them. This process of clarifying abstract concepts and translating them into specific, observable measures is called operationalization and involves *descending the ladder of abstraction.*

Clarifying concepts

Before developing indicators of concepts we must first clarify the concepts. This involves developing both nominal and operational definitions of the concept.

Nominal definitions Concepts do not have a fixed or correct meaning. Marriage breakdown could be defined in terms of the law (such as whether the decree nisi has been granted), the quality of the relationship or practical arrangements (living apart). Similarly, we need to define children. Is a child defined by a blood relationship, a legal relationship (includes adopted), a social relationship (*de facto* parents), chronological age, level of dependency or some other criterion? By deciding on the type of definition we provide a *nominal definition*: it specifies the meaning of the concept but remains abstract.

Different definitions produce different findings. Consequently, defining concepts is a crucial stage of research. It needs to be done deliberately and to be systematically and carefully justified. There are three steps in developing and narrowing down a nominal definition.

First, *obtain a range of definitions*. Look at review articles, discipline dictionaries (e.g. a dictionary of sociology), encyclopaedias (e.g. an encyclopaedia of social sciences) and journal articles. Look for both explicit and implicit definitions.

Second, *decide on a definition*. From your list either select one definition or create a better definition from the common elements of several definitions. Explain and justify your approach.

Third, *delineate the dimensions of the concept*. Many concepts have a number of dimensions and it is helpful to spell these out as they can help to further refine your definition. This can be illustrated using the concept of the *child's wellbeing*. We can think of a number of dimensions of wellbeing: emotional, psychological, physical, educational, financial, social, environmental, legal etc. If we are arguing that marriage breakdown affects a child's wellbeing, what sort of wellbeing are we talking about? All of these? Just one or two? Having delineated various dimensions you will need to decide which are of interest in the present study. You may examine all aspects or limit yourself to one or two.

A concept may have *subdimensions*. Suppose we focused on *social* wellbeing. This broad concept could incorporate subdimensions such as the level of safety in the neighbourhood, the nature of the child's relationships and her experiences of social discrimination. The subdimension of 'relationships with others' could be further divided into relationships with particular people such as mother, father, peers, siblings and grandparents. Having settled on the particular relationships with which we are going to deal, we would need to identify what *aspects* of the relationships to measure and decide how to measure them (see below). In Figure 2.7 relationships are measured according to the level of

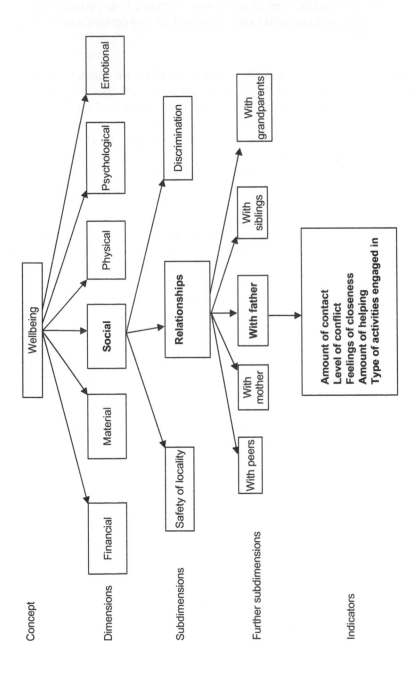

Figure 2.7 *Dimensionalizing the concept of child's wellbeing*

contact, conflict, closeness, helping and type of shared activities. These measures or indicators would then provide the core around which to frame specific questions or to focus an observational study.

In this example I have focused on one dimension at each level but I could have been exhaustive and developed measures for each conceivable dimension and subdimension. The decision of whether to adopt a focused or an exhaustive approach will depend on what you are interested in. The advantage of adopting a systematic approach as outlined in Figure 2.7 is that it helps focus and refine the research question and forces you to make deliberate decisions about how to measure a concept.

Operational definitions Having defined the concepts you will develop an *operational definition* – the observations to measure the concept. What *indicators* of marriage breakdown will you use? We might operationally define marriage breakdown according to the quality of the relationship. Using this definition we might measure breakdown according to level of conflict, type of communication, signs of lack of affection and level of cooperation or lack of cooperation.

How well such indicators tap the concept as defined will have a critical bearing on the value of the conclusions drawn from the study. If the indicators tap something other than what we claim they do then our conclusions can be easily challenged. For example, if our measures of marital breakdown simply tap social class differences in marital style rather than breakdown then our conclusions about marital breakdown will be suspect.

Once the operational definition of the concept has been developed we come to the final stage of operationalization. This entails the precise way in which the indicators will be measured. This might involve developing questions for a questionnaire or identifying what and how observations will be made. Articulating the mechanics of these strategies is beyond the scope of this book.

Concepts for research design

Two concepts, internal and external validity, are fundamental to developing research designs. Ideally research designs should be both internally and externally valid.

Internal validity

We need to be confident that the research design can sustain the causal conclusions that we claim for it. The capacity of a research design to do this reflects its internal validity.

Imagine a research project that compares the emotional adjustment of children from divorced families and intact families. It finds that children from divorced families are less well adjusted than children from intact families. Can we conclude that divorce caused emotional maladjustment? Not on the basis of these results. The design does not enable us to eliminate alternative explanations. The poorer adjustment of children with divorced parents might be due to adjustment differences that predated parental divorce.

A different research study may deal with this problem by tracking children before parents divorce and for some years afterwards. It may find that these children do show a significant decline in emotional adjustment after their parents' divorce. Does the research design show that divorce is producing this decline in adjustment? No. The decline in adjustment may simply reflect a general decline in emotional adjustment as children get older. The same decline may be evident among children from intact families.

Yet another study might try to overcome this problem by tracking changes in adjustment of children before and after their parents divorce and changes among children from intact families as well. If children from intact families show less deterioration in adjustment than children from divorcing families, this must surely demonstrate the effect of divorce. No. We would need to be sure that the two groups of children were comparable in other relevant respects (e.g. age). The different rates of change in adjustment could be because those from divorcing families were younger on average. Maybe younger children show greater changes in adjustment over a particular period than older children. It may be age differences rather than having divorced parents that account for the adjustment changes of the two groups of children.

Internal validity is the extent to which the structure of a research design enables us to draw unambiguous conclusions from our results. The way in which the study is set up (e.g. tracking changes over time, making comparisons between comparable groups) can eliminate alternative explanations for our findings. The more the structure of a study eliminates these alternative interpretations, the stronger the internal validity of the study. A central task of research design is to structure the study so that the ambiguities in the above examples are minimized. It is impossible to eliminate all ambiguities in social research but we can certainly reduce them.

External validity

External validity refers to the extent to which results from a study can be generalized beyond the particular study. A study may have good internal validity but its value is limited if the findings only apply to the people in that particular investigation. The critical question is whether the results are likely to apply more widely. The most common threat to our capacity to generalize more widely from a research study is the use of unrepresentative samples. This, and other threats to external validity, will be discussed more fully in Chapters 5, 8, 11 and 14.

Measurement error

A further threat to the conclusions that can be drawn from any study is measurement error. This occurs when we use flawed indicators to tap concepts (see Chapter 1).

TYPES OF MEASUREMENT ERROR

Indicators must meet two fundamental criteria. They must be both valid and reliable. A valid indicator in this context means that the indicator measures the concept we say it does. For example an IQ test is used to measure intelligence. If it really measures intelligence the test would be valid. If the IQ test measured something else instead, such as education level or cultural background, then it would be an invalid measure of intelligence.

Reliability means that the indicator *consistently* comes up with the same measurement. For example, if people consistently obtain the same IQ score on repeated IQ tests, then the test would be reliable. If their results fluctuate wildly depending on when they take the test, then it would be unreliable.

Validity   The earlier discussion of internal validity related to the validity of the *research design*. It addressed the question: is the research design delivering the conclusions that we claim it delivers? In addition we need to examine the validity of the *measures* used in any piece of research.

The validity of a measure depends both on the use to which it is put and on the sample for which it is used. For example, the validity of using frequency of arguments between partners to measure marital happiness turns on what we mean by marital happiness. The validity of this measure may vary for different cultural groups and for the same cultural group in different historical periods. Measures of children's emotional adjustment will vary according to their age and their cultural group.

There are three basic ways of assessing validity. *Criterion validity* is best suited to situations where there are well-established measures of a concept that need adapting, shortening or updating. It involves comparing the way people rate on the new measure with how they rate on well-established measures of the concept. If ratings on the new measure match those of an established measure we can be confident of its validity.

Criterion validity has two limitations. First, it requires that the established benchmark is valid. If the benchmark is invalid then it is of little value in assessing the new measure. Second, there are no established measures for many social science concepts.

Sometimes criterion groups can be used to assess criterion validity. Instead of comparing a measure against an existing benchmark measure, the new measure can be trialled. For example, a new measure of marital happiness could be trialled on couples who seek marital counselling. We would expect that this group of couples would normally obtain low scores on a valid measure of marital happiness. If these couples actually obtain high scores on the marital happiness measure we would probably want to question whether the measure was really tapping marital happiness.

Content validity evaluates how well the measures tap the different aspects of the concept as we have defined it. A test of arithmetic skills that only tested subtraction skills would clearly not be a valid measure of arithmetic skills. Similarly a measure of marital happiness that only asked about the frequency of arguments between partners would probably lack content validity unless we had defined marital happiness simply as the absence of arguments. Measures of marital happiness could also include the nature of the arguments, leisure activities shared by partners, communication, methods of resolving conflict, the quality of the sexual relationship etc.

Given disagreement about the 'content' of many social science concepts it can be difficult to develop measures that have agreed validity. Even if we can agree on the concept and measure it using a whole battery of questions, we then face the problem of the *relative importance* of the various components of the measure. For example, should measures of the frequency of arguments be as important as the nature of the arguments, the method of conflict resolution, the style of communication or statements about level of subjective marital satisfaction?

Construct validity relies on seeing how well the results we obtain when using the measure fit with theoretical expectations. To validate a measure of marital happiness we might anticipate, on the basis of theory, that happiness will vary in predictable ways according to stage in the life cycle. If the results of a study provide confirmation, this could reflect the validity of our measure of marital happiness. However, this approach to assessing validity relies on the correctness of our expectations. If our theory is not supported this could be for one of two reasons: the measure of marital happiness could be wrong or the theory against which the measure is being benchmarked may be wrong.

There is no ideal way of assessing validity. If a measure passes all three tests it is more likely to be valid but we cannot be certain. In the final analysis we will need to *argue* for the validity of our measures.

Reliability   A reliable measure is one that gives the same 'reading' when used on repeated occasions. For example, *assuming there was no actual change*, a reliable measure of marital happiness should yield the same 'reading' if it is used on different occasions. A thermometer that measured body temperature as 97.4 °F one minute and 105 °F the next would be useless. Which measurement is right? Does the change reflect real change or just measurement 'noise'?

Unreliability can stem from many sources. Poor question wording may cause a respondent to understand the question differently on different occasions. Different interviewers can elicit different answers from a person: the match of age, gender, class and ethnicity of an interviewer and interviewee can influence responses. Asking questions about which people have no opinion, have insufficient information or require too precise an answer can lead to unreliable data. The answers to some questions can be affected by mood and by the particular context in which they are asked.

Measures need to be both valid and reliable. Although these two concepts are related they are not the same. A measure can be reliable without being valid. That is, a measure can be consistently wrong. For example, people consistently underestimate their level of alcohol consumption in questionnaire surveys. Alcohol consumption measures are reliable but do not accurately tell us about the true level of alcohol consumed.

Measures will never be perfectly reliable and perfectly valid. These are not all or nothing concepts and the goal is to maximize the reliability and validity. If these aspects of measurement are weak then the results of the study that uses them might plausibly be attributed to poor measurement rather than telling us anything about social reality.

FORMS OF MEASUREMENT ERROR

Error can take different forms and the consequences of error will vary depending on its form. These forms of error are *random, constant* and *correlated*.

Random error is that which has no systematic form. It means that in some cases a measurement for a variable might be too low while in others it is too high. The measurement of someone's weight might display random error. Sometimes people underestimate their weight while others may overestimate it, but if these errors are random there will be the same number of over- and underestimates and the size of the overestimates will be the same on average as the underestimates. When the average (mean) is calculated for the whole group it will be accurate because the overestimates and the underestimates cancel each other out. Furthermore, these mis-estimates are not correlated with any other characteristic (e.g. gender, age) but are truly random. Because random error does not distort means and is uncorrelated with other factors, it is less serious than other forms of error.

Constant error occurs where there is the same error for every case. For example, if everyone underreported their weight by 5 kilograms we would have constant error. Such error is uncorrelated with other characteristics. Although purely constant error will be rare there will be variables for which there will typically be a component of constant error (e.g. overstatements of frequency of sexual intercourse and understatements about the amount of alcohol consumed). Because such error is constant it does not cancel out but has an effect on sample estimates. Thus the average weight of the sample would be an underestimate to the extent of the constant error.

Correlated error takes place when the amount and direction of error vary systematically according to other characteristics of respondents. For example, if women tend to overestimate their weight while men underestimate theirs then this error would be correlated with gender. If the format or language in a questionnaire is difficult then mistakes in answering questions may well be correlated with education. This would produce results that make it appear that people with different levels of education behave or think differently while in fact it is only their capacity to understand the question that differs.

A crucial goal of the design and administration of survey instruments is the minimization of the various forms of measurement error. Achieving this entails paying careful attention to question wording, indicator quality, interviewer and observer training, and to ways of identifying social desirability responses and other forms of deliberate misrepresentation by respondents. In many cases it is difficult to identify the extent to which such errors actually occur. However, this does not reduce the need to do all that one can to minimize their likelihood and to have built-in checks to identify some sources of error. Such checks include looking for inconsistencies in answers, using multiple questions rather than single questions to tap concepts, identifying social desirability response sets, making inter-interviewer checks and careful fieldwork supervision.

Summary

This chapter has emphasized the importance of clarifying research questions and concepts before developing a research design. Lack of clarity regarding the research question and the central research concepts will severely compromise any research design. Guidelines were provided to help focus both descriptive and explanatory research questions and to clarify the concepts they employ.

It is also unwise to develop a research design unless alternative ways of understanding the matter at the heart of the research question have been identified. Since one of the purposes of research design is to help identify which of a range of alternative explanations work best it is desirable that these alternative explanations be identified before the research design is developed. The design can then be structured in such a way that relevant data are collected to enable us to choose between these alternatives. Guidelines were provided to assist in identifying these alternative explanations.

Finally, three core concepts that are at the heart of good design were discussed. These were the concepts of internal validity, external validity and measurement error. Later chapters will evaluate the various designs using these concepts.

3

CAUSATION AND THE LOGIC OF RESEARCH DESIGN

Establishing causal relationships is at the heart of explanatory research design. However, it is not a simple matter to establish that one event causes another (Blalock, 1964; Hage and Meeker, 1988). The main reason why it is difficult to establish causal relationships is because we cannot actually *observe* one phenomenon producing change in another. Even though one event might always follow another we do not know that this is because one event causes the other. Causal relationships must therefore be inferred rather than observed. *The purpose of research design in explanatory research is to improve the quality of our causal inferences.*

Inferring causal relationships

Criteria for inferring cause

In Chapter 1 I distinguished between probabilistic and deterministic concepts of causation. Probabilistic approaches to causation are those that argue that a given factor increases (or decreases) the probability of a particular outcome. For example we may argue that there is a causal relationship between gender and working part time – that gender affects the probability of working part time.

In order to infer that a probabilistic causal relationship exists between two variables, two basic criteria must be met. First, there must be co-variation of causal and outcome variables (e.g. between gender and being a full time or part time worker); and second, the assertion that one variable affects the other must make sense.

Co-variation

If two factors are causally related they must *at least* be correlated: they must co-vary. If X causes Y then people who differ from one another on X should tend to differ from one another on Y. For example, if we were to argue that working in the private sector rather than the public sector makes people more achievement oriented at work we would, *at the very*

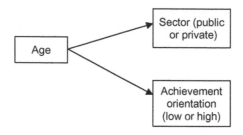

Figure 3.1   *A spurious relationship*

least, need to demonstrate that private sector workers had a higher achievement orientation than public sector workers. If two factors did not co-vary – that is public and private sector workers had identical levels of work achievement – then we would be hard pressed to argue that they are causally related.[1]

However, while co-variation is a precondition it is not enough for us to assert that the variables are causally related. Correlations can also reflect non-causal relationships. When two variables or events are correlated but not causally related the relationship between the two variables is said to be spurious (see Chapter 1). For example, the correlation between sector of employment and employment orientation might be due entirely to a third variable such as age (Figure 3.1). Younger people might be more likely than older people to work in the private sector and younger people might also have a higher achievement orientation than older people. These two patterns will mean that sector and achievement orientation are correlated (more young people in the private sector, so therefore the private sector is associated with achievement orientation). However the link between sector and achievement orientation is coincidental rather than causal.

IT MUST MAKE SENSE

Any assertion that co-variation reflects a causal relationship must be plausible. It must make sense at three levels.

Time order   If two variables are correlated the cause must come *before* the effect. Causal reasoning has no time for the assertion that a future event can have a present effect (teleological explanation). Our causal proposition must be such that the causal variable occurs before the presumed effect. The time gap between cause and effect can be minutes or may be years (e.g. the effect of education on income can take many years to show itself).

Even though two variables might be causally related it can sometimes be difficult to work out which variable comes first and therefore to establish which variable is the cause and which is the effect. For example, does sector of employment affect achievement orientation or is it the other way around? Even where we assert that one variable comes first the causal relationship may be two-way. That is, sector of employment may affect achievement orientation which in turn influences future decisions about the sector of employment in which one works. Causal relationships can be reciprocal (two-way) rather than one-way.

Dependent variable must be capable of change   If we say that a correlation between two variables is because one is causing the other, we must make sure that the dependent variable (the effect) is *capable* of being changed. If it cannot be changed then a causal account of the relationship makes no sense. For example, any causal relationship between sex and income could only be in the direction of sex affecting income. The opposite proposition (income→sex) makes no sense.

Theoretical plausibility   The causal assertion must make sense. We should be able to tell a story of how X affects Y if we wish to infer a causal relationship between X and Y. Even if we cannot empirically demonstrate *how* X affects Y we need to provide a plausible account of the connection (plausible in terms of other research, current theory etc.). For example, to support the assertion that sector of employment affects achievement orientation we might argue that the private sector fosters the development of an achievement orientation by strategies such as paying performance bonuses, developing a culture of higher expectations, providing better resources and creating less job security. When backed up by this type of reasoning, any correlation between employment sector and achievement orientation can be plausibly interpreted in causal terms.

Types of causal patterns

DIRECT AND INDIRECT CAUSAL RELATIONSHIPS

Causal relationships can be either *direct* or *indirect*. A direct relationship is one where we assert that the cause affects the outcome directly rather than via other variables. An indirect causal relationship is one where the cause has its effect by operating via its influence on another variable that, in turn, produces the effect. The variable through which the two variables are related is called the *intervening* variable: it comes in time and in a causal sequence between the initial cause and the effect. For example, we might argue that the way the private sector produces higher achievement orientation is by making employees fear for their jobs (the intervening variable) (Figure 3.2).

Indirect causal relationships may be simple (as in Figure 3.2) or consist of an extended causal chain or a number of different causal paths (Figure 3.3).

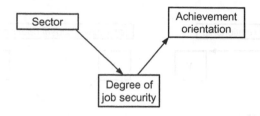

Figure 3.2   *An indirect causal relationship*

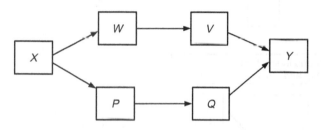

Figure 3.3   *More complex indirect causal relationships*

TYPES OF RELATIONSHIPS IN A THREE-VARIABLE MODEL

Any relationship between two variables will consist of two components – a causal component and a non-causal (spurious) component. The causal component can consist of a direct component, an indirect component or both.

It follows then that any relationship between two variables can be interpreted as:

- a direct causal relationship
- an indirect causal relationship
- a spurious relationship
- any combination of these.

Figure 3.4 illustrates the possibilities where we have three variables which, for the purpose of the example, I will call X, Y and Z. The relationship between X and Y could be any of the following:

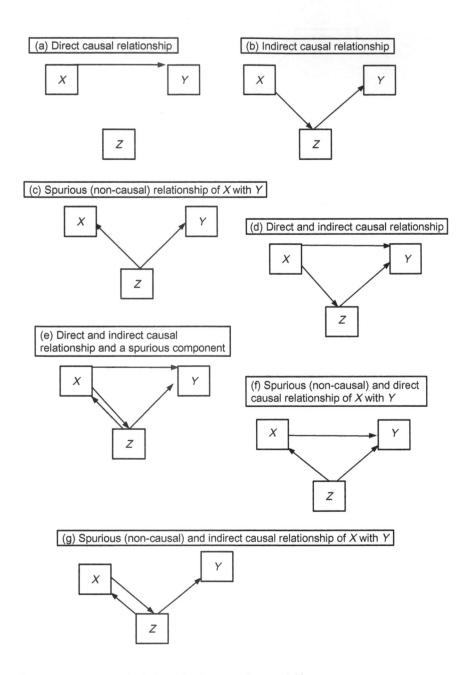

Figure 3.4   *Types of relationships between three variables*

(a) *Direct causal*   Y follows X in time, Y is capable of being changed, and it is plausible that X could produce changes in Y. In the absence of finding any other variable that is responsible for this relationship we may continue to argue that the observed correlation is direct and is causal (Figure 3.4a).

(b) *Indirect causal*   Y follows X in time, Y is capable of being changed, and it is plausible that X could produce changes in Y. However, in this case we are spelling out the mechanism by which X affects Y. We may think of Z as a single mechanism or a whole lot of intervening variables (Figure 3.4b).

(c) *Spurious*   X and Y are not causally related to one another. Even though Y might follow X in time and be capable of being changed, both X and Y are joint effects of some third variable Z. X and Y co-vary purely because Z has a simultaneous effect on both X and Y (Figure 3.4c).

(d) *Both direct and indirect*   The effect of X may be partly via its effect on an intervening variable and partly direct (Figure 3.4d).

(e) *Direct and indirect causal and spurious*   The relationship between X and Y could consist of three components: a direct causal part $(X{\rightarrow}Y)$, an indirect causal part $(X{\rightarrow}Z{\rightarrow}Y)$ and a spurious part $(X{\leftarrow}Z{\rightarrow}Y)$ (Figure 3.4e).

(f) *Direct causal relationship combined with a spurious component*   (Figure 3.4f).

(g) *Indirect causal relationship combined with a spurious component*   (Figure 3.4g).

This set of possibilities results from situations in which we have only three variables. The more variables we take into account, the more complex matters become.

When we collect and analyse data it can be helpful to draw diagrams to spell out the ways in which we propose variables are interrelated. We need to specify:

1   whether relationships are presumed to be causal or spurious
2   whether causal relationships are expected to be direct or indirect
3   the mechanisms (intervening variables) underlying any indirect causal relationships.

Resolving these matters allows us to articulate our research question and the most plausible line of explanation.

Providing a frame of reference

The logic of making comparisons is fundamental to testing causal models. Consequently a central element in designing an explanatory

Proposition Divorce leads to emotional problems in young children. [divorce → emotional problems of children]   *Observation* We find that many children with divorced parents have emotional problems.
Proposition Private schools produce high academic performance among their students. [private schools → high performance]   *Observation* There are many instances of students from private schools achieving highly.
Proposition Youth unemployment is responsible for youth suicide. [unemployment → high suicide rate]   *Observation* 50% of young people who commit suicide are unemployed.

Figure 3.5   *Propositions and observations without a comparative frame of reference*

research study is providing a comparative frame of reference. Different research designs go about the task of providing comparisons in different ways.

Comparing groups

By making comparisons we provide a frame of reference within which to try to make sense of particular findings. The importance of this can be seen in the illustrations in Figure 3.5. In these examples the observation in each case hardly provides convincing support of the proposition. One reason for this is that there is no frame of reference within which to make sense of the observations. There are no groups with which to compare and contrast the observations. It is only by making *comparisons* that our observations take on much meaning and we are able to eliminate alternative explanations.

The proposition that *divorce leads to emotional problems in young children* would encourage us to expect to find emotional problems among children whose parents are divorced. But finding such evidence will not get us very far. To go further down the path of explanation we must make comparisons. Are emotional problems greater than, the same as or less than those among children from intact families? Do the observations among children of divorced parents simply reflect that which we would find among *any* group of children?

Proposition   Divorce leads to emotional problems in young children.

Restated proposition   Children whose parents have divorced are more likely to display emotional problems *than are children whose parents have not divorced.*
[parental marital status → level of emotional problems]

Proposition   Private schools produce high academic performance among their students.

Restated proposition   Private schools will have higher levels of academic performance among their students *than will government schools.*
[school type → level of academic performance]

Proposition   Youth unemployment is responsible for youth suicide.

Restated proposition   Unemployed youth are more likely to commit suicide *than employed youth.*
[employment status → suicide rate]

Figure 3.6   *Using propositions with an explicit comparative frame of reference*

It will be recalled that when we say that two variables are related it means that *variation* or difference on one variable is linked to differences on the other variable. In this instance we have two variables: (1) parents' marital status (married versus divorced) and (2) child's emotional adjustment (low versus high). If our research design included only divorced parents we could say nothing about the impact of divorce on children. Even if 100 per cent of the children from divorced parents had a low level of emotional adjustment we could draw no conclusions about the impact of parental divorce on children's emotional adjustment. We would need to compare the adjustment of the children with divorced parents with the adjustment of children from intact families. The *difference* in adjustment levels in the two groups will provide strong evidence regarding the alleged effect of divorce on children's emotional adjustment.

The propositions in Figure 3.5 only mention one particular group (children of divorced parents; private school students; suicidal youth). It can be helpful to restate the propositions to highlight the implicit comparisons. Figure 3.6 restates these propositions using explicit comparisons.

MULTIPLE COMPARISON GROUPS

The independent variables above (parents' marital status, school type, youth employment status) have all been treated as two-category variables (dichotomies). However, we are not restricted to comparisons of just two groups. Multiple comparison groups are possible and will arise from at least two circumstances.

Independent variables with more than two categories Where independent variables have more than two categories we can compare more groups and provide stronger and subtler tests of theories. For example, in examining the effect of divorce on children we could simply classify marriages into divorced or intact, or we could classify them as single (never married), intact, separated, widowed, divorced (repartnered) and divorced (not repartnered). If we took the latter approach we could make multiple comparisons. In doing so we can get a clearer picture of what is going on. If we find that it is the children of divorced parents who have repartnered who have the most problems we achieve a more focused understanding of the impact of parental marital status on children. We have learned that it is not divorce *per se* but the arrangements that follow divorce that are critical. Had we simply compared divorced and intact marriages we might never have identified this.

Combined effects of different independent variables It is possible that it is only when people have a particular *combination* of characteristics that an effect is produced. For example, it may be the *joint* effects of gender and age rather than each independently that is linked to suicide. We may hypothesize that when a person is both male and young, the likelihood of suicide is at its highest. If, for the purpose of this example, we think of age as a dichotomous variable (15–35 = young; 35+ = old), then we can think in terms of four groups based on the combination of these two independent variables. These are illustrated in Figure 3.7.

Comparing time points

A finding that children from divorced families are less well adjusted emotionally than those from intact families *presumes* that divorce is responsible for this difference. The problem with a simple comparison between groups (divorced and intact) is that it does not tell us whether divorce has actually produced any *change* in the emotional adjustment of children. Any conclusions would be much more convincing if we could track the emotional adjustment of children both before and after divorce to see if there was any change in the emotional adjustment of children following divorce.

By tracking children over time we could see if there was a change in emotional adjustment of the children and evaluate whether this was attributable to their parents' divorce.

MULTIPLE PRE-TESTS AND POST-TESTS

In the above example the measurement of emotional adjustment at the beginning of the study is often referred to as the 'pre-test' and the

	Male	Female
Young	Group 1: young males	Group 2: young females
Old	Group 3: old males	Group 4: old females

Figure 3.7   *Multiple comparison groups created by combining two independent variables*

remeasurement at the end is called the 'post-test'. Between the pre-test and the post-test certain critical events occur – in this case parental divorce (or non-divorce as the case may be). These events serve as the independent variables in the study – i.e. the presumed causal variable behind the observed change. In some designs these intervening events are called the intervention or the treatment (see Chapter 4).

We can collect data about more than two time points rather than being restricted to simple 'before' and 'after' data collections. We might have repeated measurements over an extended period to track 'ups' and 'downs' and to track *trends* before and after any critical event. Multiple 'pre-tests' and multiple post-tests can help distinguish between short term and long term trends. They also help identify the effect of the 'intervention' or independent variable. For example, a simple measure of emotional adjustment before and after divorce might show a decline in adjustment. But what if there was strong evidence of the decline having commenced well before the divorce? Only multiple measures before divorce would show that a trend had already begun. Similarly, a simple post-test might show that adjustment is lower after divorce but multiple post-tests might show poor adjustment immediately after divorce but a steady improvement over time (see Chapter 6).

Making meaningful comparisons

Ideally the groups we are comparing should be the same in all relevant respects except in regard to the independent variable. For example, if we want to test the idea that non-government schools produce students that achieve better academically than government schools we would need to be confident that both types of schools contained comparable students. We would need this so that we could be confident that the only relevant difference between the two sets of students is in the type of school attended. If the students differed in additional ways, how would we know which of the differences was responsible for any differences in academic achievement?

Comparisons of children from divorced and intact families are complicated by the fact that typically children of divorced parents are older than children from intact families. Any differences between the level of emotional adjustment of the two sets of children could be due to age differences rather than the marital status of their parents.

The same problem can arise when looking at the same group or category of people over time. Ideally with comparisons over time the only differences between the pre-test and the post-test should be the event we are proposing as the cause of any change. However, many events can occur which can account for the change and these may confuse our comparisons and our attribution of what lies behind the change in the outcome variable (see Chapter 4 for further discussion).

Since comparisons are central to good research design we must ensure that they are meaningful. The more we can remove unintended and unknown differences between groups, the more we reduce the risk of mistaking spurious relationships for causal relationships – that is, the more we eliminate alternative plausible explanations.

There are four main strategies for maximizing the comparability of groups.

MATCHING

When recruiting the groups we can deliberately match them on relevant characteristics. Thus when comparing students attending government schools on the one hand and fee paying private schools on the other hand we should ensure that the two sets of students are similar in terms of intelligence, aspirations, parental resources, education values, family history, gender and age. By comparing like with like we should be able to isolate the effect of the type of school on academic achievement.

The problem in comparing like with like is to establish the identity of all the variables on which we need to match the groups. We can match for the characteristics that we know might contaminate our results but there may be other factors that we have not thought of.

Ex post facto matching Ideally groups should be matched at the beginning of the study before critical events (e.g. divorce, attending the school). Another approach referred to by Spector (1981: 48) as a 'patchwork procedure' involves creating matched groups from a whole pool of study participants *after* all the data have been collected. For example, we might have a large number of students from government and fee paying private schools. From this pool we could extract a group of government school students and a group of fee paying private school students who are comparable in terms of intelligence, aspirations, parental resources, values about the importance of education, family history, gender, and age. We could then compare these groups and see if there were differences in their level of academic achievement.

There are many problems with this approach. The obvious one is that we must have the relevant information on which to match. Since this will always be limited, the groups are likely to remain unmatched on important but unknown factors. Another problem is that many cases from both groups simply will not have matches from the other group and will have to be discarded. If we match on more than a small number of factors we will often end up with only a very small number of people in the study since the number of cases from both groups that match can be quite small.[2]

RANDOMIZATION

A simpler and more effective way of making groups comparable is to randomly allocate people to different groups at the beginning of a study. By randomly assigning individuals to each group any differences between groups should be random rather than systematic. So long as groups are large enough, random assignment should automatically produce groups with comparable profiles on both known and unknown factors. From a statistical perspective, random assignment of people to groups will make the groups identical for all intents and purposes and provides what Davis calls 'The all purpose spuriosity insurance of randomization' (1985: 35). We control for an infinite number of plausible rival hypotheses *without specifying what any of them are* (Campbell, 1989).

This is the approach taken in drug trials. Individuals are randomly assigned to one of several groups and each group is then given a different drug. Since the groups should have virtually identical profiles to begin with, any differences in outcomes between the groups should be due to the different treatments administered to each group. However, this approach is often not applicable in social research because practical and ethical considerations preclude us assigning people to groups and then doing something to one group to see what effect it has (see Chapter 5). Advantages and drawbacks of this approach to social research are discussed in Chapters 4 and 5.

MATCHED BLOCK DESIGNS

While randomization minimizes the chances of initial differences between groups there is still the chance that there will be differences between the groups – especially in smaller groups. Where we want to be certain that the groups are comparable on a particular characteristic we can take an additional step to guarantee that the groups are comparable at least on specific variables. This is achieved with what is called the randomized block design – a combination of both randomization and matching.

Suppose we wanted to evaluate the effect on academic performance of three methods of delivering university courses: (1) face-to-face delivery of lectures and tutorials, (2) correspondence using written materials and (3) electronically using the internet and e-mail. Further, suppose that we could assign individuals to one of these three modes. Random allocation would be the obvious way. But suppose we want to be absolutely certain that the students in each of the three modes are of comparable academic ability.

To achieve this we would do the following:

1   Obtain a measure of academic ability at the pre-test.
2   Rank all the students from highest to lowest ability.
3   Select the three students with the highest ability (because we have three learning modes). This group of three students is block 1.
4   Randomly allocate each of the three students to a group (one to face-to-face; one to written correspondence; and one to electronic learning).
5   Select the next three most able students (block 2) and repeat the random allocation to groups.
6   Repeat this until all students have been allocated to one of the three groups.

STATISTICAL CONTROLS

An alternative way of making groups comparable is to do so at the data analysis stage after data have been collected. It involves multivariate analysis that, in one respect, matches groups on specified variables (see Chapter 12 for a discussion of the logic of some of these techniques).

Although the procedures of multivariate analysis can be very complex, the essential logic is simple. Suppose we want to compare the emotional adjustment of children from divorced and intact families but we believe that any comparison would be confounded by the fact that, on average, children whose parents divorce are older than those from intact families. Any greater maladjustment among children whose parents have divorced could occur because they are older, as older children display greater maladjustment.

Multivariate analysis removes any effects that might be due to age by comparing like with like – by selecting, say, preschoolers and comparing those from divorced and intact families to see if, despite similarity of age, the children show different levels of adjustment. The same comparisons could be repeated among say 5–8 year olds, 9–12 year olds, 13–15 year olds and so on.

The obvious shortcomings of this approach are similar to that of matching. We can remove the influence of variables that we have thought of and on which we have data but we cannot remove the effects of unknown variables, or those for which we have no data. Since we can never know what factors we have missed there is always the danger that factors we have not thought of may be contributing to group differences.

Interventions and independent variables

Throughout this chapter I have used the terms 'intervention', 'treatment', 'independent variable' and 'groups' more or less interchangeably. Research designs vary in terms of the type of independent variable employed and in the number of independent variables built into the study.

TYPES OF INDEPENDENT VARIABLES

When thinking in causal terms $(X{\rightarrow}Y)$ X is the independent variable. When we conduct the research and do the analysis we compare the outcomes (Y) for different groups. The groups are defined according to which category of the independent variable they belong to. In some studies the investigator introducing an *active intervention* defines the independent variable (e.g. allocate different people to one of three modes of course delivery – face-to-face, correspondence or electronic). In other situations the independent variable is defined by a *naturally occurring 'intervention'* (e.g. a person retires or remains employed). In other situations the independent variable is determined by the relatively *fixed attributes* of participants (e.g. sex, education, race etc.) rather than by interventions of any sort.

NUMBER OF INTERVENTIONS

Research designs can also differ in terms of the number of interventions that are made. Where the independent variable involves either an active or a passive intervention we can examine the effect of single versus repeated interventions. We can see whether a single intervention has a different impact than the cumulative impact of repeated interventions. For example, we might be evaluating the impact of teachers giving students negative feedback on their work. Initial criticism of the work may boost a student's effort and performance but repeated negative feedback may lower performance as the student loses confidence. A multiple intervention design helps refine our understanding of the way in which interventions affect participants and enables us to rule out alternative ways of interpreting results.

Dimensions of a research design

The above discussion has identified six core elements of a research design. The particular mix of the elements in any study will yield different designs.

These six main elements in producing a research design are:

1   *The number of groups in the design*   Designs will vary from those with
    no comparisons (e.g. single case design of case study) to those with
    many different comparison groups.
2   *The number of 'pre-test' measurement phases*   Designs vary from those
    with no 'pre-test' (e.g. cross-sectional designs and some experimental
    designs) to those with a series of 'pre-tests' which establish pre-
    existing trends before an event.
3   *The number of 'post-test' measurement phases*   All designs require at
    least one 'post-test' – the measurement of an outcome variable. In
    some designs (e.g. cross-sectional) there will be one 'post-test', while
    other designs can have many post-tests to help distinguish between
    short and long term outcomes.
4   *The method of allocation of cases to groups*   In multiple group designs
    groups can be made comparable by allocating people to different
    groups by random allocation, 'pre-test' matching, *post hoc* matching or
    block matching or by using statistical controls in the analysis phase.
5   *The nature of the intervention*   Studies that rely on existing variation
    (cross-sectional designs and those with 'fixed' independent variables)
    have no interventions. Other designs rely on interventions between a
    pre-test and a post-test. These 'interventions' may be either active or
    natural.[3]
6   *The number of interventions*   Designs with an intervention can have
    either a single intervention or multiple interventions. Multiple inter-
    ventions can be used to identify the effect of cumulative 'treatments'.

A range of research designs

The combination of the possibilities created by these six elements of a
research design yields a large number of possible designs. A useful
summary discussion of many of these designs is provided by Spector
(1981). To impose some order on this range of possibilities it is helpful to
think in terms of four broad types of design. For each design type,
decisions taken by the investigator will produce variations within the
type. These four types provide the structure for the rest of the book. The
four broad types of design are experimental, longitudinal, cross-sectional
and case study. I will examine each of these in turn.

Experimental design

The classic version of the experimental design has the following elements:

1   One pre-intervention (pre-test) measure on the outcome variable.
2   Two groups: one group that is exposed to the intervention (the
    experimental group) and one group that is not exposed to the inter-
    vention (the control group).

Method of allocation to groups	Pre-test	Intervention (X)	Post-test
Random (experimental group)	Measure on outcome variable (Y)	'Treatment'	Measure on outcome variable (Y)
Random (control group)	Measure on outcome variable (Y)	No 'treatment'	Measure on outcome variable (Y)

Figure 3.8   *Classic experimental design*

3   Random allocation to the groups before the pre-test.
4   One intervention (test/treatment).
5   One post-intervention (post-test) measure on the outcome variable.

This design is illustrated in Figure 3.8.

The analysis of any effect of the intervention focuses on changes in the experimental group before and after the intervention and a comparison with the rate of change in the control group. If the change is greater in the experimental group than in the control group the researcher will attribute this to the impact of the independent variable (the treatment).

Longitudinal design

The basic form of this design involves:

1   One group.
2   One pre-'intervention' measurement on the outcome variable.
3   One 'intervention' where everyone receives the 'treatment'.
4   One post-'intervention' measurement on the outcome variable.

In effect, this design is similar to the experimental design except that there is no control group and typically only one 'experimental' group. The design is illustrated in Figure 3.9.

The analysis in this design compares the pre-intervention measures with the post-intervention measures. Change in these scores can reflect the influence of X on Y. However, the absence of a randomized control

Method of allocation to groups	Pre-test	Intervention (X)	Post-test
Random (one group)	Measure on outcome variable (Y)	'Treatment'	Measure on outcome variable (Y)

Figure 3.9 *Simple longitudinal design*

group makes it difficult to know whether the intervention or some other factor produces any change.

Cross-sectional design

The basic elements of the cross-sectional design are as follows:

1 Instead of interventions the cross-sectional design relies on existing variations in the independent variable(s) in the sample.
2 At least one independent variable with at least two categories is present.
3 Data are collected at one point of time.
4 There is no random allocation to 'groups'.

This design mirrors the post-intervention phase of the classic experimental design but without any random allocation to 'groups' being made. The data for this design are collected at one point of time and are analysed by examining the extent to which variation in the outcome variable is linked with group differences. That is, to what extent do those in different categories of the independent variable differ in relation to the outcome variable? Causal relationships are established by utilizing statistical controls rather than by random allocation of people to groups.

This design is illustrated in Figure 3.10. In this case the 'intervention' is simply being in a different category of the independent variable.

Case studies

Case study designs rely less on comparing cases than on exhaustive analysis of individual cases and then on comparing cases. A distinguishing characteristic of case studies is that contextual information is collected about a case so that we have a context within which to understand causal processes.

Method of allocation to groups	Pre-test	Intervention (X)	Post-test
Non-random	None	'Treatment'	Measure on outcome variable (Y)
Non-random	None	No 'treatment'	Measure on outcome variable (Y)

Figure 3.10   *Simple cross-sectional design*

Case study designs might consist of a single case study (e.g. a community study, a study of an organization) or a series of case studies with perhaps each case testing a theory from a different angle. It is useful to think of a case study in a similar way to an experiment. We do not finally reject or accept a theory on the basis of a single experiment; we try to replicate an experiment and conduct it under a variety of conditions. Similarly, a case study project that entails a single case study is analogous to a single experiment. If similar results are found in repeated case studies, or predictable differences in results are found for particular cases in the study, then we develop greater confidence in the findings of the cases in the same way that we gain confidence in experimental results that are found in repeated experiments.

Summary

This chapter has examined ways of structuring research designs to help draw convincing causal inferences from the research. Since causes cannot be observed they must be inferred from observations. However, incorrect inferences can easily be made. The chapter has considered ways of structuring research to improve the quality of these inferences. A range of ways of interpreting correlations between variables was outlined and criteria required for inferring that a correlation reflects a causal connection were provided.

The chapter emphasized the importance of making meaningful comparisons between groups as a core element of drawing causal inferences.

One of the tasks of research design is to structure the research so that meaningful comparisons of outcomes between groups can be made.

Finally, the chapter outlined six core elements of research designs: number of groups, number of pre-tests, number of post-tests, nature of allocation to groups, type of interventions and number of interventions. Research designs vary in the way these elements are dealt with. Four main types of research design – experimental, longitudinal, cross-sectional and case study – were then briefly described. These broad categories of design provide the framework for the remainder of this book.

Notes

1 There can be exceptions to this where a suppressor variable may be operating to mask a causal relationship. See Rosenberg (1968: Chapter 4).

2 We shall see later that this problem of loss of cases can be overcome with certain forms of multivariate analysis.

3 A naturally occurring intervention is an event that takes place between pre-test and post-test without the investigator initiating any intervention. An example might be a study of families over time in which some families experience parental divorce. Divorce is the 'natural intervention'.

PART II

EXPERIMENTAL DESIGNS

4

TYPES OF EXPERIMENTAL DESIGN

This chapter builds on the elements of research design outlined in Chapter 3 to introduce a variety of types of experimental designs. It outlines the different environments in which experiments can be conducted and describes both simple and more complex variations of experimental designs. This chapter does not seek to evaluate experimental designs: that is the task of Chapter 5. The discussion also provides a useful framework within which to understand some of the strengths and weaknesses of the research designs discussed later in this book.

The classic experimental design

The classic experimental design focuses on two variables: the independent variable (the cause/intervention) and the dependent variable (outcome). The purpose of the design is to remove the influence of other variables so that the effect of the intervention can be clearly seen. Since the classic experimental design was outlined in the previous chapter there is no need to repeat it here. However, an example will help clarify its elements.

Suppose we wanted to test the proposition in Figure 4.1, namely *the more difficult it is to join a group the more desirable the group will seem*.[1] In order to test this proposition it is necessary to develop measures of desirability of membership and to define what is meant by 'difficulties of joining'. The expression could refer to things such as restricted membership, long waiting periods, high fees, harsh initiation, high time commitments. For the purpose of this exercise we will use 'severity of

Figure 4.1 *Simple causal proposition*

initiation' into the group as the indicator of difficulty of joining. The classic experimental design for such an investigation entails the following steps:

1 Randomly allocating people to two groups: an experimental group and a control group.
2 Obtaining measures of perceived desirability of group membership.
3 Subjecting the experimental group to severe initiation requirements and the control group to no initiation requirements.
4 Obtaining measures of desirability of group membership from both groups after the initiation of the experimental group has been completed.
5 Calculating the *change* in desirability of membership for the *experimental group* before and after the initiation and of the control group at T_1 and T_2.
6 Comparing the level of change in the experimental group with that in the control group.

If changes in the perceived desirability of membership are different between the two groups (more than would be due to chance) this should be because one group had experienced severe initiation. This is represented in Figure 4.2. Here the symbol T_1 represents time 1 or the pre-test. E_1 represents the experimental group at time 1 and C_1 represents the control group at time 1. The amount of change in the experimental group is symbolized as E_{change} and is the difference between the group's desirability score at T_2 compared with T_1. The comparable change for the control group can be symbolized as C_{change}. The effect of the intervention is the difference between the amount of change in the experimental group before and after the intervention (E_{change}) and the amount of change in the control group (C_{change}) between T_1 and T_2 (i.e. $E_{change} - C_{change}$). If this is greater than zero then we would probably conclude that the initiation had an impact on desirability.

If the measure of desirability was measured quantitatively on a scale of, say, 0–100 with a high score indicating high desirability, we could quantify the effect of the intervention (severity of initiation). This is illustrated with hypothetical data in Figure 4.3. Using these figures we can see that:

Method of allocation to groups	Time 1 (T_1) Pre-test	Intervention (X)	Time 2 (T_2) Post-test	
Random allocation (experimental group)	E_1 Pre-test average desirability score	'Severe initiation'	E_2 Post-test average desirability score	$E_{change} = E_2 - E_1$
Random allocation (control group)	C_1 Pre-test average desirability score	No initiation	C_2 Post-test average desirability score	$C_{change} = C_2 - C_1$

Figure 4.2 *Structure of the classic experimental design*

	Time 1 (T_1) Pre-test	Intervention (X)	Time 2 (T_2) Post-test	
Experimental group	E_1 Mean score = 50	'Severe initiation'	E_2 Mean score = 75	$E_{change} = 75 - 50$ = 25
Control group	C_1 Mean score = 50	No initiation	C_2 Mean score = 60	$C_{change} = 60 - 50$ = 10

Figure 4.3 *Classic experimental design: effect of difficulty of joining a group by perceived desirability of group membership*

1 Both groups had the same level of desirability before the initiation (the result of random allocation).
2 The desirability score of the experimental group increases (by 25 points).
3 The desirability score of the control group also increases (by 10 points).
4 Therefore some change in the experimental group is not due to initiation (10 points worth since this level occurs without initiation).

5 The change in the experimental group is greater than in the control group (by 15 points).
6 Therefore severity of initiation leads on average to a 15-point increase in perceived desirability of group membership.

The logic of this experimental design is based on two conditions:

1 The groups are the same in all relevant respects before any intervention (T_1).
2 The groups experience the same conditions between T_1 and T_2 except for the specific intervention/treatment.

If either of these conditions is not met then there are *alternative plausible hypotheses* that could account for the different changes between the experimental and control groups. The different levels of change could be due to initial differences between the two groups rather than the severity of initiation. If the two groups differ in other experiences between T_1 and T_2 (e.g. mixing with different people in the group) these differences rather than severity of initiation could account for the different rates of change in the two groups.

Experimental contexts

Experimental designs can be implemented in three different ways: in a laboratory, in the field and by utilizing natural occurrences.

LABORATORY EXPERIMENTS

The laboratory experiment is designed to ensure that experimental and control groups are exposed to exactly the same environment except for the experimental intervention. This is achieved by standardizing and controlling the environment and all the events between T_1 and T_2. Maximum control over the environment is designed to ensure that the only feasible reason for group differences at T_2 is the differential treatment.

An example of a laboratory experiment is a study designed to test the effect of extremely graphic images of alcohol caused road accidents on views about drink-driving. Participants could be randomly allocated to experimental and control groups and asked about their views regarding appropriate penalties for drink-driving. The experimental group could be shown a graphic film of alcohol caused accidents. Members of the other group would not be shown the film. At a specified time after showing the film both groups would again be asked about their views regarding drink-driving penalties. If the views of the experimental group changed more than the views of the control group it would be reasonable to assume that viewing the film caused the change. The laboratory setting enabled the researcher to control everything, so the *only* difference between the groups was the exposure or lack of exposure to the film.

Laboratory experiments have been used to great effect in the physical and biological sciences. However, for a variety of methodological, practical and ethical reasons their use in social research has been limited (see Chapter 5).

FIELD EXPERIMENTS

Because of the artificiality and impracticality of laboratory experiments, social scientists have established experimental designs in real world environments. In a field experiment the investigator creates experimental and control groups through randomized allocation of participants. The experiment also involves an intervention. The intervention is implemented in the 'field' where a real life environment is treated as the laboratory. This approach has become especially popular among those evaluating policy initiatives and pilot programmes.[2]

In order to illustrate the nature of field experiments I will recount the major features of an American study of income maintenance among families of low socio-economic standing. The study is known as the Seattle/Denver Income Maintenance Experiment (Hakim, 1986). Almost 5000 low income families participated in the experiment in the 1970s. The purpose of the study was to establish the effect of the introduction of a guaranteed minimum income on the work effort and marital stability of participants. Families were randomly allocated to different versions of the scheme (no income support, short term support, through to long term guaranteed income). Among the many variables measured were work effort and marital stability. They were measured at the beginning of the scheme and then at various points throughout the experiment. While participating in the experiment these families went about their normal lives and were subject to all the varying experiences and additional changes (e.g. political and social changes) that took place over the period of the study.

I participated in a field experiment conducted by the Australian Department of Social Security (DSS). It was designed to see if the participation of welfare recipients (DSS clients) in self-help groups increased their living standards. Various self-help groups were established in 80 locations. Clients of the DSS living in those locations could choose whether or not to participate in the groups. Extensive measures of living standards were obtained before participation and 12 months later. In each of the 80 locations a random sample of DSS clients who did not participate in the self-help groups were also questioned about their living standards. These people acted as a control or comparison group.

Clearly this was an attempt to implement the logic of the experimental design in a field situation. However, the design had a serious flaw. Participants were not randomly allocated to groups, so we do not know whether those who participated in the self-help groups were initially similar to the non-participants. In addition we do not know whether participants and non-participants were exposed to comparable influences over the 12-month period. We observed that self-help group participants did better over the 12 months compared to members of the control group. However, we could not be sure whether this was due to participation in the self-help groups or whether the sorts of people who volunteered to participate were more self-help oriented prior to the commencement of the experiment. These initial differences might have accounted for their greater improvement in living standards.

While laboratory experiments suffer from problems of artificiality, field experiments encounter problems from inadequate control of events between T_1 and T_2. There is always the danger that uncontrolled events rather than the experimental intervention are producing any observed changes.

However, other factors (i.e. uncontrolled events) should not be a major problem *if both the experimental and the control groups are equally exposed to these other influences*. Total change in the experimental group between T_1 and T_2 consists of two elements: that produced by the intervention and that produced by other intervening events.[3] In the control group, total change will be due entirely to the other intervening events. If the same intervening events apply equally to both groups we can still identify experimental change by looking at the *difference* in the total change between the two groups. In the earlier example (severity of initiation) the total change in the experimental group was 25 points compared to 10 points in the control group. The difference in total change between the two groups was 15 points – the experimental effect.

We do run into problems, however, when any of these external factors influence one group more than the other. This can occur in at least two ways:

1 One group may be selectively exposed to additional factors more than the other group.
2 The external factors may *interact* with the intervention. That is, when a person is exposed to *both* the experimental intervention *and* the external factor this *combination* has a unique effect that neither the experimental nor the external factor has on its own. An example of an interaction effect is evident in the treatment of depression. Drug treatment on its own may have some limited effect on depression, and psychotherapy on its own may have some effect. But when the two approaches are used together they can have a dramatic impact on depression. The combined impact is much greater than the simple cumulative impact of each approach: it is the *mix* that has the most effect.

Natural experiments

The natural experiment relies on naturally occurring events as interventions rather than on controlled experimenter-induced interventions.

If we can anticipate that an event will occur we can collect information before and after to monitor its impact. To help interpret the results we could try to identify a comparison group that will not be exposed to the event.

A natural experiment is well suited to studying the impact of legalizing poker machines on family wellbeing. For such an experiment we would obtain measures of family wellbeing before and after the legalization of poker machines. We would obtain a comparison group by measuring family wellbeing in a comparable region, state or country in which poker machines remained illegal. Similarly, a natural experiment is well suited to examining the impact of the introduction of no-fault divorce on divorce rates. We would examine the divorce rates in a country before and after the introduction of no-fault divorce and compare the rate of change with a comparable country without no-fault divorce.

Another form of natural experiment can be achieved by constructing experimental and control groups *after* the 'intervention' has occurred. Let us assume, for example, that we want to establish how women's return to the workforce impacts on the division of housework and child-care between marriage partners. We would collect baseline information about the domestic division of labour from couples where the wife is not in the paid workforce. We could return to the same sample several years later anticipating that some wives will have returned to the workforce. These could be treated as the experimental group while those couples where the wife remained out of the labour force would constitute the control group. Changes in who did what around the home would be compared in the two groups to assess the impact of the return to the workforce.

The difficulty here is that the groups are self-forming rather than being created by random allocation. We might be able to match regions, countries or families to some extent but matching has its obvious limits (see Chapter 3). These limits mean that the groups we are comparing may be dissimilar in important ways. This necessarily compromises our ability to say exactly what is producing any change or any differences between the groups. In the gambling example the problem will be finding a truly comparable region in which gambling remains illegal; with divorce the problem will be finding truly comparable countries. The housework example would encounter the problem that the women returning to work may be different from those staying at home.

Simpler experimental designs

In many circumstances we cannot obtain all the measurements required for the classic experimental design (pre-test and post-test for both the control and the experimental groups). In some circumstances valid inferences can be drawn without all these measurement points.

Method of allocation to groups	Time 1 (T_1) Pre-test	Intervention (X)	Time 2 (T_2) Post-test
Random allocation (experimental group)	None	'Treatment'	Measure on outcome variable (Y)
Random allocation (control group)	None	No 'treatment'	Measure on outcome variable (Y)

Figure 4.4   *Post-test only experimental design with a control group*

Post-test only with control group

This design is illustrated in Figure 4.4. So long as groups are large enough, random allocation to experimental and control groups means that any differences between experimental and control groups are random and will not account for group differences in outcomes. Therefore, where we form groups using random allocation, the pre-test measurement phase can be omitted.

Campbell and Stanley argue that:

> While the pre-test is a concept deeply embedded in the thinking of research workers . . . it is not actually essential to true experimental designs. For psychological reasons it is difficult to give up 'knowing for sure' that the . . . groups were 'equal' before the differential experimental treatment. Nonetheless, the most adequate all-purpose assurance of lack of initial biases between groups is randomization. (1963: 25)

When this design is utilized analysis cannot be undertaken by examining different amounts of *change* between the groups. Rather, analysis focuses on post-test differences between groups. Because participants have been randomly allocated to their groups, post-test differences on the outcome measure should be the same as the difference in change scores of experimental and control groups in the classic experimental group.

Retrospective experimental design

This design entails constructing experimental and control groups *after* an 'intervention' (see earlier discussion of natural experiments). Since such

Method of allocation to groups	Time 1 (T_1) Pre-test	Intervention (X)	Time 2 (T_2) Post-test
Retrospective matching (experimental group)	Measure on outcome variable (Y)	'Treatment'	Measure on outcome variable (Y)
Retrospective matching (control group)	Measure on outcome variable (Y)	No 'treatment'	Measure on outcome variable (Y)

Figure 4.5 *Retrospective experimental design*

groups are not formed through random allocation any differences between the groups could simply reflect 'pre-intervention' differences. This design can be improved in two ways using retrospective data (Figure 4.5).

The two groups could be *matched* so that they are comparable in at least some relevant ways. Some of the information for matching would relate to past events. This information would have to be collected by asking about these past events. The design can also be improved by refining the measurement of *change* on the outcome variable. If we simply have 'after' measures we cannot see whether, following the 'intervention', one group has changed more than the other. To measure change we could obtain 'before' measures retrospectively and then assess the amount of change. So even if the two groups were different to start with we can see whether the amount of change in one group is greater than in the other.

For example, we might want to see whether having children encourages people to be more politically conservative.[4] To achieve this end we could compare the level of political conservatism of a group of families with children and a group without children. Since any differences between groups could be due to factors other than parenthood we would collect other information about the families and match the two groups so that we compare like with like. However, we still cannot be sure that having children has produced changes in political views. To test this proposition we could ask participants to describe their political views at some earlier point before they had children. This strategy provides us with a pseudo 'before' measure. We could use this measure to assess whether parents had changed any differently from the non-parents.

Method of allocation to groups	Time 1 (T_1) Pre-test	Intervention (X)	Time 2 (T_2) Post-test 1	Time 3 (T_3) Post-test 2	Time 4 (T_4) Post-test 3
Random allocation (experimental group)	Measure on outcome variable (Y)	'Treatment'	Measure on outcome variable (Y)	Measure on outcome variable (Y)	Measure on outcome variable (Y)
Random allocation (control group)	Measure on outcome variable (Y)	No 'treatment'	Measure on outcome variable (Y)	Measure on outcome variable (Y)	Measure on outcome variable (Y)

Figure 4.6 *Experimental design with multiple post-tests*

More complex experimental designs

We can add to the classical experimental design by introducing more than two groups, adding additional pre-test and post-test measures and including more than one independent variable.

Multiple post-tests

Since the effects of an intervention might not show up immediately or might only last for a short time, multiple post-tests can help identify the short and longer term outcomes. For example, divorce law reform designed to simplify divorce may produce a sharp increase in divorces initially (pent-up demand, formalization of family breakdown) but over the longer term the divorce rate may decline and stabilize to pre-reform levels.

A multiple post-test experimental design is represented in Figure 4.6. The same design could be modified to provide multiple *pre-tests* to estimate the extent to which change was taking place before the intervention to see to what extent the intervention accelerates or slows the rate of change.

Multiple groups

So far I have only described designs where the independent variable or intervention has two categories. However, interventions frequently have multiple variations. There may be several alternative interventions to evaluate.

For example, we may be interested in the effect of compulsory voting on electoral turnout. We might consider five conditions: (1) completely voluntary voting, (2) compulsion without sanctions for non-compliance, (3) compulsion with a warning only for the first offence, (4) compulsion with a fine of $50 for non-compliance, (5) compulsion with a fine of $250 for non-compliance. After randomly assigning individuals to one of five groups we could ask about their intention to vote in the next election. Assuming that voluntary voting is the status quo, four of the five groups will be told that voting is going to be made compulsory at the next election. Each group is to be told a different thing about the sanctions that will be imposed for non-voting. The control group will believe that voting will remain voluntary. After being given this information people in each group will be asked about their voting intention. Differences in the T_2 voting intentions of the five groups should reflect the effect of compulsion on the stated intention to vote. This design is diagrammed in Figure 4.7.

Solomon four-group design

One problem when designing experiments which have before and after measurement phases is that making measurements can produce change on its own, regardless of any intervention. This is the problem of *instrument reactivity*. To the extent that change may be attributed to the effect of measuring rather than the experimental 'treatment', the results will remain ambiguous.

The Solomon four-group design helps evaluate whether change in the outcome variable is due to instrument reactivity (Figure 4.8). In this example I describe this design for an independent variable with only two categories, but the logic of the design could easily be extended to independent variables with more than two categories or conditions.

Using this design the experimental group is split into two subgroups, as is the control group. One experimental group involves a pre-test while the other does not. The same conditions apply to the control group. If there is no instrument reactivity then the two experimental groups should score identically on the outcome measures at T_2, as should the two control groups. Any difference between the T_2 scores of the two experimental groups or of the two control groups should be attributable to instrument reactivity.

The example in Figure 4.9 illustrates this design using figures. For the sake of the example the outcome variable is measured on a scale of 0–100. In the experimental groups the pre-test group obtained a score of 80 compared with a score of 70 for the experimental group without the pre-test. If we can assume that there were no other differences between the

Method of allocation to groups	Time 1 (T_1) Pre-test	Intervention (X)	Time 2 (T_2) Post-test
Random allocation (experimental group 1)	% intending to vote	Compulsion without sanctions	% intending to vote
Random allocation (experimental group 2)	% intending to vote	Compulsion with initial warning	% intending to vote
Random allocation (experimental group 3)	% intending to vote	Compulsion with modest fine as sanction	% intending to vote
Random allocation (experimental group 4)	% intending to vote	Compulsion with heavy fine as sanction	% intending to vote
Random allocation (control group)	% intending to vote	No compulsion	% intending to vote

Figure 4.7   *Experimental design with multiple groups and one pre-test and one post-test*

two groups then the discrepancy of 10 points between the two groups is attributable to the effect of the only other difference between the two groups – being exposed to a pre-test. The same logic can be applied to the two control groups.

The real effect of the intervention would be the difference between the experimental group and the control group with the effect of instrument reactivity removed. This would give us a score of 70 for the experimental group and a score of 50 for the control group. We would conclude that the intervention had an effect of 20 points.

You might ask, why bother using such a complicated design to remove the effect of pre-testing? Could we not have achieved the same outcome by simply dropping the pre-test altogether and comparing the T_2 scores of a single experimental group and a single control group? We would have arrived at exactly the same answer. However, when we have small groups randomization may be insufficient to remove initial differences

Method of allocation to groups	Time 1 (T_1) Pre-test	Intervention (X)	Time 2 (T_2) Post-test
Random allocation (experimental group)	Measure on outcome variable (Y)	'Treatment'	Measure on outcome variable (Y)
Random allocation (experimental group)	None	'Treatment'	Measure on outcome variable (Y)
Random allocation (control group)	Measure on outcome variable (Y)	No 'treatment'	Measure on outcome variable (Y)
Random allocation (control group)	None	No 'treatment'	Measure on outcome variable (Y)

Figure 4.8   *Solomon four-group design*

between the two groups and we may wish to conduct pre-tests to measure *change*. In such cases we may need this more complex design.

Factorial designs

All the experimental designs so far have dealt with just one independent variable. However, we will often want to evaluate the effects of a number of independent variables. We could, if we had the time and resources, conduct a separate experiment for each independent variable and hopefully work out which independent variable had the greatest effect.

But separate experiments would be both inefficient and impractical. More importantly, separate experiments would not allow us to see how the various independent variables work together in particular combinations to produce unique effects. An independent variable can have an effect on its own (called main effects or direct effects) or in combination with other variables (interaction effects). A main effect is when, regardless of anything else, the variable affects the outcome. An interaction effect occurs when the effect of one independent variable is at least partly contingent on other factors also being present.

Method of allocation to groups	Time 1 (T_1) Pre-test	Intervention (X)	Time 2 (T_2) Post-test	
Random allocation (experimental group)	Mean=50	'Treatment'	Mean=80	Difference between experimental groups is 10 (80 minus 70). This is attributable to instrument reactivity
Random allocation (experimental group)	None	'Treatment'	Mean=70	
Random allocation (control group)	Mean=50	No 'treatment'	Mean=60	Difference between control groups is 10 (60 minus 50). This is attributable to instrument reactivity
Random allocation (control group)	None	No 'treatment'	Mean=50	

Figure 4.9   *Hypothetical example of the Solomon four-group design*

For example, alcohol, on its own, affects mood. On their own, amphetamines also affect mood. The effects are main effects: they each have an effect on their own. But the mixture of alcohol and amphetamines can have unique effects above and beyond either alcohol or amphetamines independently. This will be more than just an additive effect: it will be a unique effect that is only produced by mixing the two drugs. Similarly, giving workers more control over their work might improve work satisfaction for everyone (main effect) but it might have *more* effect on particular types of people such as professionals or older people (interaction effect).

The purpose of factorial experimental designs is simultaneously to examine the direct effects (main effects) of a number of independent variables and to see how various combinations of characteristics work together to produce an effect. The simplest version of this design is called the 2 × 2 factorial design, that is one based on two independent variables each with just two categories. This simple 2 × 2 design can easily be extended to more than two variables each of which might have two or more categories or conditions.

The simple 2 × 2 design can be illustrated best with an example in which we have two independent variables and one dependent variable

		Control (X_1)	
		High (a)	Low (b)
Gender (X_2)	Male (a)	Group 1 Males with high control	Group 2 Males with low control
	Female (b)	Group 3 Females with high control	Group 4 Females with low control

Figure 4.10 *Defining groups in a 2 × 2 factorial design*

(Figure 4.10). The dependent variable (Y) is job satisfaction measured on a scale of 0–100, with 100 indicating very high satisfaction. One independent variable is degree of control over one's work situation (X_1) classified simply as low and high control. The other independent variable is gender (X_2).

A factorial design entails forming experimental groups for each possible *combination* of the two independent variables. In this case the four groups are those defined in Figure 4.10. Symbolically the two independent variables can be represented as X_1 (control) and X_2 (gender). The categories of each can be represented as 'a' and 'b'. Thus males with high control can be symbolized as $X_{1a}X_{2a}$, while low control females would be symbolized as $X_{1b}X_{2b}$.

In this particular case, since gender is an independent variable but is hardly an 'intervention' we would start with a randomly selected group of males and a randomly selected group of females (Figure 4.11). To each of these groups we would introduce the 'treatment' of high and low job control. Half the males would be randomly assigned to a low control work environment and half to a high control work environment. The same would apply to females. We would thus have four groups for which we would then obtain before and after measures.

The number of groups grows if either variable has more than two categories. It is perhaps more difficult to visualize what would happen with three or more variables. We can do this symbolically where we have three independent variables with a varying number of categories: X_1 (two categories called a and b), X_2 (two categories called a and b) and X_3 (two categories called a and b). The first category of the first variable can be symbolized as X_{1a} and the second category as X_{1b}; the first category of the second independent variable is represented as X_{2a}; and so on. Table 4.1 illustrates the number of groups that could be produced by each of the possible combinations of these three independent variables.

Method of allocation to groups	Time 1 (T_1) Pre-test	'Interventions' (X_1 and X_2)	Time 2 (T_2) Post-test
Random allocation	Measure on job satisfaction (Y)	$X_{1a} X_{2a}$ Males with high control	Measure on job satisfaction (Y)
Random allocation	Measure on job satisfaction (Y)	$X_{1a} X_{1b}$ Males with low control	Measure on job satisfaction (Y)
Random allocation	Measure on job satisfaction (Y)	$X_{1b} X_{2a}$ Females with high control	Measure on job satisfaction (Y)
Random allocation	Measure on job satisfaction (Y)	$X_{1b} X_{2b}$ Females with low control	Measure on job satisfaction (Y)

Figure 4.11   *Elements of a 2 × 2 factorial design*

Table 4.1   *Defining groups in a 3 × 2 factorial design*

X_1	X_2	X_3	Group
X_{1a}	X_{2a}	X_{3a}	1
X_{1a}	X_{2a}	X_{3b}	2
X_{1a}	X_{2b}	X_{3a}	3
X_{1a}	X_{2b}	X_{3b}	4
X_{1b}	X_{2a}	X_{3a}	5
X_{1b}	X_{2a}	X_{3b}	6
X_{1b}	X_{2b}	X_{3a}	7
X_{1b}	X_{2b}	X_{3b}	8

It quickly becomes apparent that the number of groups required can explode with the addition of each additional variable and as each of those variables has additional categories. Of course we do not need to design the research with every possible combination included. For theoretical and practical reasons we might just select particular sets of combinations and examine the effect of these selected combinations.

Summary

This chapter has outlined a variety of experimental designs of varying complexity. The logic of drawing causal inferences from data obtained with experimental designs was outlined. The various experimental designs vary in terms of their use of pre-tests, the number of pre-test and post-test measurement points and the number of groups compared within the design. All experimental designs will have comparison groups and all attempt to make the groups as similar as possible except in relation to the experimental intervention. Although random allocation to groups is the favoured method, the means by which groups will be made comparable will vary depending on the circumstances of the research (see Chapter 3). The rigour of experimental designs will vary depending on the contexts within which the experiment is conducted. Laboratory settings provide maximum control of confounding external influences while natural experiments provide the least control.

Notes

1 This is a modification of an argument tested in an experiment by Aronson and Mills (1959) and discussed in Kerlinger (1979: 91).

2 Unfortunately these goals are not always specified at the beginning of the implementation of the pilot programmes and evaluation studies are all too frequently commissioned *after* the pilot programme has been developed and implemented.

3 There is also measured change that is due to various types of error (see Chapter 2).

4 The argument being that as people have children their concern for the wellbeing of their family makes them become more concerned about social and political stability.

5

ISSUES IN EXPERIMENTAL DESIGN

Experimental designs have been widely used in the natural sciences and in psychological and educational research and have provided a great deal of valuable research data. However, experimental designs have been less widely used in the social sciences. This lack of use in the social sciences stems from methodological, practical and ethical considerations. This is not to say, however, that experimental designs cannot be used in one form or another in social science research or that the logic of the experimental design cannot be invaluable in developing other research designs that are applicable in the social sciences. This chapter explores some of the strengths and weaknesses of experimental designs and the issues that must be dealt with in developing any research that uses this design.

Methodological issues

The problem of explanatory narrowness

The strength of experimental research is the ability it provides us with to say how much direct causal impact a variable has. Experiments allow us to isolate the impact of the experimental variable. This is achieved by randomly allocating people to experimental and control groups – a process that makes the groups comparable in all respects except with regard to the experimental variable. Hakim argues that:

> Experiments are appropriate when there is some argument as to the very existence of a causal relationship between X and Y (net of other contextual or related factors), or when the precise measure of the size and direction of the effect is needed. (1986: 105)

The strength of experiments gained through randomization, however, comes at a considerable cost. Experimental research is not well suited to providing an *explanation* of the results – to identifying the mechanisms by which one variable affects another. Nor does it allow us to build a picture of the complex *set* of factors that produce a given outcome. Experiments focus on the impact of just one or two factors.[1]

RANDOMIZATION MAKES IT DIFFICULT TO ESTABLISH THE ROLE OF
OTHER FACTORS

The strength of randomization is also its weakness: in removing the
effect of numerous variables it also removes too much information.
While the control that randomization provides helps to isolate the impact
of the experimental variable, it prevents us testing more complex causal
models, or working out why an intervention has an impact.

This drawback can be illustrated with the earlier example of the
impact of school type on student academic achievement. Imagine an
experiment where we could randomly allocate students to government
funded schools and others to fee paying private schools. Such a random
allocation should remove any differences between the two sets of
students in key variables such as initial student ability and home
background. At the end of the study period we could compare the
academic achievement of students in the government funded schools
with that of students in the private schools. Any differences should be
attributable to the school.

However, what we learn about actual life situations by invoking this
procedure is limited. In the real world many other factors apart from the
type of school itself may contribute to the actual differences we see. Yet
we have eliminated such relevant influences – e.g. home background –
by randomization and consequently we cannot identify their impact.

Even if we demonstrate that, despite starting off the same, private
school students perform better than government school students, we do
not know *why* the former perform better. What is it about the private
schools that produces better performance? Is it better teachers, superior
resources, an environment that emphasizes academic performance or
what? All that we know is that private school students perform better
academically.

In summary, the experimental design can be effective in identifying
what interventions will be effective but it does not help us understand
why an intervention is effective.

RANDOMIZATION CAN UNDERESTIMATE THE TOTAL CAUSAL EFFECT

Randomization can result in the underestimation of the *total causal
relationship* between the experimental variable and the outcome variable.
In the real world the total causal effect between two variables consists of
two components:

- direct causal effect
- indirect causal effect.

Randomization ensures that the groups we compare are alike in all
relevant respects. We can only look at the direct effect of the experimental variable. We cannot look at the real world effects of a variable in

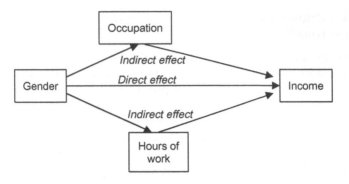

Figure 5.1   *Direct and indirect effects of gender on income*

those circumstances in which an intervention or experimental variable works indirectly.

This shortcoming can be illustrated by considering the relationship between gender and income. The direct effect of gender on income consists of the income difference between men and women who are alike in all relevant respects except their gender. It is the effect that gender has in and of itself – not because of the way in which gender might be linked with other factors such as the type of job, level of workforce participation or education level. Experimental designs are good at identifying the extent of a direct effect.

The problem, however, is that gender can also have an indirect effect – via other variables. For example, gender affects the type of occupations people choose or which they are allowed to enter. The type of occupation in turn affects their level of income. So, as well as men earning more purely because of their gender (simple discrimination), they also earn more because of factors such as the types of jobs they have, the greater likelihood of working full time and a greater opportunity to accept overtime (Figure 5.1).

If we estimated the impact of gender on income by only looking at its direct effect we would seriously underestimate the overall influence of gender on income. Ignoring indirect effects has practical implications. Gender differences in income will not be overcome simply by paying men and women the same money for the same job. Because gender is linked to income indirectly, any policy designed to increase gender equity would also need to address the mechanisms that link gender to income (e.g. the link between gender and occupational choice and between gender and hours of work).

Problems with internal validity

The purpose of design is to structure the collection and analysis of data to reach unambiguous conclusions. If we observe change in an outcome variable we want to be sure that it is due to what we think it is rather than something else. Where the logic and structure of a design are faulty and fail to eliminate competing explanations of results then the design lacks *internal validity*.

All designs face threats to internal validity. Campbell and Stanley (1963) have identified the threats discussed below.

History

If, in addition to the experimental intervention, events take place between pre-test and post-test then these events can threaten the internal validity of the research. These events, rather than the experimental intervention, could produce any change we observe. The problem of extraneous events is greatest in field and natural experiments in an unknown way. In such experiments we have less control over what happens to people. This lack of control is a great danger to the research as the time between the pre-test and post-test increases.

Experimental designs deal with such problems by using control groups. So long as the control group and the experimental group are equally exposed to these uncontrolled external events then the experimental intervention remains the only difference between the groups. Although the occurrence of such external events means that we cannot attribute *all* the change we observe to the intervention we can still attribute *differences* in the amount of change in the experimental and control groups to the intervention. For example we might observe 50 units of change in the experimental group and 30 units of change in the control group. If external events are operating and produce the 30 units of change in both experimental and control groups the remaining amount of change in the experimental group (20 units) is attributable to the experimental intervention.

Even when control groups are used these uncontrolled external influences can cause problems for experiments. We cannot be certain that both the experimental and control groups are equally exposed to the unknown and uncontrolled external influences. If, for some reason, the experimental group was more exposed this could account for any post-test differences between the control and experimental groups. Furthermore, there also may be an *interaction* effect that gets mistaken for a simple direct effect of the intervention. That is, the intervention might have its effect only because another unknown or unintended event *also* took place.

Maturation

In a study of change some of the change could be due to the passing of time rather than the experimental intervention. For example, if we wish to test the impact of a teaching method on mathematical performance of children we would have to be sure that any improvement in performance is due to the intervention (teaching method) rather than because the children are growing older. We need to ensure that we do not confuse the impact of an intervention for developmental or maturational changes that take place in the course of an experiment. Maturational effects might occur in a study of organizational change. In such studies we need to distinguish between the impact of the introduction of new ways of doing things from the changes that accrue simply because, over time, people are in the organization longer and become more experienced. In a laboratory experiment hunger, tiredness and boredom provide further examples of maturation effects.

Since both the experimental and control groups should be equally vulnerable to maturation, these effects can be largely removed by using randomized control groups. The logic for this is the same as outlined in the discussion of the influence of history. The use of multiple pre-tests and post-tests can also help detect maturation as they allow us to see if change in the experimental period is simply part of an ongoing trend that began before the intervention.

TESTING

Testing participants several times can contaminate results. A person may remember previous answers and subsequently answer questions in such a way as to appear consistent. Completing questions can sensitize people to issues about which they had previously given little thought and this, rather than any experimental intervention, can produce change. Similarly, familiarity with a test (e.g. an IQ test) can lead to better performance.

Assuming that testing will have the same effects for both experimental and control groups the effect of testing can be removed by using a control group, in the same manner as described above. The danger of interaction effects (testing and the intervention combined have a unique effect) is a danger that the Solomon four-group design (Chapter 4) can identify and enable us to remove statistically. The testing effects in a randomized experiment can also be eliminated by dropping the pre-test phase altogether. This approach is evident in the randomized post-test only design (Chapter 4).

INSTRUMENT DECAY

Measured change could be due to changes in the way pre-test and post-test measures are made. Changing the question wording, the response alternatives (e.g. adding a 'don't know' option to attitude questions), the question sequence or the data collection mode (e.g. face-to-face interview at T_1 and telephone interview at T_2) could all account for measured change. A different person collecting the information also can contaminate the procedure, as can the same person becoming more experienced and familiar with collecting the data.

Providing careful training and systematic instructions for those collecting data can reduce this problem. The introduction of control groups and the use of the same instruments for both experimental and control groups can substantially reduce the problem of instrument decay. Even if there is instrument decay, its effect can be removed by comparing *differences* between the experimental and control groups in the amount of change on the outcome variable.

STATISTICAL REGRESSION

Groups or people who register extreme scores on an outcome measure at T_1 (e.g. high or low IQ) are likely to change to a more moderate score by T_2. This statistical tendency rather than an experimental intervention can account for some change.

Statistical regression occurs because all scores are due in part to chance variations. An extremely high or low IQ score is more likely to contain an element of random error than a moderate score. The odds are against a person achieving an extreme score on two occasions due to random error. Therefore, the odds are that a fair proportion of those people who initially achieved a high score due to some random error will not be subject to the same random error a second time. Accordingly in a second test their score is likely to be less extreme than it initially was.

Statistical regression can also be due to the fact that measurement error can only change extreme scores in one direction. On a scale of 1 to 10 a score of 10 can only get *lower* due to measurement error. A score of 1 can only get *higher*. The bias, therefore, of measurement error based change will be to a more moderate score.

By utilizing control groups the researcher can deal with this problem. So long as people with extreme scores are randomly allocated to the control and experimental groups, the level of statistical regression should be the same for both groups.

SELECTION

If two groups are initially different, post-test differences between groups could be due to this initial difference rather than to the researcher's intervention. Reasonable sized randomized control groups should eliminate selection effects. Where randomization is not feasible, matching can eliminate specified selection effects but the possibility of unmatched differences influencing results remains (see Chapter 3).

MORTALITY/DROPOUT

If an experiment is conducted over time a loss of certain types of participants, rather than an experimental intervention, may be responsible for any measured change. For example, we might measure the academic grades of a group of students at T_1 and calculate the group average. We then implement an experimental intervention over a period of a year and then remeasure performance. We might observe an increase in average grades. Would this be due to the intervention? Possibly. But it could also be due to the less able people dropping out of the programme. If the less able dropped out then the increase in average marks could simply be because the less able were not being included in the calculations at T_2.

The best way of dealing with the impact of the loss of participants is to minimize selective dropout. The next best thing is to remove its effect at the analysis stage. In the above example we could recalculate the T_1 averages just for the students that remained throughout the study. Alternatively, where there is evidence of selective dropout, we could weight the samples to adjust for selective dropout (Chapter 9), introduce statistical controls (Chapter 12) or conduct analysis separately for various subgroups.

Problems with external validity

The notion of external validity refers to the extent to which we can generalize the results of the experimental sample to the population it is meant to represent. Would the experimental intervention work in a real world situation or is its effect only going to occur in an experimental setting with a particular set of participants? Campbell and Stanley (1963: 5–6) identify a number of factors that can undermine our ability to generalize experimental findings beyond the specific experiment.

REACTIVE EFFECT OF PRE-TESTING

If pre-testing itself changes behaviour or attitudes or sensitizes people so that they are more vulnerable to the effects of the intervention, then any experimental findings may be an artifact of the experimental situation and not apply to people who do not participate in the experiment. If the pre-test rather than the intervention produces the effect then the effect will not occur in a real world implementation of an intervention since the real world context will not include experimental pre-tests.

In situations where there is a chance of pre-test effects, it is best to adopt a design without the pre-test phase, or to use the Solomon four-group design so that the impact of this type of interaction can be estimated and taken into account.

UNREPRESENTATIVENESS

The fact that a study has strong internal validity does not mean that an experimental intervention will have the predicted effect in the real world. If the experimental participants are different in important ways from the 'real world' people for whom the intervention is intended we cannot be sure what the outcome will be. For example, we might use first-year university students to test the effect of seeing a film portraying graphic road accidents on driving behaviour. Can we be confident that any effect on this young and predominantly middle class group will apply to other types of people?

There are two approaches to dealing with this problem. One is to conduct experiments using large representative samples and to analyse results to see if they hold equally for all types of people. In the absence of randomly selected representative samples the best strategy is to *repeat* the experiment many times with different samples and in different contexts. This is called *replication*. If we keep getting the same results with different types of samples we can be more confident that the results apply more widely. If, however, we fail to replicate the results with particular types of people or under particular conditions it does not mean that the procedure is fundamentally flawed. Rather, it enables us to specify the limits of our generalization and the types of people to whom the results do and do *not* apply.

ARTIFICIALITY

In endeavouring to achieve internal validity and to attend to ethical and practical matters we can end up with an experiment that is elegant and ethical but is so artificial that we learn nothing of any use about real people in real social contexts. Tajfel (1984) reminds us that the typical social psychology experiment is based on

> a temporary collection of late adolescent strangers given a puzzle to solve under bizarre conditions in a limited time during their first meeting while being peered at from behind a mirror. (in Hakim, 1986: 111)

Simply being selected for a study can make people feel special and produce artificial results. A famous study of the Western Electric Hawthorne Works in Chicago in the early 1930s first discovered the importance of what has become known as the Hawthorne effect (Roethlisberger and Dickson, 1939). The researchers selected a group of workers and changed their working environment in an effort to improve productivity. They found that regardless of which interventions they made, the group became more productive. They concluded that it was not the interventions that were effective – it was being specially selected that produced the effect. Had the same changes been made without giving people the feeling that they were special we cannot be confident that satisfaction and productivity would have improved.

Practical issues

There are few simple answers to the many practical questions that arise when designing social experiments. In most cases the answer to the question is, 'It depends.'

How much do you tell participants?

Should we tell participants they are in the control group? How much should we tell them about the experimental treatment? Should they know what the research hypothesis is? While the ethical principle of informed consent (see later in this chapter) suggests that we should tell participants everything, doing so could make the study worthless. If participants know what we are looking for they might behave in such a way as to either confirm or sabotage our expectations. Telling people they are in a control group or explaining the range of experimental interventions (e.g. the range of income support levels in the guaranteed income project) may make them feel that they are missing out on the desirable interventions and create resentments and non-cooperation.

There are no hard and fast rules about how much information to provide participants, but within the requirements of informed consent it is safest to minimize the amount of detailed information provided before the experiment is completed. This minimizes the chances of contaminating the experiment. Sometimes an experiment involves explicit deception to avoid sabotage. In such cases ethical guidelines and careful debriefing need to be scrupulously adhered to.

How many participants?

The importance we attach to external validity and the approach we take to external validity will have a large bearing on the size of the sample we choose. If we want to generalize statistically to a wider population we need to use a sample that is both randomly selected and big enough from which to generalize confidently. Many books provide formulae for working out the sample size required for statistical generalization (Moser and Kalton, 1971; Kalton, 1983b). If, however, we use a replication (see above) to achieve generalization the critical factor is whether we have replicated the experiment a sufficient number of times and under a sufficient range of conditions. Theoretical considerations and common sense as to the range of conditions under which we attempt replications must guide us.

If our main concern is with internal validity we can manage with much smaller samples than are required for statistical generalization but they must still be large enough to detect an effect. That is, the sample size must be large enough to give the experiment statistical 'power'. Procedures for working out the sample size required to detect effects can be found elsewhere (Cohen, 1987). The sample size must also take into account the way in which we will analyse the data: different methods require different sample sizes.

How should participants be recruited?

External validity is best achieved by choosing a sample that is representative of the wider population to which we wish to extrapolate. A representative sample is best gained by using random sampling techniques. This requires us to select participants in such a way that each person in the wider population has an equal or a known probability of being selected. Probability theory provides us with a way of estimating how likely our results are to hold for the wider population from which the sample was selected.

Unfortunately, even if we use random sampling we will not necessarily end up with a representative sample. It can be biased because we go about our research in an ethical way. It is unethical either to pressure potential subjects to participate or to try to prevent them withdrawing from the study at any stage during the research. The extent of the bias that results will depend on how many potential participants refuse to participate, or subsequently withdraw.

Gaps between tests and interventions

How long should the gap be between introducing an intervention and the post-test? The length of the gap must depend on what our theories and previous research lead us to expect about the time it would take for an effect to be detectable. The length of the gap between intervention and post-test will also depend on whether we are looking for short term or longer term effects.

The gap between a pre-test and an intervention should be as short as possible. A short gap is desirable because it minimizes the chance of events taking place before the intervention that might make the experimental and control groups different in some way before the intervention. However, we may sometimes need to leave a gap if we suspect that the pre-test might interact with the intervention (e.g the pre-test has sensitized participants to issues).

In establishing the size of the temporal gap between the pre-test and the post-test we must be mindful of the impact of the loss of participants and its threat to both internal and external validity. Since dropouts increase the longer a study lasts, we need to set the gap with a view to minimizing their occurrence.

However, too short a time gap can produce other methodological problems. Where the gap between pre-test and post-test is short it is likely that participants will remember their pre-test responses. Their memory may influence the way they respond in the post-test phase of the experiment.

Such memory effects can be dealt with in a number of ways. Pilot testing might establish the amount of time that has elapsed before participants forget their pre-test responses. Alternatively, if we have allocated participants randomly and have a sample of sufficient size the pre-test can be eliminated altogether (Chapter 4). A third alternative is to use the Solomon four-group design. This design overcomes the problem as it enables us to assess and statistically remove pre-testing effects.

Practical matters will also determine time gaps between stages of the study. The amount of time available to complete the study and the availability of funds at our disposal to keep track of people will influence the way we finally design the experiment.

Which method of data collection?

The particular research design we adopt does not dictate a particular method of data collection (e.g. observation, interview or questionnaire). The data collection method we adopt will depend on the nature of the observations we need to make (Chapter 1). What is critical is that the method of data collection produces reliable, valid and meaningful data.

Since the experimental design relies on detecting differences over time and differences between groups it is critical that we have measures that accurately and reliably reflect change. We must be confident that measured change is real rather than just an artifact of poor methods of information collection.

The need to achieve high reliability does not point us to a single data collection method. The reliability of a method will depend on what data are being collected and on the skill of the person collecting them. In some cases we will achieve much better information by watching people than by asking them highly structured questions. Sometimes a less structured questionnaire that enables an interviewer to probe and follow up responses might be more effective than a highly structured one.

As well as yielding reliable data our data collection method must produce valid information: we must be measuring what we think we are. There is little use in collecting reliable data that are wrong. There is little merit in collecting data using very reliable instruments on, say, level of racial prejudice if the method of data collection is getting people to express socially desirable views rather than their real views.

Problems with randomized assignment

The practice of randomly assigning participants is one of the distinguishing characteristics of experimental design. For a number of reasons, however, random assignment does not necessarily achieve its goal of ensuring that the experimental and control groups are initially comparable.

LIMITS OF RANDOM ALLOCATION

Choosing a small sample can impede achieving comparability of experimental and control groups. For example, randomly assigning a sample of 10 people into two groups of five people each may easily result in dissimilar groups. As the size of the total sample increases the average characteristics of the experimental and control groups should converge. Where the sample size cannot be increased, the randomized block design can be used to ensure equivalence on specified characteristics. However, with large groups there can still be important differences between the groups on variables with low variability despite randomized assignment (Cook and Campbell, 1979: 342).

GATEKEEPERS AND THREATS TO RANDOM ALLOCATION

Random assignment can be difficult to achieve in field settings where practical realities may require negotiating with authorities and other 'gatekeepers' who control access to potential participants. Among the gatekeepers the researcher is likely to come across are school principals, managers of organizations, and professional welfare workers. Gatekeepers can cause problems by insisting on allocating people to groups themselves or by undermining the research by poor implementation. They might, for example, allocate the 'most deserving' to desirable treatment groups. Ideally the researcher should allocate people to groups but, where this is not possible, close scrutiny of those doing the allocation is required.

CONTROL GROUP RESENTMENT

If people believe that they are in a control group they can feel badly done by. The resentment that results can lead to a high dropout and produce a control group that differs in important ways from the experimental group (e.g. more negative). These perceptions, rather than the effect of any interventions, could be responsible for any final outcome differences between the groups.

One solution is to disguise the fact of being in the control group by using a 'placebo' – i.e. an irrelevant treatment. In drug research the placebo might be a sugar pill. In social research it might be a treatment that is known not to affect the outcome variables and is thus safe to use. Alternatively, we can assure control group participants that they can have the desirable treatments, should they wish, at the conclusion of the experiment.

REFUSALS TO PARTICIPATE IN THE INTERVENTION

A comparable problem can arise when people allocated to a given treatment refuse to participate because the treatment is seen to be undesirable. Dropout at this point would mean that despite initial random allocation the groups could be different *before* the intervention.

This problem can be avoided by postponing random allocation to groups (Cook and Campbell, 1979: 358). Having recruited participants we can ascertain their willingness to participate in the control or any one of a number of different experimental treatments. We could then eliminate from the study participants who were unwilling to participate in any particular group. Then we could randomly allocate the remaining willing participants to the various groups.

DROPOUTS

Since experimental designs examine change over time they face the danger of differential dropout from different groups (e.g. the less desirable interventions). This differential dropout could be responsible for any post-test group differences (see earlier in this chapter). This can be a serious problem in long term, field based social research. Furthermore, even where the dropout rate is much the same across all groups, the dropouts may differ significantly from those who remain in the experiment, thus threatening the external validity of the study.

A key thing to check for is whether dropouts are distinctive in relation to their initial scores on the outcome variable. For example, are those with low initial scores on the outcome variable more prone than others to drop out either before, during or after the experimental intervention? If they are more likely to withdraw then differential dropout rate between groups could be responsible for post-test differences. If participants with low scores drop out this will automatically boost the average score of the group, even if the intervention itself did not produce the boost in scores.

Apart from minimizing dropout the next best thing is to identify the characteristics of those who drop out and then adjust for these characteristics at the data analysis stage. We can use the information collected at the pre-test stage to help identify these dropout characteristics and then include these variables in a multivariate analysis to see if group differences would have emerged if there was no differential dropout.

Unevenness of interventions

In field based experimental social research both political and practical considerations reduce our degree of control over the intervention. When we rely on a variety of people to implement an intervention (e.g. a different person might be responsible for carrying out an intervention in different organizations) we may not be able to ensure that the intervention is consistently or properly implemented. When the intervention is unevenly carried out we do not necessarily have a good test of the impact of the intended intervention.

As far as possible the investigator should maintain tight control of the way in which interventions are implemented. Without this we cannot be confident what intervention has actually taken place and we may thus have difficulties making sense of the data.

The self-fulfilling prophecy

In any research there is always the danger that the researcher's expectations and values will inadvertently distort the way he or she collects and interprets information. For example, if we expect that a particular teaching method might improve the level of children's classroom cooperation we might 'see' more cooperation than if we did not hold this belief. A researcher's expectations can affect what they see, how they interpret it and how hard they look for evidence contrary to their expectations.

In drug experiments this problem is minimized by using a 'double-blind' approach. Neither the participant nor the investigator knows which drug or placebo is being administered to which participants. But this solution is rarely available in social research. Because of the operation of the ethical principle of informed consent (see later in this chapter) it can be difficult to use placebo treatments. Similarly, in many social experiments it is very difficult to hide which groups are subject to which intervention.

About the closest we can get to the 'double-blind' approach in social research is to ensure that the person collecting the data is unaware of the research hypotheses. But even if this condition is achieved the researcher's values and beliefs can distort what they see and how they report what they see.

We can take two approaches that can reduce the danger of only seeing what we want to see. One is to develop clear operational definitions and research protocols that reduce distortion of observations and interpretations. The second is to use multiple 'judges' and observers so that the different observers can act as a check on one another. By using multiple observers we can identify the extent to which the patterns are observer dependent.

Ethical issues

Regardless of the research design, social research should conform to four broad ethical principles (Kimmel, 1988; Homan, 1991).

Voluntary participation

A well-established principle of social research is that people should not be required or led to believe that they are required to participate in a study. Furthermore, participants should know they can withdraw from the study at any point. We should avoid people gaining the impression from the *context* in which the request is made that participation is required. In situations where there is a 'captive audience' and where there is a power differential between the researcher and the potential experimental participants (e.g. first-year psychology class, welfare recipients at a welfare agency) the researcher needs to be especially careful to stress that participation is truly voluntary.

The surest way of ensuring that people understand that participation is voluntary is to explicitly tell them. For example, at the beginning of a study participants can be told

> 'Although your participation in this study will be greatly valued, you are not required to participate. You can stop at any point or choose not to answer any particular question. Just let the interviewer know.'

Voluntary participation can produce a number of problems. It can threaten the external validity of the experiment. Since certain types of people (e.g. those with lower levels of education, those from non-English-speaking backgrounds, older people) are more likely than others to decline to participate in studies, voluntary participation can produce biased samples. It can also threaten the internal validity if we get differential dropout in the experimental and control groups (see earlier section on problems with randomization). In addition, if voluntary participation leads to high dropout rates it can lead to too few cases for meaningful analysis.

However, compulsion is not the answer. Although compulsion might reduce sample bias, unwilling participants can undermine the quality of data in a study. Since we can statistically adjust for known sample biases it is best to maximize the quality of responses and encourage voluntary participation.

It is better to *encourage* rather than require people to participate in studies. There are two main ways of doing this. One is to appeal to people's altruism by pointing to the study's possible benefits. People are remarkably generous and willing to participate in studies where they believe it will do some good. However, in our enthusiasm to recruit participants we must avoid 'false advertising' which overstates the benefits. Second, we can appeal to people's self-interest – how participation can benefit them. We might offer rewards for participating or at least compensate for their time and any costs they might incur by participating. Some studies provide token gifts and offer to provide participants with a summary of the main findings.

Informed consent

Informed consent is a close cousin of voluntary participation. Typically participants should be informed about:

1 the purpose of the study and its basic procedures
2 the identity of the researcher and the sponsor
3 the use to which the data might be put.

They should also be provided with the following:

4 an outline of reasonably foreseeable risks, embarrassment or discomfort
5 a description of the likely benefits of the study
6 a description of how they were selected
7 an offer to answer any questions
8 a statement that participation is voluntary, that each participant is free to withdraw at any time or to decline to answer any particular question.

While the issue of informed consent seems entirely reasonable and desirable it is not always straightforward. *How much* information should we provide before a participant can be considered informed? How *fully* informed should participants be? What does it mean to be informed? Providing more information need not mean that people will be any better informed. Simply providing detailed descriptions of the study does not mean that respondents will be any more enlightened as a result. Indeed, detailed technical information may confuse, distract and overwhelm rather than inform.

Furthermore, providing details about the study – especially detailed information about the study design, about the hypotheses and theories we are testing – can distort the way people answer questions and undermine the validity of the findings.

One solution is to provide basic information and to offer to answer further questions. If this information could distort the way people behave we can tactfully explain that this is a concern and offer to deal with the questions *after* the experiment is over. In some psychological research participants are deliberately deceived since accurate knowledge would invalidate the study (Homan, 1991: 96ff). Where this is warranted it is critical that participants be fully debriefed after the study.

This raises the question of when consent should be obtained. Most ethics committees[2] require that consent be obtained *before* participation. However, a case can be made that participants do not really know what they are agreeing to until they have participated, and that they can only provide *informed* consent *after* they have participated.

Who should give consent? Who should give permission in research of young children, the intellectually disabled and others who may not be in a position to fully understand the implications of participating in a survey? Participation still ought to be voluntary but consent may need to be obtained from other people such as parents and guardians as well as the participant. In hierarchical organizations gatekeepers may grant permission for junior people to participate and thus, in some sense, oblige junior people to participate. In such situations we should ensure that we gain consent from both the gatekeepers and the actual participants.

No harm to participants

In some experimental studies participants are potentially exposed to harm. For example, in medical experiments in which a new drug is trialled, participants are potentially endangered. In psychological experiments participants might be given stimuli or be induced to behave in ways that they later regret and find distressing.[3]

Where there is any danger of harm to participants the principle of informed consent requires that participants be told of the dangers before participating in the experiment. Where there is potential for harm and the person still agrees to participate there is the need for careful debriefing after the experiment. Depending on the type of potential harm there may be the need for long term follow-up to ensure that any potentially harmful side effects are monitored.

Unlike other designs, many experimental designs involve the investigator actively doing something potentially harmful to the participants. While it should be obvious that we must not subject people to potentially harmful interventions, it seems reasonable to set up experiments where the interventions will benefit the participants. For example the guaranteed income experiments described in Chapter 4 could be justified because the intervention of providing a guaranteed income would only benefit participants (Hakim, 1986: 102).

However, the argument that an intervention will be beneficial presumes that we know the outcomes of the intervention. We may *believe* that income maintenance will, at worst, be harmless, but *we do not know this ahead of time*. Even with the best of intentions there can be unintended harmful effects. There is also the issue of 'beneficial to whom?'. Hakim (1986) notes that the income maintenance experiments led to an increase in divorce, as some women became financially more secure. This *may* have benefited the women but the husbands (and children) may have held very different views.

When there are perceived benefits to participating in an experiment (e.g. an income maintenance experiment, medical trials) we may face the opposite problem – that of *withholding* a beneficial treatment from the control group. Is it fair to deny some people the potential benefit of the treatment? Random allocation can reduce some of the ethical problems in this regard. We can also undertake to provide the control group with access to the treatment once we know it has been successful (or a modification of the treatment on the basis of what was learned from the experiment).

Anonymity and confidentiality

An obvious way in which participants can be harmed is by failure to honour promises of confidentiality. People participating in experiments are entitled to expect that they cannot be identified as the source of any particular information. Frequently, social science experiments entail the collecting of personal information which, if made public, could be embarrassing or humiliating or cause harm to participants in one way or another.

It is essential therefore that information be collected in such a way that confidentiality can be guaranteed. It is also essential that the people involved in collecting, analysing and reporting the findings respect scrupulously the confidentiality requirements.

In order to protect participants, data must be stored in such a way as to preclude any unauthorized access. This may mean storing data in locked cabinets and removing all identifying information. If the data are stored electronically then passwords and encryption can help ensure privacy. It is highly desirable that personal identifying details and the responses relating to participants be kept separately. Information about a person's name and address should be stored in one file and all their answers to questions should be stored in a different file. Identification numbers for cross-referencing must be stored in such a way that only authorized people can make the matching.

Providing assurances of confidentiality is important for methodological as well as ethical reasons. If participants are confident that their responses are truly confidential (or even better if they are anonymous) we can expect that people are more likely to participate in the study – especially if it is about private matters. We can also expect that if a person feels that their answers are truly confidential they will be more likely to provide frank and honest answers.

One should not make promises of confidentiality unless they can be kept. In a study of school children you might learn of the identity of a drug pusher or a teacher who is sexually molesting students. In a study of prisoners you might learn of plans for an escape or of the identity of a person who murdered an inmate. In such cases you face the problem of weighing your promise of confidentiality against the harm caused to others by respecting that promise. Make sure that you do not make unrealistic promises of confidentiality.

In promising confidentiality be aware of the legal ramifications of your promise. Depending on the context in which data are collected, they may be subject to freedom of information legislation. In many countries research data collected with the guarantee of confidentiality do not enjoy legal privilege and could be subpoenaed by courts. Given such a situation it is important to clarify your rights to maintain the confidentiality of data when working in government agencies or under a contract. Contracts frequently make explicit statements about the ownership of data and it is important to ensure that these provisions do not compromise your undertakings regarding confidentiality.

Summary

Experimental designs are valuable for isolating the causal impact of specific variables. This is especially the case when they are conducted in highly controlled environments. The structure of the design, especially the use of good control groups, helps maximize the internal validity of experimental research. However, the artificiality of such research and the narrowness of the designs often mean that, for social science research, experimental designs yield only limited information that frequently has poor external validity. This chapter has discussed some of the threats to internal and external validity of research and has outlined the ways in which experimental designs overcome these threats. In social science research practical and ethical matters also mean that experimental designs often cannot be used. This chapter has outlined these practical and ethical issues.

Notes

1 These weaknesses of randomization are most evident with simple experimental designs in which there is only one independent variable. They can be reduced somewhat in more complex experimental designs that include several independent variables (see discussion on factorial designs in Chapter 4).

2 Most institutions (e.g. hospitals, universities, research organizations, government departments) have institutional ethics committees which must approve projects from an ethics perspective before funding is released for the study.

3 The Milgram experiments on obedience are classic examples of this. See Baumrind (1964) and Milgram (1964).

6

ANALYSING EXPERIMENTAL DATA

There are a large number of statistical techniques that can be used for analysing experimental data. The purpose of this chapter is to provide some guidance in selecting from among these many different ways of analysing experimental data.

The core of experimental analysis is the *comparison of groups*. Do groups that differ in terms of the independent variable also differ on the dependent variable? Do groups that have different 'treatments' perform differently on the outcome variable? In a well-designed experiment the only difference between the groups should be the different 'treatments' to which they are exposed. The more we can be sure that our groups are similar except in terms of the independent variable (intervention) the more we can be confident that the group differences on the outcome variable are due to the intervention.

In making comparisons three things need to be stressed.

1   The comparison focuses on *groups* – not individuals.
2   We need ways of working out how much difference there needs to be between experimental and control groups before we attribute any importance to the differences. For instance, we might observe small but important differences or we might observe substantial differences that might be simply due to sampling and measurement error.
3   We compare groups in terms of the outcome variable.

Selecting the method of analysis

There are so many techniques for analysing experimental data. The range of techniques is because of the range of types of variables and diverse forms of the data that are collected. To analyse experimental data we need to match the method of analysis to the characteristics of the data.

What kind of analysis is required: description or inference?

Statistical analysis serves two main purposes: description and inference. Descriptive statistics summarize patterns in a *sample* while inferential statistics establish if the findings for a sample can be extrapolated to the wider *population* from which the sample is drawn. For example, we might find among members of the sample that people who are unemployed have worse health than employed people. How likely is it that the same link between unemployment and health would be found in the wider population that the sample is meant to represent? Inferential statistics provide a way of estimating whether sample patterns will hold in the wider population.

Ideally, analysis should involve both descriptive and inferential analysis. We should carefully describe the extent of any differences between groups and then work out whether any differences are likely to be found in the wider population.

What sort of sample do we have?

Inferential statistics can only be used to generalize findings if a *probability sample* is used. A probability sample is one of two broad types of samples. The other is a non-probability sample. A probability sample is one in which each person has an equal or at least known chance (probability) of being selected. The surest way of obtaining such a sample is to randomly select sample members from a known and defined population.

When we have a probability sample we can only legitimately generalize to the specific population from which the sample is drawn. A probability sample of a country which systematically excluded people aged under 18, those without telephones or those living in institutions would yield findings that could only be generalized to the population of non-institutionalized adults with a telephone. If an experiment is based on a probability sample of students in a first-year psychology class in a particular university then we can only confidently generalize to this population (unless we can demonstrate that these first-year psychology students at the particular university are representative of some wider population).

If we do not have a probability sample there is little point in using inferential statistics to generalize to some wider population. We should limit ourselves to descriptive statistics that summarize patterns in that sample. Many researchers are unable to recruit random samples. Nevertheless they continue to use inferential statistics inappropriately in their analysis. Where probability samples are not feasible the most appropriate way to test for generalizability is to repeat the experiment in different contexts and with different samples.

What level of data do we have?

In statistical analysis the *level of measurement* of variables is critical in selecting particular statistical analysis. There are three main levels at which variables are measured: interval/ratio (also called continuous), ordinal and nominal (also called categorical or qualitative). These can be best explained with three examples.

INTERVAL/RATIO VARIABLES

An interval/ratio variable is one in which the categories can be ranked from *low to high* in some meaningful way. In addition to ordering the categories from low to high it is possible to specify the *amount of difference* between the categories. Age, when measured in years, is an example of an interval variable. We can rank order the categories of age (years) from youngest (lowest) to oldest (highest). Furthermore, we can specify the amount of difference between the categories. The difference between the category '20 years old' and the category '25 years old' is 5 years. Variables such as the weekly number of hours of paid work, IQ, height, weight, income (in dollars) are all variables where the categories are numeric and where the intervals between the categories can be specified precisely.

ORDINAL VARIABLES

An ordinal variable is one where we can rank order categories from low to high. However, we cannot specify in numeric terms *how much* difference there is between the categories. For example, when the variable age has categories such as 'child', 'adolescent', 'young adult', 'middle aged', and 'elderly' the variable is measured at the ordinal level. The categories can be ordered from youngest to eldest but we cannot specify precisely the age gap between people in different categories. If we measured level of workforce participation as full time, part time and not in the labour force this variable would be an ordinal variable. If we asked the precise number of hours worked each week the variable (hours of work) would be measured at the interval level.

NOMINAL VARIABLES

A nominal variable is one where the different categories have no set rank order. With a nominal variable it makes no sense to say that the categories can be ordered from low to high in some sense. Religious affiliation is a nominal variable where we can distinguish between categories of affiliation (e.g. Jewish, Roman Catholic, Orthodox, Protestant, Islamic, no religion). These categories have no natural rank *order*.

When selecting a method of data analysis we must first identify the level of measurement of each of the variables in our analysis. To work out the level of measurement of any variable, ask the questions in Table 6.1.

In selecting appropriate methods of analysis the level of measurement of *both* the grouping variable (independent or intervention) and the

Table 6.1   *Determining the level of measurement of variables*

| | Level of measurement | | |
	Nominal	Ordinal	Interval/ratio
Are there different categories?	Yes	Yes	Yes
Can I rank the categories from low to high?	No	Yes	Yes
Can I specify the amount of difference between the categories?	No	No	Yes

outcome variable are relevant. The selection of particular methods will depend (in part) on the combination of levels of measurement across the two variables and on which variable (dependent or independent) is at which level of measurement. Figures 6.5 to 6.8 demonstrate how this affects the choice of statistical methods.

Type of comparisons required?

Groups are compared in terms of the outcome variable. These comparisons might examine the amount of pre-test and post-test *change* in the experimental and control groups or the absolute differences between the groups at the post-test stage. There are different aspects of the outcome variable that can form the focus of the comparisons.

DIFFERENCES IN CENTRAL TENDENCY

Groups can be compared in terms of their averages on the outcome variable. Different types of averages (mean, median or mode) can be used depending on the level of measurement of the outcome variable.

The most widely used comparison technique is to compare the means of groups, but this requires that the outcome variable is measured at the interval level (see below). At the descriptive level this simply requires comparing the means. However, these differences in the sample may not hold in the population: they may simply be the result of sampling error. We could use an inferential statistical technique to work out whether the difference between the means is likely to reflect a real difference in the population or is simply due to chance (sampling error). To do this we could use a technique such as a *t*-test, an *F*-test or analysis of variance.

Unfortunately, averages can hide important information. For example, we can get identical averages between two groups yet the two groups can differ sharply. The example in Figure 6.1 illustrates this point. In this example the experimental and control groups are identical at time 1. Each person in both groups achieved an identical score on the outcome variable (5) and the average for each group was 5. At time 2 the control group remains unchanged and maintained an average score of 5. How-

Case	A	B	C	D	E	F	G	H	I	J	Average (mean)
Time 1	Score on outcome variable										
Control group	5	5	5	5	5	5	5	5	5	5	5
Experimental group	5	5	5	5	5	5	5	5	5	5	5
Time 2	Score on outcome variable										
Control group	5	5	5	5	5	5	5	5	5	5	5
Experimental group	0	0	0	0	0	10	10	10	10	10	5

Figure 6.1   *Problems with comparing averages*

ever, the experimental group has changed a great deal. All individuals have changed: half have much lower scores and half have higher scores. However, the average score for this experimental group remains at 5. The averages of the two groups at time 2 remain the same. Consequently, a simple comparison of the two averages without looking at other elements of the distributions would lead to a false conclusion that the intervention had no effect, since the averages reflected neither change nor differences between experimental and control groups.

DIFFERENCES IN VARIABILITY

An alternative way of comparing groups is to measure the degree of diversity within each of the groups. Are some groups more uniform than others? Do some groups change to become more uniform or less uniform than others? The impact of an intervention may be not to increase the scores overall but to make a group more uniform or more diverse (as in Figure 6.1). There are statistical measures such as range, variance and standard deviation that provide summaries of the degree of uniformity (homogeneity) in groups and there are tests which measure whether the levels of homogeneity in groups differ. Graphical techniques such as histograms and box and whisker plots can also be used to examine whether groups are equally diverse. Which tests of variation are used in part depends on the level of measurement of the variables concerned.

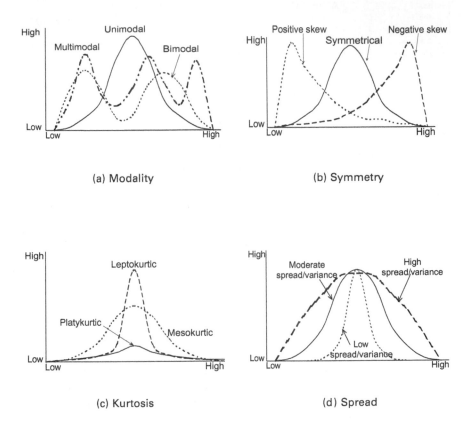

Figure 6.2   *Shapes of distributions*

SHAPE

The impact of an intervention may be seen in its effect on the *shape* of the
scores on the outcome variable. Comparisons of group homogeneity are
one form of comparing shapes of distributions. Other aspects of the
shape of a distribution can also form the basis of group comparisons and
reveal the impact of an intervention.

Apart from comparing the degree of sameness or difference within a
group we can also compare the distributions using other dimensions of
the shape of a distribution. These different dimensions are illustrated in
Figure 6.2.

- *Modality* Distributions can be unimodal, bimodal, or multimodal (Figure 6.2a). An experimental intervention might change a unimodal distribution to a multimodal distribution.
- *Symmetry* Distributions of ordinal or interval variables can be symmetrical or skewed (Figure 6.2b). Skewed distributions can be positive (cases clustering around the low end of the outcome variable or negative (cases clustering around the higher end of the outcome variable. An intervention might change the symmetry of the distribution.
- *Kurtosis* Distributions can vary in terms of how clustered they are around the centre of the distribution. This is called the kurtosis Figure 6.2c. The distribution can be very clustered or peaked (leptokurtic), bell-shaped (mesokurtic) or fairly flat (platykurtic).

These different ways of thinking about distributions all provide different ways of examining the impact of an intervention on an outcome variable. Rather than focusing narrowly on the impact on the average score of a group we can look at other dimensions of the outcome variable to detect an effect.

PROPORTIONS

Another approach to comparing groups, best used for categorical (nominal) outcome variables or variables with few categories, is to compare the proportion or the percentage from each group giving a particular response.

For example, imagine that we wanted to examine the effect on university course completion rates of different methods of delivery of a course. We examine completion rates of those who are taught in face-to-face situations with those who take their course over the internet. We might find that in the face-to-face group 75 per cent successfully completed compared to 60 per cent of the members of the internet group. These percentages provide a description of the different outcomes in the two groups (descriptive statistics). We could then undertake an analysis that would tell us whether these differences between the groups (75 per cent and 60 per cent) are likely to be due to chance or whether they are likely to reflect real differences in the population from which the sample was drawn (inferential statistics). In the example just provided, the two-samples test for difference between proportions would fulfil this function (Loether and McTavish, 1974a: 189ff).

ASSOCIATION BETWEEN VARIABLES

Groups also can be compared usefully by examining the association or correlation between variables. Statistical measures of association test the extent to which two variables co-vary. When we say that gender and income are associated we mean that knowing someone's gender helps predict their income better than if we did not know their gender.

A simple experimental design has two variables – the intervention variable (independent variable) and the outcome variable. If the intervention has an effect on the outcome variable then the two variables – the intervention and the outcome – will be associated statistically. That is, if those people in the group that received the intervention (experimental group) scored differently on the outcome variable than those who did not receive the intervention, the two variables – intervention and outcome – would be statistically associated. Such an association can be displayed using cross-tabulations, graphs or statistical summaries such as correlation coefficient.

In addition to describing the extent to which there is an association between the experimental intervention and the outcome, we should use an inferential statistic to determine whether the association is likely to hold in the wider population. Different inferential tests have been developed for different correlation coefficients.

What type of display is required?

Since the purpose of analysis in experiments is to compare groups, we must decide how to *show* any group differences. Our choice is between using tables, graphs or summary statistics. Which one(s) we choose will depend partly on the audience and the complexity of the data.

The three forms of displaying results can be illustrated with an example. Suppose we had an experiment examining the impact of different forms of rewards on workplace productivity. The three experimental conditions would be: (1) standard fixed rates of pay regardless of productivity, (2) a productivity bonus for the whole group at the end of the year depending on group output, (3) individual productivity bonuses depending on the individual's productivity. The outcome variable would be the percentage change in the productivity of each individual.

Examples of tabular, graphical and statistical methods of displaying results are illustrated below.

Tabular

Table 6.2 provides an example of how results from a study might be presented in tabular form. In this example the degree of productivity change is reported for each of the three bonus schemes. The cells in the table indicate the number of people from each bonus scheme exhibiting various levels of productivity change. To look for differences in the effect of the three bonus schemes we need to look at the pattern and spread of numbers for each of the three schemes.

Table 6.2 *Productivity change according to incentive scheme*

% change in productivity	Fixed rate group (no.)	Group bonus group (no.)	Individual bonus group (no.)
100 or more	–	2	7
75 to 100	–	5	1
50 to 74	–	6	2
25 to 49	2	10	1
1 to 24	5	6	14
No change	19	3	1
–1 to –24	5	1	2
–25 to –50	2	–	5
–50 or less	–	–	–
N	33	33	33

GRAPHICAL/CHART

When deciding to display data with a graph we must also decide which type of graph to use. In Figure 6.3 just three of many possible graphical displays are provided: histograms, stem and leaf plots and box and whisker plots. All three graphs are based on the same data and provide different ways of thinking about and visualizing the distributions.

SUMMARY STATISTICS

Alternatively, we could avoid the use of tables and graphs altogether and simply demonstrate group differences by using averages, percentages or some other form of statistical summary. Figure 6.4 provides a set of summary statistics in relation to productivity change in the three groups. This is a comprehensive statistical description of the changes in the three groups. However, much of the same *picture* can be gleaned from the graphs and table.

How many groups are to be compared?

Another determinant of the way we analyse our data is the *number of groups* we compare. Some statistical techniques are limited to comparisons of two groups (e.g. *t*-test) while others are appropriate for multiple groups (e.g. *F*-ratios and analysis of variance). Some correlation coefficients are designed for a small number of groups (Kendall's tau, eta) while others are appropriate for independent variables with a large number of categories. Similarly, the appropriateness of tabular and graphical display techniques will depend on the number of groups in the analysis.

ONE-GROUP COMPARISONS WITH A KNOWN VALUE

The simplest form of comparison is where we have only one group and we wish to compare the results in this group with a known value. These methods of analysis are referred to as *one-sample* designs.

(a) Histograms

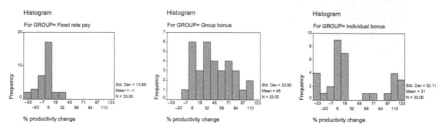

(b) Stem and leaf plots

```
% productivity change Stem and Leaf Plot for:
GROUP= Fixed rate pay
Frequency      Stem &  Leaf
    5.00 Extremes   (=<-17)
    1.00          -0 .  9
     .00          -0 .
    2.00          -0 .  45
    3.00          -0 .  223
    1.00          -0 .  1
   10.00           0 .  0000000001
    2.00           0 .  23
    3.00           0 .  445
     .00           0 .
    2.00           0 .  89
    4.00 Extremes   (>=17)
GROUP= Group bonus
Frequency      Stem &  Leaf
    1.00          -0 .  0
   19.00           0 .  0000111222233333444
   11.00           0 .  55667778899
    2.00           1 .  03
GROUP= Individual bonus
Frequency      Stem &  Leaf
    7.00          -0 .  0123334
   16.00           0 .  0000000111112222
    3.00           0 .  569
    7.00           1 .  0111122
```

(c) Box and whisker plots

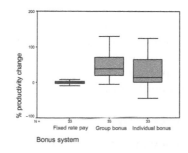

Figure 6.3   *Graphical representations of productivity changes by bonus system*

Descriptives

Bonus system			Statistic	Std. Error
% productivity change	Fixed rate pay	Mean	−.5455	2.3769
		Median	.0000	
		Variance	186.443	
		Std. Deviation	13.6544	
		Minimum	−30.00	
		Maximum	30.00	
		Range	60.00	
		Interquartile Range	7.5000	
		Skewness	−.161	.409
		Kurtosis	1.078	.798
	Group bonus	Mean	45.4848	5.9012
		Median	39.0000	
		Variance	1149.195	
		Std. Deviation	33.8998	
		Minimum	−5.00	
		Maximum	130.00	
		Range	135.00	
		Interquartile Range	53.0000	
		Skewness	.567	.409
		Kurtosis	−.261	.798
	Individual bonus	Mean	31.1515	9.0712
		Median	14.0000	
		Variance	2715.445	
		Std. Deviation	52.1099	
		Minimum	−45.00	
		Maximum	125.00	
		Range	170.00	
		Interquartile Range	79.5000	
		Skewness	.679	.409
		Kurtosis	−.822	.798

Figure 6.4 *Summary statistics: productivity change by bonus scheme*

Say for example we wanted to establish what connection there was, if any, between having a child with a disability and the likelihood of the child's parents divorcing. Let us suppose that we know that the national divorce rate in any one year for couples with a child in the household is 12 per 1000 married couples. We then find from our research that in a sample of families in which there was a child with a serious disability the divorce rate was 14 per 1000. The rate of 14 for the disability sample is certainly higher than the national overall figure, but is the difference likely to reflect a real difference or simply be due to sampling error? An inferential statistic can answer this question. The same logic of comparing a single sample group with a known comparison figure can be applied to analysis in which we focus on the mean, proportion or variance of a single group (see Loether and McTavish, 1974a: Chapter 7).

Two groups

The classic experimental design comprises two groups – the experimental group and the control group. In experimental designs with an interval level outcome variable the *t*-test is used to establish the statistical significance of intergroup differences. It indicates whether the difference between the means of the two groups is likely to be due to chance or whether it reflects true differences in the population. The use of this test depends somewhat on the distribution of the variable (see below). Other tests, such as the critical ratio, can be used to establish the significance of group differences for large samples where the assumption of normality is not satisfied (Mueller et al., 1977: 422).

There is nothing about the logic of the experimental design that restricts us to interval level outcome variables. Where there are only two groups and the outcome variable is either nominal or ordinal we might use a measure of association as a summary statistic to describe the link between group membership and outcome.

Alternatively, we might use cross-tabulations or graphs to display the differences between two groups. If we needed to generalize about whether any such relationship shown in tables or graphs was likely to hold in the wider population we could use an appropriate inferential statistic. *Chi square* is one widely used statistic that is especially useful when outcome variables are measured at the nominal level. This tells us whether the two variables are independent of one another – that is, whether group membership makes any difference to the outcome variable.

Three or more groups

Some experimental designs require three or more comparison groups. For example, we may want to compare a range of interventions as well as having a control group.

When the outcome variable is nominal or ordinal we will largely be restricted to tables, graphs, measures of association and other ways of comparing distributions. These methods are satisfactory so long as there are sufficient numbers of people in each group and there are not too many groups to compare. When there are more than six or seven groups to compare the comparisons can become very difficult.

If the outcome variable is an interval level variable the analysis is most effectively made by comparing the means of the different groups. *A one-way analysis of variance* is frequently used for this purpose.

A one-way analysis of variance will tell us whether there are differences within a set of means. For example, in the earlier illustration of the impact of bonus schemes on productivity there were three groups: fixed rate of pay, group bonus and individual bonus. Let us suppose the results outlined in Table 6.3 were obtained in this study.

Table 6.3 *Mean percentage change in productivity by bonus scheme*

Bonus group	Mean % change in productivity
Fixed rate of pay	-0.55
Group bonus	45.48
Individual bonus	31.15

An analysis of variance may show that, overall, productivity change varies according to group membership. However, the problem with this analysis is that we do not know *which* group differences are important. Fairly clearly both the group bonus and individual bonus groups do better than the fixed pay group, but is the difference between the group and individual bonus systems statistically significant? Could the difference between the 45.48 per cent improvement and 31.15 per cent improvement be simply due to chance?

To find out *which* groups have means that are statistically different from one another we need a multiple comparison procedure. In such a procedure all possible *pairs* of groups are compared and it can be established which pairs of groups, if any, have means that are significantly different from one another. One widely used multiple comparison technique is the Scheffé test.

The Scheffé test gives us an estimate. It does so by looking at the differences in means between the following pairs of groups:

1 fixed pay versus group bonus
2 fixed pay versus individual bonus
3 Group bonus versus individual bonus.

It can be shown that the differences in the first two pairs (fixed pay versus group bonus and fixed pay versus individual bonus) were unlikely to be due to chance. However, the difference between the productivity increases in the group and individual bonus schemes was probably due to chance. This means that if the observed differences in productivity improvement of those with individual bonuses and those with group bonuses is due to chance then essentially the two schemes are equally effective. It does not matter which bonus scheme is used.

Are the comparison groups independent samples?

INDEPENDENT SAMPLES DESIGNS

The simplest and most effective way of making groups initially comparable is to randomly assign individuals to experimental and control groups. This is called an *independent samples design*. Random allocation to experimental and control groups should ensure independence *between* the groups. There should also be independence between cases *within* groups. Since the selection of one sample element should be independent of the selection of every other element, a group consisting of, say, husband and wife pairs does not produce an independent samples design.[1]

PAIRED SAMPLES DESIGNS

In a *paired samples design* groups are made comparable by pairing sample elements rather than simple random allocation. Here the selection of people in one group is not independent of selecting people for other groups. For example, we might have a group of identical twins and assign one twin to the experimental group and the other to the control group. Alternatively, we might simply administer different experimental treatments to the *same* group at different times. By using the same group we theoretically remove any other differences between the groups (except of course later treatments might be contaminated by earlier treatments to the same group). In effect people in one experimental group are paired with themselves for the next treatment.

Some inferential statistics need to take into account the way in which people were allocated to the different experimental conditions. Were they *paired* in some way or were they *randomly* (independently) selected?

Is the dependent variable normally distributed?

Some inferential statistics, called *parametric* statistics, require *interval* level outcome variables that are normally distributed in the population. Unfortunately often either outcome variables are not normally distributed in the population (in the statistical sense) or their population distribution is unknown.

When the outcome variable is not normally distributed or we cannot reasonably assume a normal population distribution we have three main options (Loether and McTavish, 1974a: 268ff).

1 We can 'normalize' the distribution by transforming it (Marsh, 1988: Chapter 11).
2 We can violate the assumption of normality and use the parametric statistic anyway. It is argued that some of these statistics are *robust* and yield very similar results regardless of whether their assumptions are met.
3 We can use a *non-parametric* statistic that does not assume a normal distribution.

How can we tell whether the outcome variable is normally distributed in the population? Given a sample of sufficient size a line graph or a histogram can give a visual idea of whether the distribution is a bell-shaped, unimodal distribution. A normal curve will also have a skewness of 0 (i.e. symmetrical) and a kurtosis of 3 (i.e. mesokurtic) (Loether and McTavish, 1974b: 162). When the sample is small (e.g. less than 50) and is not randomly drawn from the population, and its population distribution is unknown, the safest strategy is to use either non-parametric statistics or a robust parametric statistic.

Is the variance on the dependent variable similar between each comparison group?

Group comparisons can be usefully executed by comparing the typical response for each group. However, comparisons of what is typical can be invalidated if the groups have very different variances. Comparing the means of groups with very different variances makes it difficult to establish whether any differences in means are due to differences in central tendency or not (Loether and McTavish, 1974a: 176).

Some statistical techniques require that we establish that the variance in the (two) groups is similar. This is particularly important for *t*-tests of differences between the means. In the case of *t*-tests there are different forms of the test depending on whether there is equality of variances between the groups. Most statistical packages include statistical techniques to test for this condition.

How many independent variables?

The simplest experimental designs have just one independent variable. However, many designs include several independent variables. Factorial and Solomon four-group designs examine the impact of each of the experimental variables on the outcome variable. They also identify the impact of interactions between these independent variables on the outcome variable. In field experiments where random allocation is not possible we need to estimate and statistically remove the effect of known group differences so that we can examine the 'pure' effect of the experimental variable.

When multiple independent variables are used the analysis strategy will depend on:

- the level of measurement of all the variables (both independent and dependent)
- whether we want to examine the *relative impact* of each independent variable (including interaction effects) or
- whether we want to look at the effect of a single independent variable with the effect of other variables controlled.

INDEPENDENT IMPACT OF MULTIPLE INDEPENDENT VARIABLES

When a design uses multiple independent variables and an interval level outcome variable, *two-way* or *factorial analysis of variance* is a common method of analysis This method enables the investigator to look at the impact of each independent variable with the effects of the other independent variables removed. That is, the analysis can isolate the 'pure' effect of each independent variable and each possible interaction effect.

This approach can be illustrated by employing a chemical analogy in which there are three chemicals A, B and C. The question is, 'What is the corrosive effect of these three chemicals on steel?' We could look at the effect of chemical A alone, chemical B alone and chemical C alone. We might also want to know what happens when we combine the three chemicals in different ways: A with B; A with C; B with C; and A, B and C combined. Factorial analysis of variance enables us to answer these sorts of questions.

Multiple regression is another approach employed for analysis involving an interval level outcome variable and multiple independent variables. Multiple regression provides a way of examining the effect of each independent variable minus the effect of every other independent variable, and of the interactions between the independent variables. Where the *independent* variables are not measured at the interval level (normal multiple regression analysis assumes that all the variables are measured at the interval level) we can use a modified form of regression analysis called *dummy variables* (see de Vaus, 1996).

If the *dependent* variable is nominal or ordinal in character, analysis of variance or standard regression analysis cannot be used. There are, however, other forms of regression analysis such as logistic regression that can be used for these situations.

REMOVING THE EFFECTS OF OTHER VARIABLES

If we are interested in the effect of just one independent variable we may need to statistically remove the effects of other group differences on the outcome variable. Analysis of variance and regression achieve this. However, with nominal and ordinal outcome variables we can also use cross-tabulations to remove the effect of 'contaminating' variables. To do this we would use elaboration analysis (see pp. 203–210). There is insufficient space to describe this approach here, but clear explanations are readily available (Rosenberg, 1968; Johnson, 1977). Another way of removing the confounding effects of other variables is to use an average partial table (Loether and McTavish, 1974b: 290).

Summary process for selecting the right measure

Figures 6.5 through 6.8 are designed to help you select an appropriate form of statistical analysis given different types of experimental situations

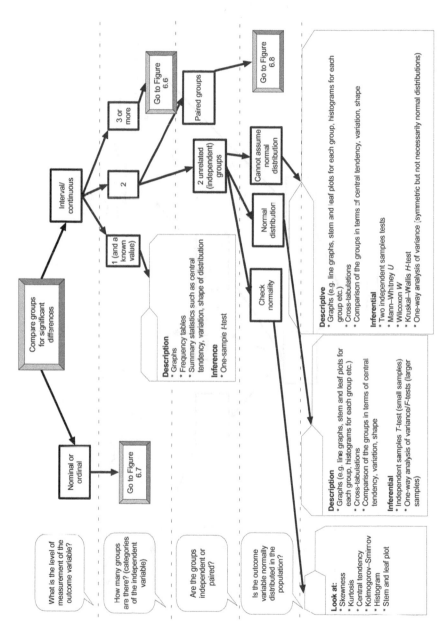

Figure 6.5   *Selecting statistical methods of analysis, part 1*

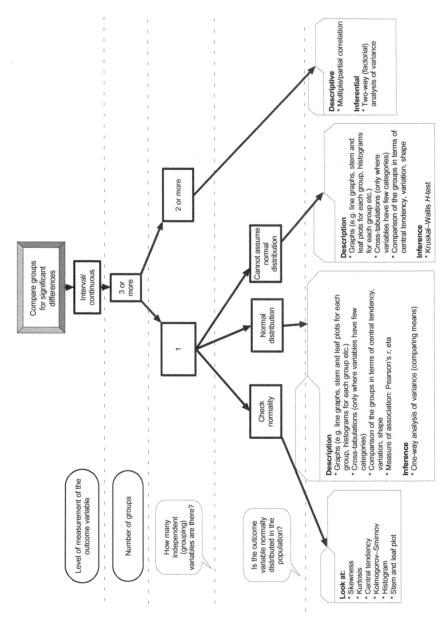

Figure 6.6   *Selecting statistical methods of analysis, part 2*

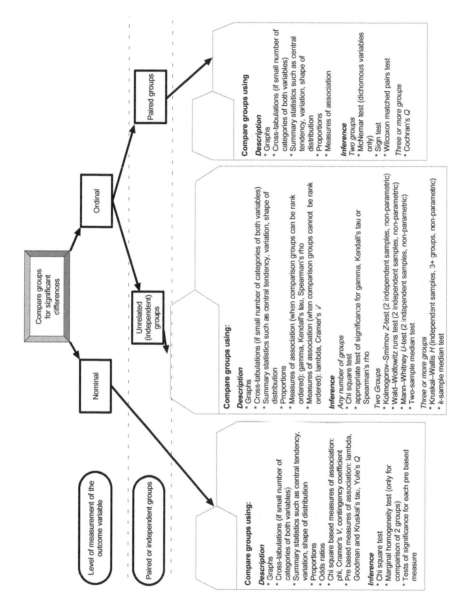

Compare groups for significant differences

Level of measurement of the outcome variable

Paired or independent groups

Nominal — Ordinal — Unrelated (independent) groups — Paired groups

Compare groups using:

Description
* Graphs
* Cross-tabulations (if small number of categories of both variables)
* Summary statistics such as central tendency, variation, shape of distribution
* Proportions
* Odds ratios
* Chi square based measures of association: phi, Cramer's V, contingency coefficient
* Pre based measures of association: lambda, Goodman and Kruskal's tau, Yule's Q

Inference
* Chi square test
* Marginal homogeneity test (only for comparison of 2 groups)
* Tests of significance for each pre based measure

Compare groups using:

Description
* Graphs
* Cross-tabulations (if small number of categories of both variables)
* Summary statistics such as central tendency, variation, shape of distribution
* Proportions
* Measures of association (when comparison groups can be rank ordered): gamma, Kendall's tau, Spearman's rho
* Measures of association (when comparison groups cannot be rank ordered): lambda, Cramer's V

Inference
Any number of groups
* Chi square test
* appropriate test of significance for gamma, Kendall's tau or Spearman's rho

Two Groups
* Kolmogorov–Smirnov Z-test (2 independent samples, non-parametric)
* Wald–Wolfowitz runs test (2 independent samples, non-parametric)
* Mann–Whitney U-test (2 independent samples, non-parametric)
* Two-sample median test

Three or more groups
* Kruskal–Wallis H (independent samples, 3+ groups, non-parametric)
* k-sample median test

Compare groups using

Description
* Graphs
* Cross-tabulations (if small number of categories of both variables)
* Summary statistics such as central tendency, variation, shape of distribution
* Proportions
* Measures of association

Inference
Two groups
* McNemar test (dichomous variables only)
* Sign test
* Wilcoxon matched pairs test

Three or more groups
* Cochran's Q

Figure 6.7   Selecting statistical methods of analysis, part 3

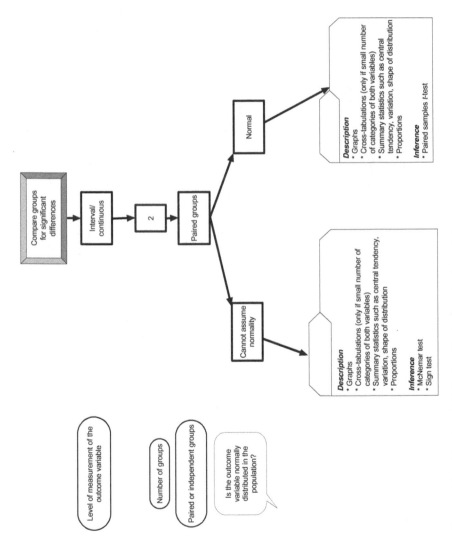

Figure 6.8   *Selecting statistical methods of analysis, part 4*

and different types of data. These figures cannot cover all possibilities but provide guidance for a fair range of typical situations. Most of these statistics are easily computed using packages such as SPSS or SAS.

TEN QUESTIONS

Selecting the appropriate method of analysis essentially involves asking a series of questions:

1 What sort of sample do you have?
   • Probability.
   • Non-probability.
2 What is the level of measurement of the outcome variable?
   • Nominal.
   • Ordinal.
   • Interval.
3 How many groups are you comparing?
   • One (against a known standard).
   • Two.
   • Three or more.
4 How were people allocated to each group?
   • Are samples (groups) independent?
   • Are the samples (groups) paired or matched in some way?
5 How is the outcome variable distributed in the population?
   • Normal.
   • Not normal or cannot assume normality.
6 Do the groups have similar variance on the outcome variable?
   • Equal variance.
   • Unequal variance.
7 What group comparisons are required?
   • Central tendency.
   • Variability/shape.
   • Proportions.
   • Association.
8 What type of way do you want to display your comparisons between groups?
   • Tabular.
   • Graphical.
   • Use of summarizing statistics.
   • Mixture.
9 How many independent variables do you have?
   • One.
   • Two or more.
10 Are you mainly concerned with description or inference?
   • Describe patterns in the sample?
   • Generalize from the sample?
   • Both.

Not all these questions are appropriate in all circumstances. Some are appropriate depending on how earlier questions are answered (e.g. if you do not have a probability sample then you cannot use statistical inference and will thus be restricted to description).

Other issues

Change scores

The logic of the classic experimental design would lead us to use change scores. When we have a pre-test we can examine how much each group changes on the outcome measure before and after the intervention. Since we recognize that the control group may also exhibit change due to factors such as maturation we would simply hypothesize that change will be greater in the experimental group than in the control group. For example:

Experimental group: $T_1 = 100$ $T_2 = 120$ change score = 20
Control group: $T_1 = 100$ $T_2 = 105$ change score = 5

We can then undertake an analysis of variance to see if this degree of difference in change scores (20 compared to 5) could have occurred due to chance (sampling error). If the difference could be due to sampling error we would assume that there would be no difference in the population from which the sample was drawn.

There are several problems with using simple change scores to detect change and these will be discussed in Chapter 9.

Truncation effects (floor and ceiling effects)

In designs where scores for a group cluster around the top or bottom end of a scale (i.e. the measure of the outcome variable) we must remember that change can only be detected in one direction. This fact can introduce a bias in the nature of the observed change.

For example, we may use a 0 to 10 scale to measure happiness where a score of 0 indicates unhappiness. Suppose that we had people in our groups that scored 0, i.e. were at the extreme of unhappiness *as measured by our scale*. However, if these people became even unhappier over time there is no way of detecting this with our measure. Such people would be identified as not changing. We could only identify people who became happier. The same thing would apply to those who scored 10. We could only detect those who became less happy.

Even those who are not at the extreme end of a scale but are near the end present a problem. For example, although the person who obtains a score of 1 in the pre-test can go lower (they can get a 0) they cannot change to the same *extent* as someone who obtained an initial score of say

3 or 4. If the analysis measures degree of change rather than simply change *per se* the 'floor' of the scale can lead us to underestimate the degree of change.

This is a problem with many measures that have upper and lower limits. It introduces a bias in terms of the type of change that we can measure at the individual level (see Chapter 9) and thus can underestimate the extent of change and wrongly estimate the direction of change overall.

It is difficult to deal with this problem of data drawn from scales with strict upper and lower limits at the analysis stage. The problem of truncation effects is best handled at the design stage where we need to ensure that our measures are designed in such a way that people are not clustered at one end of a scale. We should employ measures that have high ceilings and low floors and where people do not cluster toward either end.

Trend analysis

In order to identify short term and long term effects (see Chapter 4) some experimental designs require multiple before and after measures. These designs can present particular problems of analysis and can involve quite complex analyses if we are trying to compare two trends (as opposed to say two means). There is a range of what are called time series analysis methods that are beyond the scope of this book.

However, a useful initial approach to analysing these sorts of data is to draw simple line graphs. These may or may not reveal a clear long or short term effect or indicate that the intervention has no distinctive effect (Figure 6.9). The pattern in the experimental group(s) can then be compared with that of a control group.

The difficulty, however, is that with multiple observations the patterns are frequently not as clear-cut as those in Figure 6.9. We can observe differences at different time points simply due to chance and measurement error. The problem then becomes one of what constitutes a real difference between different time series lines. This issue is too large to be dealt with definitively here. If you plan to do this type of analysis ensure that you obtain good statistical advice before undertaking the analysis.

Summary

This chapter has examined the logic of the analysis of experimental data. For the most part the basic logic is that of comparing groups in relation to how each group performs on the outcome variable. The basis of the comparison can be averages, whole distributions, variance or many other characteristics of distributions. There is a bewildering array of statistics that are available for the analysis of experimental data. In order to assist

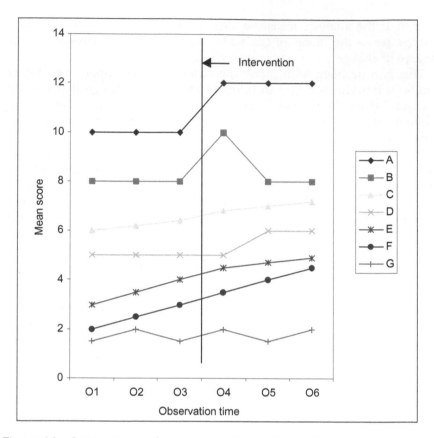

Figure 6.9   *Some outcomes of an experimental variable on a time series*

with the selection of the appropriate statistics this chapter has outlined the main considerations that need to be taken into account when selecting the particular method of comparison. Finally, since experimental designs normally involve the analysis of change the chapter discussed a number of issues about the measurement of change: the use of change scores, truncation effects and trend analysis. Further problems with measuring change will be considered in Chapter 9.

Note

1 This is true if individuals are the units of analysis in the experiment. If the couple was the unit of analysis then having the couple would not violate the requirements for independence.

PART III

LONGITUDINAL DESIGNS

7

TYPES OF LONGITUDINAL DESIGN

You will find a wide variety of longitudinal designs in the literature. However, they all share the common goals of measuring change over time and of doing so by collecting data concerning at least two time points. In both respects they are similar to the classic experimental design that has a pre-test and a post-test. However, longitudinal designs do not typically have a randomized control group.[1]

Developing longitudinal designs involves a number of critical decisions. The decisions taken will determine just what type of longitudinal design evolves.

1   *Will the same cases be followed over time?*   Here the choice is between *trend* studies and *panel* studies. Trend studies (or repeated cross-sectional studies) entail collecting information from comparable samples over time but not from the same people. Annual surveys such as the General Social Survey in the US, the British Social Attitudes Survey, the Eurobarometer surveys and the International Social Science Program Surveys are examples of trend studies in which similar questions are asked of a new sample each year. This design allows the tracking of changes in attitudes and behaviour over time. A panel design involves repeated surveys of the same people. This design allows the tracking of change at both the aggregate level and the individual level (see Chapter 9).

2   *Will data be collected at one point of time?*   Although panel designs involve collecting data concerning at least two time points, they do not necessarily require that these data be collected on two different occasions. The *prospective* longitudinal design entails collecting data on several different occasions. In such a design a group of people will

be interviewed, tracked and reinterviewed at least once at some future time. The *retrospective* panel design can entail collecting data on only one occasion. The time and change dimensions to the study are obtained by asking people to recall what things were like at some earlier point of time as well as at the present. In this way we can obtain some indication of the extent to which the person has changed over time.

Longitudinal designs can vary on many other dimensions as well. These include the following:

- *Setting*   The logic of the longitudinal design can be applied in settings ranging from the highly controlled laboratory situation, smaller scale groups (e.g. school classes, parts of an organization) to large scale national surveys.
- *Time scale*   The gap over which change can be measured can vary from a very short period (e.g. a before and after measure of attitudes after seeing a film) to many years. The National Child Development Study is an example of a long term panel survey. The study began in 1958 and included all children born in Britain between 3 and 9 March. These children have been tracked and involved in subsequent follow-up data collections in 1965, 1969, 1974, 1981, 1991 and 2000.
- *Number of time points*   Longitudinal studies will vary in terms of how many times information is collected from the same set of people in a panel study or different sets of people as in a trend study. The famous '7-up' TV programme, which has followed a group of children over a long period to see what changes have taken place in their lives, is an excellent example of a panel design. It commenced with children who were seven years old and has revisited the children every seven years since. These children are now in their 40s. The British Household Panel Survey provides an example of a panel study with more frequent data collections. It revisits its national sample every year.
- *Planned interventions*   Longitudinal surveys will also vary in terms of whether they involve planned 'interventions' or whether they rely on observing the results of naturally occurring events. Where there are planned interventions the longitudinal design is similar to the classic experimental design except that there will be no randomized control group.

Purposes of longitudinal design

Describing patterns of change and stability

The purpose of longitudinal designs can vary from the descriptive to the explanatory. As a descriptive tool the value of the longitudinal design resides in the fact that it enables us to examine change or stability. Used in this way a longitudinal study can reveal a great deal about the direction of change at a societal, organizational or individual level.

Establishing temporal order

Causal analysis entails establishing the temporal order of events. This is necessary because a basic tenet of causal reasoning is that a cause must precede its effect in time. In cross-sectional research where all data are collected at one point of time it can be difficult to establish the order in which events occur (see Chapter 10). However, longitudinal designs, particularly prospective designs, enable tracking the order in which events take place. For example, a cross-sectional study might establish a correlation between unemployment and mental health but would have difficulty establishing whether unemployment affected mental health or vice versa. A longitudinal design, however, could measure the mental health of a sample of employed people and then see what changes to mental health, if any, occur among those that subsequently become unemployed. Alternatively, we could study unemployed people and observe changes in mental health among those that get a job.

Establishing developmental (age) effects

In certain studies of change it can be difficult to establish what sort of change occurs. For example, age and political conservatism are correlated: political conservatism is more pronounced among older people than among younger people. However, this correlation in itself does not explain the link. Is it, for example, because people become more conservative as they grow older, or does the correlation reflect something about the era in which the older people grew up and formed their political views? For example, the economic insecurity experienced by the generation growing up during the Great Depression of the 1930s may be responsible for the political conservatism of the older generation.

Then again, the conservatism of older people may be due to a *developmental* effect: people may become more conservative as they grow older. They may become less adventurous, need greater certainty or become more sceptical of those who promise that change will bring a better world. The only reliable way to establish whether political conservatism is the result of a developmental effect is to track the same individuals over time and see if they change as they age.

Establishing historical (period) effects

There is a problem with adopting a tracking strategy. If we track a group of young people over time and observe that they become more conservative we cannot be sure that the change in attitudes is the result of

Table 7.1   *Age cohorts over time*

Cohort	Age in 1980	Age in 1990	Age in 2000
Born 1920–9	51–60	61–70	71–80
Born 1930–9	41–50	51–60	61–70
Born 1940–9	31–40	41–50	51–60
Born 1950–9	21–30	31–40	41–50
Born 1960–9	11–20	21–30	31–40

growing older. Everyone in the society, regardless of age, might be becoming more conservative.

What it is necessary to do to answer our question is to track different age groups over time. Doing this would enable us to look at ageing or developmental effects. Table 7.1 represents the way in which we could track a range of age cohorts over time. For each age cohort (those born in a specified period) we could look at any changes in political conservatism over the 20-year period (1980–2000). If *each* cohort grew more conservative over the 20-year period and if they did so at the same rate we could conclude that the change to a more conservative position is a *developmental* effect. That is, growing older results in people becoming more politically conservative.

In this example, Table 7.2 shows that each cohort becomes more conservative by 10 points each decade. Furthermore, regardless of the decade, people aged 51–60 have a conservatism score of 50. In other words, regardless of the period or time in history, people of a given age obtain a particular level of conservatism. Furthermore, all cohorts display a similar level of change that is independent of the particular historical period. Quite simply, time, not historical period, produces change.

Had only one cohort been tracked (e.g. those born in the 1950s) we would have observed that as they grew older they became more conservative. However, we would not know whether this was because of ageing or because this particular cohort was somehow distinctive and became more conservative because of some peculiar effect of growing up in the 1960s and 1970s. To distinguish between developmental (ageing) effects and historical (cohort/period) effects we need to examine multiple cohorts over time. In some ways having multiple cohorts is comparable to using an experimental design where the control group provides a point of comparison to help interpret changes in the experimental group.

If the cohorts did not become more conservative as they grew older this would indicate the absence of a developmental effect. However, in Table 7.3 conservatism scores depend on when people were born. Those born in 1920–9 obtained a conservatism score of 50 in 1980 and *remained* that conservative through 1990 and 2000. Those born in the 1960s obtained a conservatism score of 10 in 1980 and *remained* at that level

Table 7.2 *Development effects: changes in political conservatism from 1980 to 2000 by age cohort*

Cohort	Age group in 1980	Conservatism score	Age group in 1990	Conservatism score	Age group in 2000	Conservatism score
Born 1920–9	51–60	50	61–70	60	71–80	70
Born 1930–9	41–50	40	51–60	50	61–70	60
Born 1940–9	31–40	30	41–50	40	51–60	50
Born 1950–9	21–30	20	31–40	30	41–50	40
Born 1960–9	11–20	10	21–30	20	31–40	30

Table 7.3 *Period effects: changes in political conservatism from 1980 to 2000 by age cohort*

Cohort	Age group in 1980	Conservatism score	Age group in 1990	Conservatism score	Age group in 2000	Conservatism score
Born 1920–9	51–60	50	61–70	50	71–80	50
Born 1930–9	41–50	40	51–60	40	61–70	40
Born 1940–9	31–40	30	41–50	30	51–60	30
Born 1950–9	21–30	20	31–40	20	41–50	20
Born 1960–9	11–20	10	21–30	10	31–40	10

through 1990 and 2000. Differences in the conservatism of the age groups in, say, 2000 is because of *period* effects rather than because some people are older. The older group in 2000 has 'always' been more conservative.

Life course 'career' analysis

Longitudinal studies can help researchers study 'careers' (Menard, 1991: 15). At a purely descriptive level we frequently do not know how various 'careers' develop. Obtaining an accurate sequence of the way 'careers' unfold can be crucial in developing sensible explanations of these careers. For example, in the 'career' of a drug user what is the sequence of events? Do people start off using soft drugs and go on to hard drugs, or is there no progression? Do people mix with drug users and then begin to use drugs, or does drug use lead to participation in a drug subculture? Understanding the order of events is critical to understanding the pathways into drug use and developing intervention strategies.

Work histories can be tracked with longitudinal studies. We might look at the age at which people move in and out of the workforce, and the types of job changes they make, and plot this history onto other events such as life stage events including marriage, having children, divorce.

Types of longitudinal design

Prospective panel designs

SIMPLE PROSPECTIVE PANEL DESIGN

This simple design (Figure 7.1) requires the collection of data at two points of time from the same sample. We may make an active intervention or we might simply observe the effect of naturally occurring events between time 1 and time 2.

The simple prospective panel design is very much like the top row of the classic experimental design (Figure 4.2). That is, the design has an 'experimental group' in which change can be measured. However, the design lacks a randomized control group, which produces the problem of not knowing whether any change is due to any 'intervention' by the researcher, the elapse of time or some other influence.

The problem of not having a control group can be alleviated somewhat where a sufficiently large and diverse sample is used in the study. Such a sample allows us to determine if, over time, some people experience 'interventions' while others do not. Adopting this approach can produce comparison groups that provide a useful, but limited, way of examining the effect of specified 'interventions'. For example, we may be interested in establishing whether or not having children leads to an increase in the gendered division of labour in the home. We would begin with a sample

Figure 7.1 *Simple prospective panel design*

of childless couples and observe the extent to which men and women share the domestic work. We could track changes over a period of time during which some couples would have children while others would not. We could then group the sample into those who became parents and those who remained childless and see whether those who became parents showed a greater move towards a gendered division of labour. We may find that the parents did adopt a more gendered division of labour.

The problem with this approach, however, is that it does not take into account the fact that the two groups may be different in many ways – not just parenthood (e.g. age, ethnicity, level of workforce participation). Because we have not controlled for these possible differences we cannot be sure what is responsible for the final differences in the division of labour. However, if our sample is sufficiently large and diverse and we collect the relevant information we can statistically remove the impact of known differences between the groups and at least eliminate some of the alternative explanations for the group differences.

MULTIPLE POINT PROSPECTIVE PANEL DESIGN

This design is similar to the simple two-point design but simply involves more data collection points (Figure 7.2).

We might have specific interventions between any set of data collection points or simply collect information about relevant intervening events between each measurement point. Theoretical considerations and previous research would affect what are considered 'relevant' intervening events.

Like the simple panel design this multiple point design requires sufficient variation in the initial group and sufficient diversity in intervening experiences to enable us to construct comparison groups in the analysis stage.

The purpose of multiple data collection points is to:

- examine long and short term effects
- track when changes occur (e.g. in 'career' analysis)
- plot the 'shape' of any change
- identify factors that precede any change (or non-change).

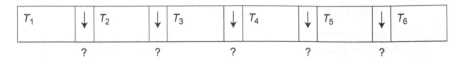

Figure 7.2   *Multiple point prospective panel design*

For example, we may wish to track the way in which marriages change over time. We could look at these changes along any number of dimensions such as levels of intimacy, who exercises power, the way in which domestic labour is shared, happiness, levels of conflict and so forth. We could track changes in these aspects of the relationship from when a couple begins to live together and at regular intervals thereafter – say every two years. We would also find out about other changes occurring between our tracking visits (e.g. level of workforce partici-pation, birth of children, new people such as a parent or parent-in-law joining the household, or changed economic circumstances).

If we wanted to explore the effect of having a child on marital happiness we could, by tracking couples regularly over a long period, distinguish between short, medium and long term effects. We could see the ups and downs that a two-point design simply would not permit.

SINGLE PANEL DESIGN WITHOUT REPLACEMENT

Whether or not a simple two-point (pre-test, post-test) or a multiple point design is used, a decision will need to be made about what to do concerning dropouts. The more points at which data are collected and the longer the duration of a study, the more dropouts become a problem.

Figure 7.3 illustrates a panel design without replacement. There are two key problems with this design. One is that in a multipoint study the cumulative dropout of respondents can result in an unacceptably small final sample. The other is that the final sample can become unrepresen-tative and thus threaten external validity. Unrepresentativeness stems from two sources: first, the people who drop out are normally different in particular ways from those who remain in the study; second, in many populations new members join and old members depart. Even if the original panel remains representative of the population as it was *when the panel was first recruited*, as the population itself changes it may become unrepresentative.

SINGLE PANEL DESIGN WITH REPLACEMENT

One way of addressing these problems is to employ some form of replacement for sample dropouts and to include new types of members of the population. In this way sample size and, hopefully, representa-tiveness are maintained. This type of design is illustrated in Figure 7.4.

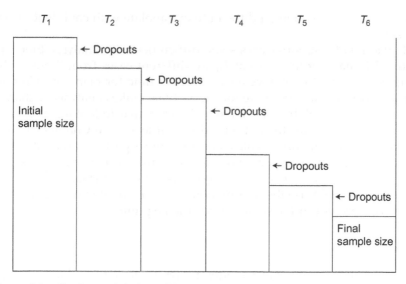

Figure 7.3   *Single panel design without replacement*

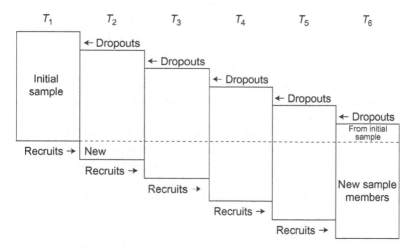

Figure 7.4   *Single panel design with replacement*

Over time, and depending on the level of dropout, the panel will become composed increasingly of different individuals to those who were initially selected. Whether the panel maintains the initial representativeness depends on the method of replacement. Given that people do not drop out randomly, recruits should be matched, where possible, with dropouts. This can be done at a broad level by ensuring that replacements are of the same age, sex, race and class. However, such matching will always be less than perfect and will lead to a loss of randomness, thus making it difficult to extrapolate with confidence from the sample.

Replacement also introduces some difficulties with analysis. Since, in Figure 7.4, many of the cases at T_6 are different cases from those in the sample at T_1, we do not have measures over time for many individuals. This absence of data over time for individuals makes analysis of change *at the individual level* difficult. We may be restricted to looking at change at an aggregate rather than at an individual level (see Chapter 9). This can be overcome in part by collecting some retrospective information for some variables (see below). We can also use certain procedures to estimate what we are likely to have been like at earlier stages. To achieve this end we would use the information we have about similar cases that have been present in the sample from the beginning.

ROTATING PANEL DESIGN

This is a further design that provides a more systematic and randomized way of dealing with sample dropout and in so doing maximizes the external validity of the design. It is called a rotating panel design.

This design is widely used in studies that require frequent measures. Labour force surveys provide such an example. Panel data of this kind enable the researcher to see what happens to the employment patterns of an *individual* (e.g. how long it takes to find work, efforts to find work, movements in and out of jobs etc.) at frequent intervals (e.g. monthly). The rotating panel design also minimizes the problem of dropout (and the consequent problems with representativeness) and burnout (demanding too much of the same people).

With a rotating panel design a series of panels is established. Each panel begins at a different time but overlaps temporarily with at least some of the other panels. Essentially a set of panels is created that have staggered starting and finishing times. But the same information is collected from each panel. The logic of this design is illustrated in Figure 7.5.

In this example the first panel (row 1) is retested each month for six months. After this panel has commenced another panel begins a month later and is followed through for six months. Testing of the second panel will be completed a month after the first panel. A number of staggered panels can be run simultaneously.

Each *panel* has a limited life, so hopefully participants are not exhausted people. However, the *study* can extend indefinitely. By tracking a particular panel individual change can be studied over that period. Consequently, we obtain a series of short term panel studies. By maintaining the study over a very long period, albeit with different cases, aggregate change over time can be studied.

The advantage of having overlapping panels is that at any point of time the information from all the panels can be pooled for cross-sectional

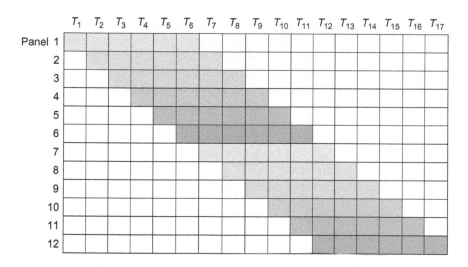

Figure 7.5   *Rotating panel design*

analysis (see Part IV). The particular advantage of this approach is that it enables the researcher to increase the sample size and thus minimize sample error. By providing a large pooled sample the design also provides more cases of hard to find groups (e.g. lone mothers). In labour force surveys the precision of sample estimates can be particularly important. So, the advantages of pooling the panels for cross-sectional analysis cannot be overemphasized.

By employing a series of overlapping panels the researcher can smooth out the impact of factors such as dropout and panel conditioning (see Chapter 8). Even though panel 1 will suffer some dropout and conditioning after the first data collection, the impact of these factors can be assessed by comparing estimates from the second panel that will not be subject to the effects of dropout or conditioning. The same logic applies at T_3 and throughout. Since fresh samples are being obtained continually the effects of burnout and dropout in the older panels can be adjusted for. Furthermore, in any cross-sectional analysis of the pooled samples the inclusion of newer panels can moderate the biasing effects of dropout.

SINGLE COHORT DESIGN

In all the panel designs discussed so far a single cohort could be used. Using a single cohort involves selecting a group of similarly aged people at one point of time and following it over an extended period. They might consist of people born in a particular year, the class of 2000 or those who had their first child in 2001.

The problem with using a single cohort, as identified earlier, is that it is impossible to tell whether this change in the group is because the group is getting older or because everyone is changing. Suppose that a study on the sexual behaviour and knowledge of a group of 20 year olds commenced in 1980. The study collected information about matters such as the level of sexual activity, number of partners and knowledge and practice of safe sex. Had these 20 year olds been tracked over the next 15 years the study probably would have found that these young people became more moderate and 'conservative' sexually with the passage of time. For example, the study would probably find that over time these young people had less sex with fewer people and adopted safer sex practices.

To what is this change to be attributed? Is it simply a matter of getting older? It might partly be that: as people grow older they settle down with one partner. But it could also be due to historical effects. During the historical period in which they are growing older, AIDS is discovered. This discovery gives rise to numerous media campaigns designed to change sexual practices. It is impossible to tell how much the change is due to ageing effects and how much is due to period effects unless changes among a range of age groups are simultaneously examined. Multiple cohort designs overcome this problem.

MULTIPLE COHORT DESIGN

The main feature of the multiple cohort design is the spread of cohorts. This spread permits comparisons between cohorts and thus helps distinguish between ageing and period effects.

It is not necessary to establish separate cohorts at the beginning of a study. So long as the sample has a sufficient diversity of age groups the cohorts can be established subsequently at the data analysis stage.

COHORT SEQUENTIAL DESIGN

A less common but potentially powerful design is one that uses multiple cohorts and has a form of panel renewal over time (Figure 7.6). One of the shortcomings of the panel design is that if the panel lasts for an extended period the whole panel ages and the panel will not include younger people. Consequently, as the panel ages nothing is learned about contemporary young people. For example, we might conduct a longitudinal study of ageing. We want to know what is it like to grow old. How do older people think about ageing and mortality? Do people's views, experiences, perceptions and fears change as they grow older? We have plenty of time to track changes and decide to include cohorts who, in the year 2000, are aged 50, 55, 60, 65, 70 and 75. We can afford to track people through to the year 2025. Since we have different cohorts we can compare changing attitudes between the cohorts. The problem is that by

Years of surveys

Age in 2000	2000	2005	2010	2015	2020	2025
25	–	–	–	–	–	50
30	–	–	–	–	50	55
35	–	–	–	50	55	60
40	–	–	50	55	60	65
45	–	50	55	60	65	70
50	50	55	60	65	70	75
55	55	60	65	70	75	–
60	60	65	70	75	–	–
65	65	70	75	–	–	–
70	70	75	–	–	–	–
75	75	–	–	–	–	–

Figure 7.6   *Cohort sequential panel design*

the year 2005 those who were 50 year olds in 2000 are now 55 years old. The sample can tell us nothing about the new 50 year olds: those who turn 50 in 2005.

The distinctive aspect of the cohort sequential design is that over time cohorts drop out of the study. This is similar in ways to the panels in the rotating panel design except that it is cohorts that are replaced rather than whole panels. In the example in Figure 7.6 we drop a cohort after they reach the age of 75.

As the oldest cohort drops out of the study they are replaced with a new, young (50 year old) cohort. This new cohort in effect substitutes for what at the first stage was the youngest cohort.

This design enables us to do three things:

1   It enables us, in each five-year survey, to have a new cross-sectional sample of people aged 50, 55, 60, 65, 70 and 75. Each column in Figure 7.6 represents a separate cross-sectional sample. We could analyse

this in the same way as we would analyse any cross-sectional survey (see Chapter 12).

2   Over time we would build up panels for each cohort. We could track through those who were 50 in the year 2000. By the year 2025 we would have tracked this cohort right through. We can do the same thing for those who were older except that the panel for that cohort would run for a shorter time. These panels are represented by each row in Figure 7.6. These panels allow for the standard analysis of individual change. The multiple panels also provide multiple cohorts to explore the effect of ageing as distinct from wider societal changes (see earlier discussion on the advantages of multiple cohort studies).

3   It enables us to plot the changing experience of an age group over time. Because we have rolling cohorts (i.e. we have information on 50 year olds in the year 2000, 2005, 2010, 2015, 2020 and 2025) we can track how the experience of being a 50 year old changes over time. Similarly, we can track what it is like to be 75 years old over time. Does the experience of this age group change over historical time?

Retrospective designs

RETROSPECTIVE PANEL DESIGN

So far all the designs have involved following a sample forward over a period of time. This approach has many advantages as will be shown in Chapter 8. But it also has disadvantages to do with matters such as cost, sample attrition and the delay in obtaining useful data about changes in the sample. The primary advantage of longitudinal designs is that they enable us to establish the sequence of events which, in turn, enables us to make stronger assertions about causal order and causation.

In some studies it is possible to reconstruct data over time by collecting all the information at one point of time. It is possible to reconstruct the degree of change and the sequence of events by asking people to *recall* what happened, and when it happened.

We might, for example, ask people about their current situation or attitudes and then ask them to provide similar material about an earlier point in their lives. We might, for argument's sake, want to know how the birth of a first child affects marital happiness. A retrospective design would ask a sample of people who have had their first child about their current level of marital happiness and ask them to recall how happy they were beforehand. This design is represented diagramatically in Figure 7.7.

The same approach could be applied in the study of the experience of growing older described earlier. We might take a group of 75 year olds and ask them to recall how optimistic they felt about the future when they were 50, 55, 60, 65, 70 and how they currently feel. This design is represented diagramatically in Figure 7.8.

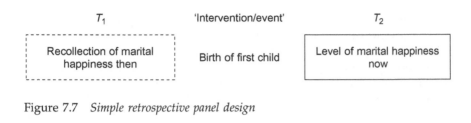

T_1	'Intervention/event'	T_2
Recollection of marital happiness then	Birth of first child	Level of marital happiness now

Figure 7.7   *Simple retrospective panel design*

Age

50	55	60	65	70	75
Recollection of optimism at age 50	Recollection of optimism at age 55	Recollection of optimism at age 60	Recollection of optimism at age 65	Recollection of optimism at age 70	Optimism now at age 75

Figure 7.8   *Multiple point retrospective panel design*

The problems with this sort of design for these sorts of matters are obvious. There will be a great deal of distortion (deliberate and otherwise) in those recollections. Not only will people not be able to recall accurately how they felt, but we know that recollections of past experiences are interpreted in the light of subsequent events and experiences. All that these sorts of designs would tell us is how people construct their past.

But this problem is not grounds to condemn all retrospective studies. When dealing with certain events, quite good and reliable information can be obtained about the sequence of past events – especially if they are significant events in the person's life. From these accounts of the sequence of past events we can reconstruct 'careers' and in so doing solve some of the problems of temporal order so necessary to developing causal explanations.

For example, we might want to examine the influence of family life stage on the workforce participation of women. We can ask women retrospectively about the timing of particular events. We would ask about the timing of their marriage, birth of first child, birth of subsequent children, divorce etc. We could also ask about any changes in levels of workforce participation such as when they entered the workforce, whether and when they left the workforce, any changes in workforce status (part time/full time/casual) or the timing of work (weekend, evening etc.). We could then plot changes in family life stage and changes in workforce participation to help identify the sequence of events. Given that such events are significant events for most people we can reconstruct the temporal order reasonably well and build up a picture of work and family careers for women. The study could also ask these women to recollect why their workforce participation changed at given points. This would provide further insight into any causal links between life stage and workforce participation among women.

This retrospective approach is most reliable when we are dealing with memorable events. Various devices can be used to help people reconstruct the order in which things took place. We can work back from the present to the past or focus on 'anchor events' and then question around these. For example we might ask the questions: 'When was your first child born?', 'Were you working at the time?', 'How much before having the baby did you stop work?', 'Did you go back to work after the baby?', 'How long after was it?'

RECORD LINKAGE DESIGNS

Although a record linkage design is not necessarily a retrospective design it usually is. It is a design where data are collated from official records. Where these records have been collected over time (usually for official purposes) we can construct a temporal sequence of events. In order to implement this type of design we would need to have personal identifiers on the records so that we can make sure that we link records for the same person over time. Examples of such records might be income tax returns, social security records, medical records and police records. By linking these records we can build up a life history or 'career' for that person.

The main shortcoming with a record linking design is the difficulty of obtaining such data. In many countries confidentiality provisions preclude accessing such data. The other main difficulty is that such records typically only collect limited information and may not contain key information necessary for developing an explanation for the sequence of events. Nevertheless record linking can help us accurately map out a temporal sequence of certain events and the nature and extent of changes over time. In this respect these records can help test whether the sequence is at least consistent with our theory.

Quasi-longitudinal designs

All the longitudinal designs described above are panel designs and involve tracking the same people over time. By so doing, changes at both an aggregate and an individual level can be plotted to resolve issues about the sequence of events.

However, panel based longitudinal designs are not the only way of obtaining data over time – at least at the aggregate level. These alternative types of longitudinal designs entail collecting data at different points of time so that changes can be plotted, but these data are collected from different individuals at each time point. When, at each time point, the samples are representative of the population the approach of using different samples at each time point can effectively track changes at the

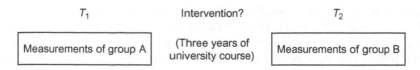

Figure 7.9 *Simulated before–after design*

aggregate level. However, since the data are collected from different individuals this type of design cannot be used to track change at the individual level.

SIMULATED BEFORE–AFTER DESIGN

The simple prospective panel design described earlier entailed measuring a group before an intervention and again afterwards. This design is similar to the classic experimental design but without a control group.

In the *simulated* before–after design, measures are obtained from one group at T_1 and then from a comparable group at T_2 after some event or intervention has taken place. By comparing the two groups after the 'intervention' the impact of the intervention is estimated.

For example, we may be interested in the impact on religious beliefs of attending university. We could establish the impact by measuring the religious beliefs of a sample of first-year and final-year students at the one point of time (i.e. a cross-sectional study). But we would not know whether any differences between first-year and final-year students were due to initial differences (i.e. the final-year students may have been different even when they were first-year students).

The simulated before and after design would entail measuring the religious beliefs of a sample of first-year students when they commenced university. Then, say three or four years later, the religious beliefs of a sample of final-year students would be measured. The two samples would include different people. The pattern of beliefs of the first-year students could be compared with the belief patterns of the sample of final-year students taken four years later.

The simulated before–after design is represented in Figure 7.9.

REPEATED CROSS-SECTIONAL DESIGN

Another way of obtaining data over time that allows us to track change at an aggregate level is the repeated cross-sectional design. This is discussed fully in Chapter 10.

Summary

Longitudinal designs provide a means of tracking change over time and of establishing the sequence in which events take place – an important matter for any causal analysis. This chapter has outlined a range of different ways of constructing a longitudinal study as a means of tracking change. These include prospective and retrospective designs, designs that follow the same people over time (panel studies) and those that look at different people at different time points (trend studies). Within each type of study there are a number of decisions that need to be made about the structure of the study. These include matters such as the setting, the number of times a group is followed up, the overall duration of the study, the gap between waves, the use of active interventions, the way in which attrition is dealt with, and the use of multiple panels. The way in which these various matters are resolved in any particular study results in a variety of different forms of longitudinal design. The main types of longitudinal designs were outlined. Chapter 8 considers some of the strengths and weaknesses of these designs and the issues that need to be considered when implementing longitudinal designs.

Note

1 However, the analysis of longitudinal data will typically create statistical control groups. See Chapter 9.

8

ISSUES IN LONGIDUTINAL DESIGN

A number of the methodological, practical and ethical issues that apply to experimental designs can also apply to longitudinal designs. This chapter focuses on matters that arise most sharply in longitudinal designs, although many of these matters are not unique to this design.

Methodological issues

Issues of internal validity

ABSENCE OF RANDOMIZED CONTROL GROUPS

In the previous chapter I indicated that panel designs are marred by their failure to include randomized control groups. This shortcoming is managed, however, by utilizing variation within the panel to construct groups, at the analysis stage, for comparison purposes. For example, the purpose of a longitudinal study might be to examine the impact of unemployment on the mental health of young people (Graetz, 1993). The initial wave of the study could include both employed and unemployed young people. By the time subsequent waves occur a number of developments will have taken place: some of those who were employed in the first wave will have become unemployed; some unemployed will remain unemployed; some employed will remain employed; and some of the unemployed will have become employed. These four possibilities are illustrated in Table 8.1. The more waves we have, the more varied will be the range of possibilities.

So long as measures of mental health are available for both waves we can get some idea of the impact of employment/unemployment and changes thereof on mental health. The obvious problem is that because the groups are not formed by random assignment they may be different in critical ways other than their employment status. These other differences may be responsible for any differences in mental health outcomes. This problem can be reduced somewhat with multivariate analysis because it allows the researcher to control for known differences between the groups.

Table 8.1 *Creating groups from panel variation*

'Groups'	Wave 1	Wave 2
1	Employed	Employed
2	Unemployed	Unemployed
3	Employed	Unemployed
4	Unemployed	Employed

HISTORY

In any study that extends over time, many events may take place in the world in which people live, and it can be difficult in panel studies to isolate which events are having an impact.

For example, we might want to examine the impact of introducing a scheme where unemployment benefits are only available to unemployed people who engage in unpaid community projects for two days a week. We could measure the work seeking behaviour before the introduction of the scheme and again, say, 12 months later. The problem with this design is that any changes in work seeking behaviour could be due to other events taking place in the 12-month period. For example, the economy might improve and increased job prospects could increase work seeking behaviour. The weather might be better. Unless the impact of all these sorts of factors can be isolated it is difficult to tell how much change in work seeking behaviour is due to the introduction of community work requirements.

MATURATION

Changes can also be due to people simply growing older (developmental effects). For example, a study of the effect of unemployment on the mental health of young people will encounter the problem that late adolescence is a period when mental health problems such as depression and schizophrenia are more likely to develop anyway. If we simply track the incidence of mental health problems among a group of young people who become unemployed we risk overestimating the effect of unemployment on mental health. It is probable that some of the incidence in mental health problems would be due to a common increase in problems in this age group regardless of employment status.

In order to identify any distinctive contribution that becoming unemployed made to mental health we would need to track several groups of young people: those who remained employed; those who became employed; and those who remained unemployed.

TESTING OR PANEL CONDITIONING

Panel conditioning occurs when panel participants respond to questions in ways that are influenced by their previous exposure to the same questions. When people remember how they previously answered questions it may influence the way they respond on subsequent occasions. Participants may respond so that they appear consistent over time. Alternatively, they may respond in a particular way because they have learned to avoid an extended series of follow-up questions. Panel conditioning can contaminate the responses of panel participants and either underestimate or overestimate the degree of real change over time.

Experimental studies can minimize testing problems by avoiding the pre-test stage altogether or by using designs such as the Solomon four-group design (Chaper 4). Unfortunately it is difficult to eliminate this problem when using a prospective panel design since, by definition, at least two tests are required. However, there are some ways of estimating the effect of testing.

One way is to employ either the rotating panel design or the cohort sequential design or other designs that have replacement strategies. These alternative designs provide a means of estimating testing effects. Using these alternative approaches we can compare the responses of new participants or panels with responses of panel members who are similar in all other relevant respects. With these comparisons we can evaluate whether the 'experienced' members are answering questions in a distinctive way.

In some studies that have many waves we also can experiment to estimate the effect of testing. For example, we can vary the frequency with which particular questions are asked. For example, we could ask a particular set of questions of some people in *every* wave but ask the same questions less frequently of other people. By comparing the responses of people who have answered the questions in each wave with those who have been asked the questions irregularly we can estimate the extent of testing effects.

INSTRUMENTATION

In a panel survey changes over time can also be due to changes in the way data are collected in each wave (Chapter 5). Varying question wording, order, interview length, interviewer, methods of collecting data (e.g. face-to-face at wave 1 and telephone at wave 2) can produce apparent but not actual changes in attitudes.

The more the data collection method is open to the subjective interpretations of the people collecting the data, the greater the danger that apparent changes could reflect observer differences rather than changes in that which is being observed. Even where the same observer is involved that person is subject to changes and can be affected by historical and maturational factors. Over time observers may see the same things differently because they, as observers, have changed in some way. There are famous examples in anthropology where different anthropologists have 'seen' the same community in very different ways. Redfield (1930) and Lewis (1951) both conducted ethnographic studies of a Mexican village 20 years apart and 'saw' the community totally differently. Similarly, Mead (1943) and Freeman (1984) both studied Samoans some years apart but observed the culture totally differently. Given the unstructured nature of the anthropologist's methods in these cases it is difficult to be certain to what extent the different observations reflect changes in the communities or simply reflect the different ways the observers interpreted their observations.

MEASUREMENT ERROR

Since a key reason for conducting longitudinal studies is to measure change it is crucial that we observe real change rather than simply measurement error. Using unreliable measurement instruments will cause us to detect 'change' where there really is no change. For example, we might measure a person's level of prejudice at T_1 and again at T_2. If, however, the measure of prejudice is unstable, how can we tell whether any change is due to the unreliable instrument or real change? Equally, if the measure of prejudice is insensitive it may fail to detect change even though there has been change.

Measurement error can lead to serious overestimates of the amount of change at the individual level (i.e. identifying individuals that change). Using unreliable instruments cause many individuals to appear to change at least marginally. In descriptive analysis the problem will not be as pronounced at the aggregate level. If we look at the mean scores of a panel or of subgroups of the panel then the effect of *random* measurement error will be muted. Those who appear to change in one direction will cancel out error caused by people who appear to change in the other direction. For example, in a panel of 1000 people the average score on a measure of prejudice that ranges from 0 to 10 might be 5. If, due to measurement error, 200 people show up as becoming less prejudiced and 200 show up as becoming more prejudiced (and the degree of change in one direction is the same as the other) then the average prejudice score will remain unaffected.

By graphing the change scores one can see if the observed change is due to random measurement error. If the observed change is due to random measurement error the change scores should form a normal distribution each side of no change.

REGRESSION

The concept of statistical regression of extreme scores to less extreme scores over several measurement waves was discussed in Chapter 5. Regression is no less a problem with longitudinal designs than with experimental designs. In other words individuals with extreme scores on wave 1 will tend, at wave 2, to 'regress' to the mean. High scores will tend to get lower and low scores will tend to get higher. When analysis of change is conducted at the *individual* level rather than at the *aggregate* level we will mistakenly attribute some individual changes to an intervention or some other factor when it is simply an artifact of statistical regression. At the aggregate level we should not make this mistake since movement from low to moderate scores will balance movement from high to moderate scores (see discussion of truncation effects in Chapter 6).

In experimental designs it is relatively easy to distinguish change due to statistical regression from change due to other factors. Since both the experimental and the control groups will be equally liable to statistical regression, it will be the *difference* in the level of change (rather than the absolute amount) that will reflect the influence of other factors. In panel studies the absence of strictly comparable control groups makes it more difficult to measure the extent of regression.

Mortality/dropout

The concept of mortality – the differential dropout in the experimental and control groups – was discussed in Chapter 5. Different outcomes for the two groups can be due to differential dropout at some stage between pre-test and post-test rather than the intervention.

The same problem arises in panel studies since dropout will not be consistent for all categories of people. The importance of the problem depends on the particular analysis (comparisons) undertaken. Identifying the biases introduced by the dropout and then statistically removing the effect of such biases can minimize the impact of differential dropout.

Issues of external validity

Panel attrition

A major potential threat to external validity in panel studies is the loss of cases over time (attrition). The longer a panel study exists and the more waves it has, the greater the danger of attrition. Attrition is a threat to external validity because it is not random. Some types of people are more likely to drop out than are others. As dropout is compounded across waves the sample becomes increasingly unrepresentative.

There are several ways of responding to attrition and its threat to external validity. One way is to replace dropouts with people with similar characteristics so that the known biases are redressed. This is more easily said than done. We may not know what biases are introduced by dropout. Also it may not be possible to recruit the appropriate new sample members. If we use replacements then the data for these new recruits will be incomplete, thus limiting analysis to aggregate level analysis (see Chapter 9).

This problem can be addressed by weighting the sample to take account of attrition. Weighting entails statistically boosting the proportion of under-represented groups in the sample so that their proportion reflects their proportion in the population (Chapter 9). If the sample is weighted accurately then it can still provide a useful basis for generalization.

The problems caused by sample attrition also can be addressed by acknowledging the biases exist and accepting that they will affect significantly our capacity to generalize at the descriptive level. However, at the explanatory level bias might not matter. If, for example, a panel study is biased because of the disproportionate dropout of younger people (they move around more and are therefore harder to keep track of over time), this age bias only matters if age is linked to the variables that are being examined. If X affects Y, regardless of age, then the age bias due to attrition does not matter. We can confidently expect that the relationship between X and Y will exist in the wider population, despite the differences in the age profiles of the sample and population.

In those circumstances in which a sample bias which is produced by attrition may affect the patterns we are examining, we need to remove statistically the effect of this bias and see if the relationship between X and Y remains (see Chapters 9 and 12). If the relationship between X and Y remains after removing the effect of any variable on which there is sample bias, we can safely generalize to the wider population despite sample bias.

PANEL CONDITIONING

The earlier discussion on the effects of testing and its implications for internal validity (attributing change to an intervention or other factor when it is really due to simply being studied) also has implications for external validity. If *participation* in a longitudinal study produces change (because it alerts participants to matters they would otherwise not think about) it is difficult to say that changes observed in the study will take place in the wider population.

However, this is more of a problem at the descriptive than at the explanatory level. If participating in a panel study affects the behaviour and attitudes of participants it will make it difficult to generalize from the panel to the population. However, conditioning should not affect the way factors are linked to one another. For example, in order to explore the impact of the breakdown of marriage on the wellbeing of children we might track families who are experiencing marriage breakdown. If being part of the study makes parents and children more alert to matters of adjustment and wellbeing then the levels of adjustment we observe in the study might not be comparable to those among children of marriage breakdown more generally.

However, there is no reason why conditioning should affect the *relationship between variables*. We might want to see if high conflict divorces produce poorer adjustment among children than low conflict divorces. While participation in the study may moderate the level of conflict between divorced parents and may affect the adjustment of children there is no reason why participation will alter the *link* between conflict and adjustment. Even though the absolute levels of conflict and adjustment may not reflect the levels in the wider population of divorces the relationship between conflict and adjustment should remain unaffected. Consequently, *this relationship* can be generalized to the wider population.

In those circumstances where panel conditioning is likely to become a serious problem for the external validity of a study it may be appropriate to use a different design. A repeated cross-sectional design may offer a suitable alternative. A rotating panel design also provides a way of estimating the extent to which conditioning might be affecting results. It does this by comparing results in new panels with those of 'experienced' panels.

Inmigration and outmigration

Panels can become unrepresentative if the population from which the panel is drawn changes. Certain types of people may leave the area where the study is being conducted. As a result the panel may over-represent these leavers (outmigrants). Similarly, new types of people may move in to the area and the panel will consequently under-represent these inmigrants.

Where population changes are creating a substantial problem for the project the solution is to use dynamic samples. Dynamic samples can be achieved in several ways. They are: rotating panel designs; designs that allow for replacement or sample supplementation; and repeated cross-sectional surveys.

If we use dynamic panels we need to be clear about the source of any change in our dependent variables. Changes on the aggregate level in a dynamic panel may reflect one of two things: change in *individuals*, or changes to the composition of the panel. For example, we might be tracking levels of life satisfaction in a particular local region and observe that, over time, the average level of life satisfaction declines. This decline may be due to individuals becoming less satisfied *or* to people who had high levels of life satisfaction leaving the area (and thereby the panel). At the same time people with low levels of satisfaction may move into the area (and thus are recruited into our dynamic panel). Declining aggregate levels of life satisfaction could be due entirely to changes in the composition of the panel and not to changes in the levels of life satisfaction experienced by individuals.

Practical issues

In both the design and execution stages of a longitudinal study there are many practical matters to solve. Some of these are to do with maximizing internal and external validity. Others have more to do with the cost of implementing different designs and the practicalities of getting the study completed.

Standardization of instruments

Since change is the core focus of longitudinal studies we need to be sure that observed change reflects real change rather than changes in the way data are collected. It is essential therefore to standardize the way data are collected for the various waves of the study. It is necessary to standardize the method by which data are collected, the way questions are asked, the order in which they are asked etc. We need to develop clear and consistent rules about what to do in particular situations and religiously follow them. The time of year at which data are collected may need to be consistent for each wave. Busy times, gloomy times of the year, times of stress (e.g. Christmas, end of financial year), vacation time may all affect the kinds of responses we get.

It is not always possible to achieve standardization. The less structured the data collection method the more difficult it is to standardize procedures. Where more qualitative and subjective techniques such as observation and unstructured interviews are called for, the greater the possibility that changes may be due to the people collecting the data and the methods themselves.

Complete standardization is not always desirable. For example, it can interfere with our research goals in life course studies in which people are tracked as they grow older. In longitudinal studies people's circumstances change so we may need to adapt our indicators to reflect such changes. In the same way that the indicators of intelligence are age specific, so our indicators of change may also need to be life stage specific. Measures of family wellbeing and cohesion may well need to be adapted according to the stage in the family life cycle.

In ongoing panel studies there is often a core of standard measures collected in each wave of the study. In addition modules which change from time to time are also frequently included.

Panel attrition

Sample attrition produces problems with both sample size and representativeness and therefore must be minimized.

To minimize attrition we must keep track of panel members. Tracking demands considerable resources. A range of techniques is used to assist with tracking people. Additional information is collected about parents, children or workplace so that if the respondent moves we can contact these other backup contacts to find the respondent. Public records can also be used. Telephone directories, electoral rolls and publicly available records from local councils can help locate respondents who have moved. Of course, it is easier if panel participants tell us they have moved. At each interview and any other contact it is helpful to provide change of address notification cards to participants to mail back to the study managers if they move. Keeping up contact between survey waves is another helpful strategy. A useful tracking device is to send a birthday card to participants. If this card is 'returned to sender' we are alerted to the need to start tracking them down immediately. The card also provides an opportunity to send a change of address card and acts as an acknowledgement of appreciation for participating in the study.

To reduce attrition it is essential to maintain the respondents' motivation to continue to participate in order to reduce attrition. Providing incentives such as money for the time people spend on the study, small tokens of thanks or summaries of key survey results can help achieve this goal. While material incentives can help maintain participation, probably the most effective incentive is for people to feel that their participation is both important and constructive. The more people feel they are participants and partners in research rather than 'subjects' the better. The overriding goal should be to make participation in the study a positive experience rather than an unwelcome burden and intrusion (Dillman, 1978).

Attrition is a bigger problem in some kinds of studies than others. Studies of people who are highly mobile, marginal or members of 'extreme' groups can experience high attrition rates. For example, studies of parents after divorce invariably create the problem of maintaining contact with non-resident parents – especially non-resident fathers. Longitudinal studies of groups such as criminals, drug users and some sorts of unemployed people have very high attrition rates induced by high levels of mobility, illness and death. Panel studies of people experiencing life transitions can also have higher than average attrition rates. Researchers investigating young people becoming adult, young people entering the labour market, people after divorce, or those people who leave the labour force all face the problem that people experiencing these transitions are highly likely to change address. As a result they can be lost to the panel study.

Respondent burden

Panel surveys can impose a considerable burden on participants. This is especially so if each wave of the study is close together or if interviews/questionnaires are lengthy or intrusive. Heavy respondent burden is a problem because it can produce high attrition and a loss of data quality as the burden increases.

There are a number of ways of reducing respondent burden. Some questions do not need to be asked at every wave: every second or third wave may be sufficient for some questions. Alternatively, a set of questions might be asked of only half the panel and a different set of questions put to the other half. Although we have fewer people answering the questions we may still have sufficient numbers for meaningful analysis.

Respondent recall

Retrospective panel designs rely on respondent recall. This has two problems. The first is that people will reconstruct past events in the light of subsequent events. This can result in distortion and reinterpretation by which recalled events bear little resemblance to actual events. For example, a study that asks people who have divorced to describe aspects of their marriage will be affected by the divorce – by the nature of the divorce, who initiated it etc.

The second problem with studies requiring respondent recall is telescoping and reverse telescoping (Menard, 1991). People can misremember and think that events happened more recently than they actually did (telescoping) or longer ago than they really did (reverse telescoping). A number of techniques can be used to reduce this problem. Getting people to focus on certain memorable events and constructing a calendar of these key events can provide anchor points to help remember the sequence of events more accurately. For example, we might be interested in the link between family life stage and the work patterns of mothers. To provide anchor points we could first ask mothers to provide key dates such as the year of their first job, the date of birth of each child and so forth. Since these are likely to be dates that can be accurately remembered we can then, piece by piece, reconstruct how long after these memorable events other, perhaps less memorable, events took place.

Cost

Panel studies are typically much more expensive than a single cross-sectional study. The expense of panel surveys stems from the use of multiple data collections and the cost of tracking and maintaining the panel.

However, if the choice is between say a five-wave panel study and five repeated cross-sectional surveys the cost disadvantage of the panel design is less obvious. There is some evidence (Buck et al., 1995) that the cost of panel maintenance may be no more than the cost of recruiting new samples. Furthermore, the cost of collecting the same background data in each cross-sectional survey will limit the amount of other information that can be collected. In a panel design most background information needs only to be collected once (in the first wave) thus enabling us either to collect extra information in subsequent waves or to reduce the length (and cost) of subsequent data collections.

Ultimately the cost efficiency of the panel design will depend on the difficulty of maintaining the panel – how much time is needed for tracking and the effort required for 'call conversions' (convincing panel members who initially refuse to continue).

The cost will also depend on the method of collecting the data. Of the three main methods of collecting data in panel studies – face-to-face interviews, telephone interviews and self-administered postal questionnaires – face-to-face interviews are the most expensive. However, they tend to yield the best response rates. National panel surveys typically rely on some form of cluster sampling (Moser and Kalton, 1971; de Vaus, 1996) where sets of interviews are concentrated in a number of geographical areas. By this means it is financially feasible to conduct a number of face-to-face interviews in the one area at the same time as maximizing response rates and minimizing attrition.

Over the course of a panel study face-to-face interviews may become less financially feasible. Despite clustering interviews initially, in particular areas high rates of geographical mobility can lead to 'declustering' or scattering of the sample, thus increasing interviewing costs considerably. Fortunately, developments in telephone based interviewing (see next section) can alleviate declustering problems (Buck et al., 1995). However, changing from face-to-face to telephone interviews can introduce instrumentation problems as discussed earlier.

Method of data collection

There is nothing intrinsic in any research design that dictates that the researcher use a particular method of data collection. In principle, data can be collected using structured questionnaires, observation, structured or unstructured interviews or any other method.

However, when it is proposed to utilize a panel design there are real advantages in using computer assisted interviewing techniques. Here there are two alternatives available: computer assisted telephone interviewing (CATI) and computer assisted personal interviewing (CAPI).

There are two advantages to using computer assisted methods in panel designs. First, these designs can involve extremely complex sets of questions, with many questions being relevant to only small subsets of respondents (depending on their characteristics or the patterns of change we have observed). For example, we may require a special module of questions for families that had experienced divorce between waves and require different questions for resident and non-resident parents. With computer assisted interviewing methods all the possible questions are programmed into the interviewing package. On the basis of answers to earlier questions the computer selects which questions the interviewer needs to ask. This simplifies the task of administering complex questionnaires and reduces recording and interviewing errors.

A further advantage of computer assisted interviewing is that in the second and subsequent waves the answers from previous waves for that respondent can be fed into the interview. These can serve as excellent prompts that provide respondents with reminders as to how they have previously responded. For example the CATI or CAPI interviewer can say, 'Last time you said . . .' or 'Last time you indicated that you were planning to retire. Have you actually retired yet?' Not only does this provide respondents with a reminder of how they were feeling last time, but it personalizes the interview and makes the respondent feel that their previous answers have been taken seriously.

Number of waves

The number of waves utilized will partly depend on the purpose of the study. If we are interested simply in 'before' and 'after' a particular event, two waves should be sufficient. If we are trying to track a process of change, multiple waves may be needed. For example, if we simply wanted to know how well people have adapted to retirement, say two years after retirement, two waves may be all that is required. If we wanted to track stages of adaptation to retirement we might require multiple waves to detect the ups and downs of the process (see Chapter 7).

The number of waves will also depend on funding since each wave adds considerably to the cost of the study. Respondent burden must also be considered when planning the number of waves.

Many large scale prospective panel surveys adopt an open ended approach. Funding is available for an initial set of waves and decisions about how long to continue with the panel will depend on the capacity to secure further funding for subsequent waves.

Gap between waves

Setting the gap between waves will be affected by 'political' considerations such as the pressure to come up with some results. The nature and content of the study will also be crucial in setting the gap between waves. Studies of high frequency events or processes of relatively rapid change may require only small gaps between waves. The theoretical model being tested will also dictate the gaps. For example, in a study of adaptation to retirement that anticipated different phases in the retirement transition (e.g. honeymoon in first 3 months; distress by 6 months; rebuilding new identity by 12 months; stabilization by 18 months) the model would dictate the gaps between waves.

Where changes are expected to be gradual there is little point in frequent revisits. The famous '7-UP' series, which tracked a group of people every seven years from the age of seven, is an example of a long term study with large gaps between waves.

In establishing the gap between waves, respondent burden and panel conditioning must be considered. Short gaps can exacerbate these problems. On the other hand long gaps can create tracking problems and increase attrition.

Sample error

Sample error is, in part, a function of sample size. The smaller the sample the greater the chance of sample error. In prospective panel surveys (without replacement) sample error will occur when the initial sample is selected. Subsequent attrition may produce bias and will increase sample error as a result of reduced sample size. If the sample is replenished sample error due to overall sample size will be controlled. However, replacement will be based on new mini samples and these replacement mini samples will be subject to sampling error and can therefore affect the precision with which we can confidently generalize our result beyond the panel.

Sample size

Sample size creates a problem with any type of design. Small samples encounter problems with sampling error and with insufficient cases in special subgroups to allow meaningful analysis.

In studies of change and transitions, for which longitudinal studies are especially useful, the actual number of people in a panel who experience a particular change or transition can be quite small. For example, we might want to use a panel design to examine the effect of divorce on children. If we used a general population panel of households the number of households that actually experience divorce in a given period will be quite small. For example, on the basis of the Australian annual divorce rate of 12 per 1000 couples (i.e. in any given year 12 out of every 1000 married couples will divorce) we would require a very large panel indeed to have enough couples divorcing in a year to allow meaningful analysis. Even if we had a panel of 5000 couples only 60 couples would divorce in a year. If we followed the panel over a five-year period this would increase to something approaching 300 couples. But even this number may constitute too small a sample if we wanted to look at divorcing couples with young children. The numbers would be even smaller if we wanted to look at fathers of such children who had primary responsibility for caring for the children.

Where our interest is in small groups we may need to refine the initial panel more (e.g. just couples with young children rather than a random sample of households). Alternatively it may be possible to oversample certain types of people (e.g. couples with young children) to maximize our chances of obtaining sufficient numbers of people who subsequently experience the changes in which we are interested.

The size of the initial sample will also need to take account of the likely attrition. Since attrition will depend in part on the duration of the study and the number and frequency of waves, the initial panel size will need to take account of estimated attrition rates.

Instrument design

On the first wave of a prospective panel survey we will typically spend quite a bit of time obtaining information such as socio-demographic, household and historical information. This would include such things as year of marriage, age at obtaining first job etc. In subsequent waves we will need to check whether some things have changed (e.g. marital status, any changes to household composition, changes in job etc.).

The design of instruments will vary depending on the method of collecting data. Computerized methods allow for complex questionnaire structures with subgroup modules (see discussion of CATI and CAPI above) while self-administered questionnaires need to be simple. Instrument design will also be affected by decisions about the use of core questions, rotating modules and sets of questions given to only half the sample (see earlier discussion)

Staffing

A longitudinal study will benefit greatly from the employment of well-trained staff who have an ongoing involvement with the study. If a person is interviewed by the same interviewer over time there is more chance of the respondent continuing in the study because of a feeling of commitment to the person as much as to the study (Rose et al., 1991).

A well-conducted panel study will require people who are particularly skilled at convincing panel members who may be inclined to drop out of the study to continue. Persuading panel members who initially refuse to continue in the study is called 'converting' refusals. It takes particular skills to undertake this task successfully without contravening the ethical principles of voluntary and informed consent.

Data management is also critical to the success of a large scale panel study. Skilled data managers who store data, properly match data from successive waves and develop transparent data management protocols are essential. Finally, the analysis of longitudinal data can become very complex and project members who can properly handle the analysis will be important.

Ethical issues

Longitudinal designs confront the same ethical issues as any other design. That is, the matters of voluntary participation, informed consent, no harm to participants and confidentiality/anonymity must be implemented. Since these principles were discussed in Chapter 5 this section simply highlights matters that arise particularly with longitudinal designs.

Voluntary participation

Given the need to minimize panel attrition there is the danger that undue pressure or unethical means are employed to convince people to continue to participate in each wave. As the 'investment' in each person grows as they participate in more waves, the 'cost' of people dropping out increases. Nevertheless, voluntary participation must remain the basis on which people continue to participate.

The question also arises as to what to do with people who refuse to participate in one wave. Should that preclude trying to recruit them again in a subsequent wave? At what point does returning to prior refusers become harassment?

Informed consent

At what point should participants be asked for their consent? In a study that can extend for many years, does consent at the beginning last for the remainder of the study regardless of how many waves it eventually has? Or is informed consent required at each wave?

An interesting question arises in designs involving record linkage. Although privacy laws in many countries prevent such linkage, these designs also potentially contravene the principle of informed consent. Even though a person may have given informed consent when they provided each separate set of information, this is not the same as agreeing that the data be linked since this is a very different use of the data and is unlikely to be what the individual consented to.

Harm to participants

In experimental designs in which there is an active intervention there is an ethical requirement that this intervention does not expose participants to harm. The same concern can arise in panel designs that involve an active intervention. However, panel studies more typically rely on the effect of 'naturally occurring' events and thus do not confront the problem of harmful interventions in the same way that the experimenter does.

However, the researcher may well confront situations in which they learn of individuals who are exposed to harm. For example, the study may identify a person who is suicidally depressed or they may come across cases of child abuse. The researcher must decide what to do in such cases. There may be the temptation to do nothing since any onward referral for other help may jeopardize the ongoing participation of the person in the panel. Furthermore, such intervention may 'contaminate' the research by changing behaviour. My own view is that the wellbeing of participants should take priority and that, by inviting people to participate in a study, the researcher takes some responsibility for the safety and wellbeing of the participants – even where it is people other than the investigator causing the harm.

Confidentiality and anonymity

Since we need to be able to match cases between waves and to track cases it is impossible to assure participants of anonymity. However, it is necessary to ensure confidentiality. Apart from normal guarantees not to divulge information that would compromise any person's privacy, there is a need to ensure that data are securely stored. Since we need to be able to match responses with information that can identify respondents, it is important that data are stored in such way that no unauthorized person can match this identifying information with other responses. This can be achieved by storing the information in separate files with only a very limited number of people who have the information necessary to match the two files.

Summary

While experimental designs are frequently not feasible in social science research, longitudinal designs provide an important way of tracking and understanding change at the individual and societal level. While longitudinal designs can encounter some problems with internal validity because of the absence of randomized control groups, there are ways of minimizing these effects. These have been discussed briefly and will be developed more fully in Chapter 9. Other potential problems with internal validity have been discussed and ways of structuring longitudinal designs to overcome these problems have been outlined in this chapter. As a general rule, longitudinal designs tend to have better external validity than experimental designs but the threats to external validity remain and must be eliminated. The chapter outlined these threats and indicated strategies for minimizing them.

Longitudinal designs can be quite complex to implement and involve a wide variety of practical decisions. The practical issues and ethical issues that are particularly pertinent to panel designs were outlined.

9

DATA ANALYSIS IN LONGITUDINAL DESIGN

Many of the matters discussed in Chapter 6 in relation to the analysis of experimental data also apply to longitudinal analysis. Rather than repeat that discussion, this chapter focuses on a number of analysis issues that are particularly pertinent to longitudinal analysis.

Missing data

Missing data are a problem for any sort of analysis but are particularly problematic in panel analysis. There are two types of missing data: item non-response and unit non-response.

Sources of missing data

ITEM NON-RESPONSE

Item non-response occurs where individuals do not respond to a particular question. In some cases this is because they are not required to respond to the item (e.g. questions about a spouse for people who are not married) while in other cases some people may refuse to respond to a question (e.g. income).

UNIT NON-RESPONSE

This is a problem that is peculiar to panel studies.[1] Since panel designs involve collecting data from the same individuals on several occasions and measuring change over that time, we encounter difficulties if we fail to collect data from the case on the second or any subsequent occasion.

There are two forms of unit non-response. One is where people drop out of the study altogether. The other occurs in multiwave panel studies where some people miss some waves but are not permanently lost to the panel. This is called *wave non-response* (Rose et al., 1991).

Why a problem?

Missing data represent a problem for two main reasons.

SAMPLE SIZE

Item non-response can lead to a substantial loss of available sample size for data analysis. This is especially a problem when constructing scales or doing multivariate analysis where missing data on any one of a set of variables leads to the loss of that case for the analysis. This problem may quickly compound to produce an unacceptable loss of cases. For example, suppose that we are conducting analysis using only three variables and that for each of the three variables 10 per cent of people had not answered the question. Suppose that for each variable a *different* 10 per cent of people had not answered. We would then have a loss of 30 per cent of cases.

The problem of item non-response can compound over waves. This can be illustrated with an extreme example. Imagine a five-wave panel study in which an individual participated in each wave. We may have a set of 10 questions that form a prejudice scale administered in each wave. If a person failed to answer just one item in one wave we may be unable to construct a scale score for that person in that wave. We would therefore have incomplete data for that person which could force us to eliminate that case from the analysis. Because of one piece of missing data a great deal of data about a particular person would need to be discarded. Attrition of this extent can lead to a severe loss of cases and data. As a panel matures the problem created by missing data can worsen since the chance of an individual having missing data on a relevant variable at some point increases as the number of waves increases.

BIAS

Missing data can also introduce bias into the sample. Where item non-response is systematic rather than random (i.e. certain sorts of people are more likely than others to refuse to answer questions) unrepresentative samples can be the outcome. For example, if higher income earners are more likely than lower income earners to refuse to reveal their income we are left with inaccurate income estimates. Consequently, any analysis in which income is a variable will be affected by the loss of cases due to item non-response.

Unit non-response will introduce other sample biases. Those people who drop out of a panel are unlikely to be the same as those who remain. Loss of panel members may be due to death, geographical mobility, changed family status, or some other type of change in a person's circumstances.

Identifying missing data bias

In dealing with the problem of item non-response we can check whether non-responders are different from responders simply by comparing them on other variables. For example, we could check whether non-responders to a particular question were any different from responders in terms of age, income, education, sex, ethnicity or their attitudes on particular issues. We can also check for bias due to unit non-response. One of the advantages of panel studies is that when a person does not respond in a particular wave or drops out altogether we still know a great deal about that person from previous waves. We can use this information to see if those who drop out are different from those who continue. If they are we can employ various strategies during the data analysis to make adjustments.

Even if we identify bias it is not necessarily a problem. Bias is a problem if we wish to make generalizations and arrive at population estimates for the variables on which there is bias. However, in explanatory research the bias will not always matter. If the characteristic on which there is sample bias is not related to the variables that make up the explanatory model then the bias will not affect the patterns in the explanatory model (Chapter 8).

Dealing with missing data

Missing data create a problem because of their effect on sample size and on sample bias. The strategies for dealing with missing data will depend partly on which problem we are trying to minimize.

Of course, we should try to minimize the problem at the data collection stage, but there are three ways of addressing the problem during data analysis: imputation, weighting and statistical controls (Rose et al., 1991: 19).

IMPUTATION

Essentially imputation involves constructing responses for the questions which people do not answer. There are a number of forms of imputation, some of which are discussed by Hertel (1976) and by Kalton (1983a; 1986). These include the following.

Sample mean approach   If we do not know the value of a person on any given variable, a reasonable guess for that person is the average response by other sample members for that variable. With interval level variables we could replace missing values with the mean for the variable. We could use the median for ordinal variables and the mode for nominal variables. Although we will make errors in our guesses this method produces fewer errors than guessing any other value. Where the sample is relatively homogeneous this approach may result in few bad 'guesses'.

The problem with adopting this approach, however, is that it reduces sample variability on the variable for which the missing data are being estimated. This, in turn, reduces the correlation between this variable and other variables.

Group means approach   One way of overcoming this problem is to use group means rather than the overall sample mean. To do this we would divide the sample into groups on the basis of a background variable (e.g. sex, age and ethnicity) that correlates well with the missing value variable. We would then obtain the mean for the missing data variable for each of these subgroups. For example, if we wanted to estimate the income for people who declined to answer the income question we might divide the sample into groups according to their education level and then, within each education level, further divide the sample into males and females. For each education level and gender subgroup we could obtain the mean income level for those who did answer the income question. We might find that the income level for tertiary educated females is $30,000 p.a. while tertiary educated males earned, on average, $35,000 and so forth. Using the group means approach we would simply substitute these mean values for missing values for people according to the group into which they fell.

The disadvantage of this approach is that it exaggerates the degree of homogeneity within groups and thus can overestimate the variance between groups and for the sample overall. This error, in turn, can inflate the correlations when using the variable for which the missing data have been estimated.

Random assignment within groups   This approach is similar to the group means approach in that it relies on dividing the sample into groups on the basis of other characteristics that are likely to be correlated with the missing data variable. But it differs in that it does not involve substituting the group mean for any missing data. Instead, when we locate a case with missing data on a particular variable we would look at the value on the same variable of the nearest preceding case in that group and give that same value to the case with the missing value. This means that the missing values are replaced with a variety of different values randomly chosen from within that subgroup of cases. This approach does not affect sample or group variability: it has no effect on the strength of correlations and avoids any loss of cases. Despite being somewhat more complex to execute, this is a highly desirable method of handling missing data.

Average of span   A related approach requires that we calculate the mean or the median (as appropriate) of the cases within a given span of the case with missing data and substitute this value for the missing data value. This approach is relatively simple and avoids deflating variance (and correlations) which is a problem of the simple means substitution approach.

Regression analysis   This is a more complex method of imputation that involves the use of regression to predict the value of the person on the missing values variable. On the basis of a whole set of characteristics we can estimate how, on average, a person with those characteristics would answer the question on which they have missing data. In this respect it is comparable to the group means approach. The problem with the method is that since regression is based on a correlation matrix in which the pairwise method of handling missing data (see below) is used, there will normally be some loss of cases.

Imputing from earlier waves   For some stable characteristics we can 'carry over' values from an earlier wave (Rose et al., 1991) or check back from subsequent waves. However, for variables that are likely to be subject to change and for numeric variables in particular it can be incorrect to 'carry over' responses from a previous wave. Over time it may be possible to fill in some gaps caused by wave non-response by looking at the previous wave and the subsequent wave and imputing a midpoint value for the missing wave.

Ignoring the missing data   This is not an imputation approach but provides a way of managing with missing data when constructing scales. It entails calculating scale scores by calculating a person's mean score *for the variables for which they have provided answers.* Suppose we were constructing a scale from 10 questions each having possible scores ranging from 0 to 4. A person who obtained a score of 2 on all 10 items would achieve a total score of 20 over all 10 items and a mean score of 2. A person who obtained a score of 2 on each of eight items but did not answer the remaining two items would obtain a total score of 16 but a mean of 2. Calculating a scale score in this way avoids the problem of missing data when constructing scales.

WEIGHTING

Weighting is a way of adjusting a sample to allow for possible bias due to unit non-response. Weighting a sample should make it more representative of the population it is designed to represent so that reliable estimates can be made from the sample to the population. For example, imagine a situation in which 50 per cent of the population are male and 50 per cent are female. However, when a sample of this population is drawn it is found that, either because of non-response or because of dropout, 60 per cent of sample members are female and 40 per cent male. Since gender will be related to many other variables this bias will affect estimates of other variables from the sample to the population.

To adjust for the bias we would need to weight each of the females to count for less than one person while each male would be weighted to count for more than one person. In this way their proportions in the sample are adjusted to equate with their proportions in the population.

To achieve this end we weight each case by a specific weight. A weight is achieved by dividing the population percentage for a category by the sample percentage. In this case the formula ratio for males would be 50/40 which gives a weight of 1.25. For females the ratio would be 50/60 which gives a weight of 0.83 (de Vaus, 2001).

In wave 1 of a panel study we would need to weight the sample on the basis of what we know about the characteristics of the population and the characteristics of those who respond at the first phase (e.g. sex, region, ethnicity). This requires that we have reliable knowledge of the population characteristics.

In subsequent waves we will need to make further weighting adjustments to take account of biases that may creep in because of attrition. Given the amount of information available from the first wave we will have a great deal of information that can be used to calculate weights. In these cases the weight would be achieved by dividing the wave 1 percentage by the wave 2 (or 3, 4) percentage. This will enable the waves after wave 1 to remain representative of wave 1. So long as wave 1 is representative of the population then these weightings can help each wave remain representative of the population.

Analysis can become quite complex when multiple waves are analysed at once since each wave may need to be weighted differently. These strategies for weighting within panel surveys are discussed in detail in Kalton (1983a; 1986), Lepkowski (1989), Lynn et al. (1994) and Buck et al. (1995).

INTRODUCING STATISTICAL CONTROLS FOR BIASING VARIABLES

Not only does bias affect our ability to make reliable estimates from a sample to the population but it can also distort the patterns of relationships we find between variables within a sample. It is not always possible to reweight samples reliably. However, we can ensure that the pattern of relationships we find between variables is not due to the effect of the variable for which we have biased information.

To do this we control statistically for variables where we either know or believe there may be a bias. By using statistical controls (Chapter 12) we can look at relationships with the effect of other variables removed. By removing the effects of other variables we can eliminate the effect of a variable where sample bias is evident.

Measuring change

Aggregate level versus individual level change

In studies that extend over time we can think of change at two levels: aggregate and individual.

Change at the aggregate level is also referred to as net change or macro change, while change at the individual level is also referred to as gross change or micro change. The meaning of the two ways of thinking about change can be most easily described with an example. In wave 1 of a study about people in the paid workforce we might identify the percentage of people working full time and the percentage working part time. At wave 2 we collect the same information and find that exactly the same percentages of people work full time and part time as in the first wave.

While it would be correct to conclude that at the aggregate level there has been no change between wave 1 and wave 2, it does not follow that no individuals have changed their level of workforce participation. If 20 per cent of full time workers had changed to part time and 20 per cent of part timers had become full timers we would have a large number of *individuals* who in effect had changed their level of workforce participation, but at an aggregate level it would appear that there was no change. At the aggregate level changes by individuals in one direction can be cancelled out by changes in the opposite direction.

Distinguishing between aggregate and individual change is important both at a theoretical level and at the research design level. It is easy to misinterpret low levels of aggregate change. If we interpret low aggregate change as the absence of individual change we will arrive at different conclusions about the phenomenon. For example, the percentage of people who receive welfare and the characteristics of such people are fairly stable over time. This has led some people to believe that welfare recipients are a stable and unchanging group. In reality, there is a large turnover of those on welfare with relatively few continuously dependent on welfare over time (Hakim, 1986). Stability at the aggregate level will indicate something about the nature of the macro system (i.e. there is something about the structure of the social and economic system that produces a given level of people on welfare). However, it does not tell us about the individuals and the nature of changes they experience.

The type of research design we adopt will depend on whether our focus is on the aggregate or the individual level of change. A series of repeated cross-sectional surveys is quite appropriate for tracking aggregate change. Since such a survey measures change at a group level we need comparable groups over time. However, if we are interested in change at the individual level we have to use a panel design because the same individuals are involved in each wave.

Data will be analysed differently depending on whether we are examining aggregate or individual level change. When dealing with aggregate level change we are restricted to aggregate measures. For example, when examining aggregate change we will compare *group* means over time, changes in *group* variance, overall percentages in particular *categories* at different time points (e.g. percentage unemployed, percentage on welfare etc.). When adopting an aggregate change strategy we can compare subgroups to see if the extent and direction of aggregate change differ between subgroups. For example, we might track changes, at an aggregate level, in the level of optimism of business owners and employees before and after the election of a labour oriented government. By comparing the differences in aggregate change for the different groups we can begin to identify some of the factors that affect optimism *at the aggregate level*.

However, none of these strategies allows us to identify the extent and multidirectional nature of change at the individual level. We cannot identify the degree to which individuals change, the number who change in one direction or another, or the multidirectional nature of change (inflows and outflows). When we can identify *individuals* who change then our analysis can focus on identifying the characteristics of changers: those who change to small and large extents, and those who change in opposite directions. To conduct analysis at this level we require panel data for individuals.

Qualitative versus quantitative change

The type of analysis undertaken will depend on the *type of change* being considered. This relates to the level of measurement of the dependent variable.

If the dependent variable is nominal (categorical, qualitative) then change will simply consist of whether people have changed from one state to some other state (e.g. married to divorced; employed to unemployed). With qualitative dependent variables we will use analysis methods that can cope with this type of dependent variable. The particular form of analysis will also depend on the level of measurement of the independent variables. Menard (1991) has summarized the main forms of analysis appropriate to different circumstances and these are provided in Table 9.1. A description of each of these forms of analysis is beyond the scope of this book.

When dependent variables are measured at the interval level we can measure the *amount* or quantity of change rather than simply whether they have changed or not. We can do this at both the aggregate (group) and individual levels. For example, we might measure the degree to which economic wellbeing changes over time. Assuming that we can accurately measure economic wellbeing (e.g. income level, net worth of assets in dollars) we can quantify how much better (or worse) off people are over time. Appropriate methods of analysing change when the change variable is quantitative are outlined in Table 9.1.

Table 9.1   *Methods of analysis for panel data*

Dependent variable	Independent variable	Method of analysis
Interval (continuous)	Interval (continuous)	Differential equations; regression; multivariate ARIMA time series analysis; latent variable structural models
	Mixture of nominal and interval (continuous and categorical)	ANOVA with ANCOVA; regression with dummy variables
	Nominal (categorical)	ANOVA; non-parametric ANOVA; dummy variable regression
Nominal (categorical)	Interval (continuous)	Discriminant analysis; logit or probit analysis; logistic regression; hazard/survival/ event history analysis
	Mixture of nominal and interval (continuous and categorical)	Log-linear analysis; logistic regression; hazard/survival/ event history analysis
	Nominal (categorical)	Log-linear analysis; multistate life table models; hazard/ survival/event history analysis

Source: adapted from Menard (1991)

Measuring change in panel designs

This chapter will discuss only measuring change in panel designs. Chapter 12 will consider ways in which change is analysed in repeated cross-sectional designs.

In panel designs we have to work out how change will be measured. This could be limited to examining aggregate change, in which case aggregate measures of the dependent variable would be compared at each wave. For example, we would compare means, variances or proportions at each wave and see how much these differed between waves (Table 9.2).

However, if this is the only way in which panel data were analysed there would be little point in using a panel design. A repeated cross-sectional design would do just as well.

When panel data are available they will normally be analysed to identify change at the individual level as well as the aggregate level. The question then is how change at the individual level is to be measured.

MEASURING CHANGE

Raw change scores   One simple way of measuring change when the dependent variable is quantitative is to calculate *change scores* for each person. This is done by subtracting wave 1 scores from wave 2 scores (or

Table 9.2   *Ways of examining aggregate change over two waves*

	Wave 1	Wave 2	Change
Mean	25	35	+10
Variance	62	50	−12
Percentage in category X	45%	49%	+4%

whatever waves are being compared) and treating the difference as reflecting change. However, there are several problems with this approach.

The first is that any measure will have a degree of error. By using a measure twice (wave 1 and wave 2) and computing a change score, the unreliability of each test will be compounded in the change score. Great care should be taken in using change scores unless the measure of the outcome variable is known to be highly reliable.

Another related problem is that extreme scores are more likely to change due to the phenomena of regression to the mean and truncation effects (Chapters 5, 6). It can therefore be difficult to tell to what extent the change score reflects real change and how much it reflects measurement error.

Residual change scores   A problem with raw change scores is that the amount of change may not be independent of the initial scores. For example, we might expect more change among those who had extreme scores initially or, for some other reason, we might anticipate greater change among people who score in the middle of some scale. Certainly the *direction* of change is likely to be different depending on where a person lies on some scale. Those at the extreme ends of a scale can only change in one direction.

One way to remove the effect of the initial score is to use residualized or regressed change scores (Kerlinger, 1973: 337; Menard, 1991: 45). These identify cases where a person has changed more than would have been expected on the basis of their initial score. Using this procedure we use regression analysis to predict wave 2 scores from wave 1 scores on the basis of the correlation between wave 1 and wave 2 scores. We then subtract these *predicted* wave 2 scores from the *actual* wave 2 scores. What remains is the residual gain score – the amount of gain that is *not due* to the influence of the initial wave 1 score.

Percentage change   Another way of measuring change at the individual level is to calculate the percentage change in the initial score. This approach is only appropriate for ratio scale variables where there is a non-arbitrary zero (this includes most continuous variables in social science research). Here we subtract the wave 1 score from the wave 2 score and divide the answer by the wave 1 score. To convert it to a percentage change we would multiply the answer by 100.

For example, a person's wave 1 score might be 30 and their wave 2 score 40. Then:

$$\frac{\text{wave 2 score} \;-\; \text{wave 1 score}}{\text{wave 1 score}} \times 100 = \frac{40 - 30}{30} \times 100$$

$$= \frac{10}{30} \times 100 = 33\%$$

The wave 2 score represents a 33 per cent increase over the wave 1 score.

Distinguishing between real change and lack of reliability   All these ways of measuring change have a common problem: they all rely on possessing reliable measures of the dependent variables. Meeting with this condition can be especially problematic when using numeric dependent variables.

One approach that can be used to help distinguish between real change and 'change' produced by unreliable instruments is to replicate the analysis using different measures. If the same patterns persist when a number of different measures of the underlying concept are used it is less likely that the measured change is due mainly to measurement error. The achievement of consistent patterns when different measures are employed suggests that the pattern is not dependent on the particular measures and is not simply an artifact of unreliable measures.

How much change is change?   Given that there will always be some degree of measurement error, how is change to be defined? The problem of specifying how much measured change has to occur before we are prepared to treat it as real change is a difficulty regardless of whether raw change scores, residualized change scores or percentage change are used. If, for example, on a scale of 0–20 a person changes by 0.5 of a point, or if a person changes by 1 per cent, do we treat this as change, or is this degree of change likely to be due to measurement error? Should we employ a minimum cutoff point and only define change of more than a certain predefined level as constituting change?

There is no simple or clear-cut answer to these questions. The basic rule should be that the more reliable the measures the more we can treat small changes as real changes. Since many variables in social science are prone to measurement error we should be cautious in what we define as change.

STANDARDIZATION AND SCALING

Adjusting for 'inflation'   Some measures (e.g. income) have to be adjusted over time before we can measure change. In some cases the actual

Table 9.3   *Adjusting for inflation*

Expressed in 1990 dollars

Year	$	Inflation rate (%)	1990 $	
1990	1000	8	1000	
1991	1000	8	920	$1000 × 0.92 (i.e. 100–8%)
1992	1000	6	846	$920 × 0.92 (i.e. 100–8%)
1993	1000	8	796	$846 × 0.94 (i.e. 100–6%)
1994	1000	5	732	$796 × 0.92
1995	1000	4	695	$732 × 0.95
1996	1000	6	668	$695 × 0.96
1997	1000	3	628	$668 × 0.94
1998	1000	3	609	$628 × 0.97
1999	1000	2	590	$609 × 0.97
2000	1000	2	579	$590 × 0.98

Expressed in 2000 dollars

Year	$	Inflation rate (%)	2000$	
1990	1000	8	1673	$1549 × 1.08
1991	1000	8	1549	$1434 × 1.06
1992	1000	6	1434	$1353 × 1.06
1993	1000	8	1353	$1253 × 1.08
1994	1000	5	1253	$1193 × 1.05
1995	1000	4	1193	$1147 × 1.04
1996	1000	6	1147	$1082 × 1.06
1997	1000	3	1082	$1051 × 1.03
1998	1000	3	1051	$1020 × 1.03
1999	1000	2	1020	$1000 × 1.02 (i.e. 100 + 2%)
2000	1000	2	1000	

instrument may change (e.g. questions may need to be changed to match the age or life stage of respondents). For other variables, such as income, where the meaning of the categories changes (e.g. income needs to be adjusted for inflation) the variable itself needs to be rescaled to make measures comparable over time.

For example, we may be looking at changes in income among men and women between 1990 and 2000. Before we can make meaningful comparisons between income levels in 1990 and 2000 we need to know how much the same dollar amount is worth over time, after adjusting for inflation. Because of inflation $1000 in 1990 is not the equivalent of $1000 in the year 2000. In Table 9.3 income has been adjusted by the inflation rate. The income in each year has been expressed in 1990 dollars. Thus, after adjustments for inflation, $1000 in 2000 is the equivalent of only $579 in 1990 dollars after inflation. In the second example, the opposite calculations have been made with the worth of $1000 in each year being expressed in year 2000 dollars. Thus $1000 year 2000 dollars would buy $1673 worth of goods if that $1000 was spent in 1990.

Standardization: z-scores and percentile rank Another form of adjusting scores is to express all scores in terms of where they lie on a distribution. That is, we can *standardize* scores and, rather than looking at change in *absolute* values, we look at changes in a person's score *relative to other people* (see Marsh, 1988 for an accessible discussion of a range of methods of standardization). We look at changes to where a person lies in a distribution. When looking at change, in relative rather than absolute terms, we would only count a person as changing if they changed their position relative to others, that is they moved more (or less) than some other people. To express change on an interval level dependent variable in relative terms we can express each person's score at wave 1 and wave 2 as a z-score. With an ordinal dependent variable we can use a person's percentile rank. We would then measure change by looking at changes in z-scores or percentile rank.

For example, if we were looking at changes in income over time we could convert each person's income into a z-score which would tell us about that person's income relative to other people's income. If we had these z-scores for the same individuals over two waves we could identify those whose z-score increased and those for whom it decreased. We could also quantify how much the person's relative income position changed (Table 9.4). Alternatively, we could calculate their percentile rank in the income stakes and see how they changed over time in rank. This method of measuring change in relative terms is valuable when we need to adjust for changes in the way in which the dependent variable is measured over time. However, it is a method that can be used even when we do not need to adjust for the way in which the variable is measured.

Since the z-score indicates the number of standard deviations a person lies above or below the sample mean we can usefully compare changes in their position over time. In Table 9.4, case 1 remains below the sample mean at wave 2 but has drawn close. Case 2 has deteriorated relative to others by 0.4 of a standard deviation. Case 7 has improved her relative position considerably. By using z-scores we automatically adjust for differences in actual income due to inflation and the overall increase in mean income. This approach enables us to focus on changes in how people are doing relative to others.

Alternatively, we could examine the relative change of *individuals* by examining change in rank (Table 9.5). This is comparable to looking at changes in z-scores but does not quantify the amount of difference between individuals. It is therefore useful with ordinal level dependent variables. In Table 9.5, the relative position of case 1 has improved, that of case 7 has deteriorated sharply while that of case 9 has improved markedly.

Table 9.4   *Changes in z-scores of individuals*

Case	Raw score 1990 (income)	z-score 1990	Raw score 2000 (income)	z-score 2000	Change in z-score
1 (female)	$35,000	−0.38	$45,000	−0.18	0.20
2 (male)	$40,000	0.04	$41,000	−0.48	−0.52
3 (female)	$20,000	−1.64	$32,000	−1.16	0.48
4 (male)	$60,000	1.72	$65,000	1.35	−0.37
5 (female)	$37,000	−0.21	$40,000	−0.56	−0.35
6 (female)	$28,000	−0.96	$33,000	−1.09	−0.13
7 (male)	$45,000	0.46	$39,000	−0.63	−1.09
8 (male)	$42,000	0.21	$69,000	1.65	1.44
9 (female)	$33,000	−0.55	$49,000	0.13	0.68
10 (male)	$55,000	1.30	$60,000	0.97	−0.33
Mean	$39,500		$47,300		
Standard deviation	$11,918		$13,140		

Table 9.5   *Changes measured by changes in rank*

Case	Raw score 1990 (income)	Rank	Raw score 2000 (income)	Rank
1	$35,000	4	$45,000	6
2	$40,000	6	$41,000	5
3	$20,000	1	$32,000	1
4	$60,000	10	$65,000	9
5	$37,000	5	$40,000	4
6	$28,000	2	$33,000	2
7	$45,000	8	$39,000	3
8	$42,000	7	$69,000	10
9	$33,000	3	$49,000	7
10	$55,000	9	$60,000	8

We can also use z-scores (or percentile rank) to see if some *groups* change more than others. For example, if we were examining whether the income gap between men and women had narrowed between 1990 and 2000 we could obtain the z-scores of all men and all women at wave 1 (from a pooled sample of both men and women) and do the same at wave 2. Using aggregate level analysis we could then see if the *mean z-score* of men at wave 2 has changed more than the mean z-score of women at wave 2. In Table 9.6, women, on average, have an income of 0.75 (1990) and 0.57 (2000) standard deviations *below* the mean while men, on average, have an income of 0.75 (1990) and 0.57 (2000) standard deviations *above* the mean. Men continue to do better but the gap has narrowed slightly between 1990 and 2000.

Another approach to adjusting for 'inflation' or other change over time is to change values into proportions (Table 9.7). Absolute figures might indicate a widening of the income gap between men and women. For

Table 9.6   *Mean z-score for men and women, 1990–2000*

	1990	2000	Change
Males	0.75	0.57	−0.18
Females	−0.75	−0.57	+0.18

Table 9.7   *Female earnings as a proportion of male earnings*

Year	Column 1 Average FT male $ pa	Column 2 Average FT female $ pa	Column 3 Female as proportion of male (column 2/column 1)	Column 4 Absolute $ gap
1970	$5,000	$3,400	0.68	−$1,600
1980	$15,000	$10,500	0.70	−$4,500
1990	$25,000	$18,000	0.72	−$7,000
2000	$35,000	$26,950	0.77	−$8,005

example, the average income gap in weekly income between men and women might have been $25 in 1970. In 2000 this might have increased to $150 per week. However, 1970 dollars are not comparable to 2000 dollars. We could use any of the above approaches to make the necessary adjustments to facilitate comparison. Alternatively, we might express female earnings *as a proportion of male earnings* in each year. In this way we automatically remove the effect of inflation. Thus although the dollar gap between the average incomes of men and women is increasing in Table 9.7, the relative position of women is improving.

We can also approach the problem of standardization by adopting some other base. For example, we might want to see if the income gap is widening between the lower and higher income earners. We could take the bottom 25 per cent of income earners and express their average income as a proportion of the average income of the top 25 per cent. In this example we see in Table 9.8 that in 1970 the top 25 per cent of income earners, on average, earned five times more than the average of the lowest 25 per cent of income earners. In this hypothetical example the disparity increases over the years so that by 2000 income earners in the top 25 per cent earned 7.7 times more than the average income earner in the bottom 25 per cent.

EXPLAINING CHANGE

Assuming that the issues of how to measure change have been dealt with and we are reasonably confident that real change is being measured, we will probably also want to explain the change.

The theories and propositions around which the research is designed will provide guidance as to how to go about testing explanations.

Table 9.8   *Changes in proportions: bottom income quartile as a proportion of the top income quartile*

Year	Column 1 Average income of bottom 25%	Column 2 Average income of top 25%	Bottom 25% as a proportion of top 25% (column 2/column 1)
1970	$2,000	$10,000	5.0
1980	$5,000	$30,000	6.0
1990	$8,000	$60,000	7.5
2000	$11,000	$85,000	7.7

However, the problem in any explanation is that we cannot be certain what factors have produced the change. Because we lack the level of control of an experimental design, any change could be due to unknown factors that occurred between the waves.

When explaining change the analysis will be based on comparing different groups of people. We will see whether the extent and nature of change in one group are different from other groups. Any differences in change patterns of groups is attributed to other differences that may exist between the groups. Take, for example, a study examining the impact of paid employment on the self-esteem of young people. Using a panel design we could measure self-esteem at two or more waves. To test the effect of employment on self-esteem we would identify those young people who gained employment between waves, those who became unemployed, those who remained employed, and those who have remained unemployed. We might find that those who gained employment showed a real improvement in self-esteem, and those who lost their job showed a loss in self-esteem, while the stable employed and unemployed showed no self-esteem changes. It would be tempting to conclude that it is the differences in employment that account for the different changes in self-esteem of the groups.

The problem, however, is that we do not know that changes in employment status are the only changes these people are experiencing. Nor do we know that the four groups are comparable in other ways (e.g. gender, age and education). In experimental designs this problem is handled by random allocation to groups. Typically in panel designs this is not possible.

The main way of responding to the problem of comparability is to use statistical controls to establish comparability among the groups. This goal can be achieved by using one form or another of multivariate analysis. This strategy enables us to remove the effects of known differences between the groups. Once it is established that the groups are similar in the specified respects it is then possible to establish how much the groups differ in regard to self-esteem changes. The logic and techniques of this approach will be discussed more fully in Chapter 12.

Describing change

Once change has been conceptualized and measured, decisions must be made about how to represent this change. There are various mathematical and statistical ways of doing this (Menard, 1991: 49ff) but here I will only mention briefly some ways of displaying change in tabular and graphical form.

Tables

Change over time can be presented effectively in tabular form. The particular form will depend on the number of time points over which change is being tracked and whether change is being considered at the aggregate or the individual level.

The earlier tables provide illustrations of some of the ways in which tables might display change. These tables will usually have years on one axis – either across the top (e.g. tables on cohort analysis in Chapter 12) or down the side (e.g. Tables 9.3, 9.7 and 9.8). The way in which change is indicated will vary depending on whether aggregate or individual change is being considered. Some of the vast range of possible ways of reporting change is provided in Table 9.9.

When dealing with change at the individual level, similar approaches apply. Periods over which individual change is being tracked (e.g. year) will be indicated either across the top of the table or on the side. The other axis will represent the particular way in which individual change is being conceptualized. Again, a wide range of possible ways of representing individual change is possible. Some common approaches are illustrated in Table 9.10.

Graphs

Graphs are a good way to represent change. The most common type of graph for displaying change is the trend graph. This section will provide a brief introduction to trend graphs. A fuller discussion of these graphs and other ways of displaying change graphically can be found in Henry (1995).

The simple trend graph will have two axes: the X-axis across the bottom and the Y-axis on the side. The X-axis will represent time while the Y-axis will reflect a quantity on the variable that is being examined for change. Figure 9.1 illustrates a simple trend graph.

The Y-axis can be measured using a wide range of measurement units. In Figure 9.1 it is measured as a rate – the number of divorces per 1000 population aged 15 or over. However, the Y-axis could have denoted the *number* of divorces, or some other way of indicating the prevalence of divorce.

Figure 9.1 provides trend data for the population at large. Trend graphs can also represent trends for different subgroups separately.

Table 9.9   *Examples of tabular ways of presenting data about aggregate change*

	Year		
	1998–9	2000–1	2002–3
Mean	5	10	15
Variance	80	80	80
% change (in mean) from previous period		100%	50%
Rate	12 per 1000	12.8 per 1000	13.6 per 1000
Gaps (e.g. between male and female average income)	$10,000	$7,500	$5,000
Proportion (e.g. female average income as proportion of male average)	0.80	0.82	0.84

Table 9.10   *Examples of tabular ways of presenting data about individual change (living standards)*

	Year		
	1998–9	2000–1	2002–3
% improved (from previous period)	5%	15%	2%
% stable	85%	80%	78%
% declined	10%	5%	20%
% change	15%	20%	22%
% changing by X amount	10%	5%	7.5%
Mean improvement of improvers	25 points	35 points	40 points
Mean decline of decliners	10 points	10 points	10 points

Figure 9.2 shows the different trends in employment levels for men and women aged 55–59 over the years 1975–2010 and compares these with the overall trends for the age group. By reporting the trends separately for the different subgroups (men and women) we can obtain a more fine-grained picture than the trend line for the age group as a whole provides.

The way in which the X-axis and the Y-axis are scaled can distort the trend in the data. Each graph in Figure 9.3 has the same information as Figure 9.2 but stretching or contracting the scales provides a very different impression of the trend in the employment levels of older men and women. In Figure 9.3a the changes in employment levels appear modest because the X-axis has been stretched and the Y-axis contracted. This has the effect of flattening out the trend line. In Figure 9.3b the X-

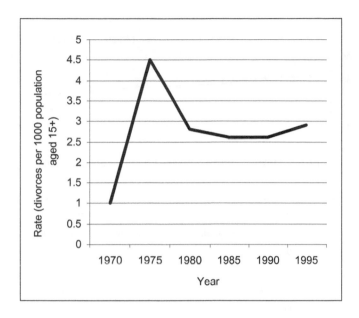

Figure 9.1   *Crude divorce rate, Australia, 1970–95* (de Vaus and Wolcott, 1997)

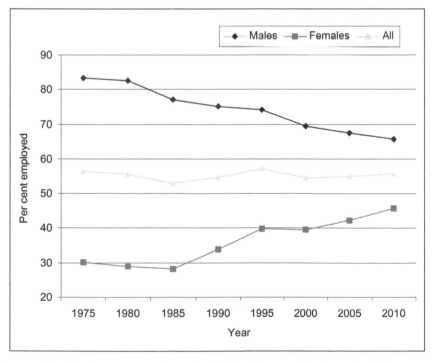

Figure 9.2   *Employment rate of people aged 55–59 by gender, Australia, 1975–2010 (actual and predicted)* (de Vaus and Wolcott, 1997)

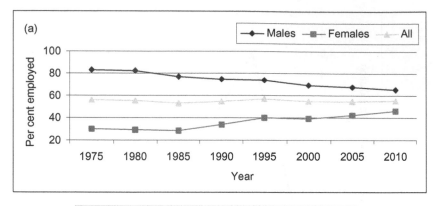

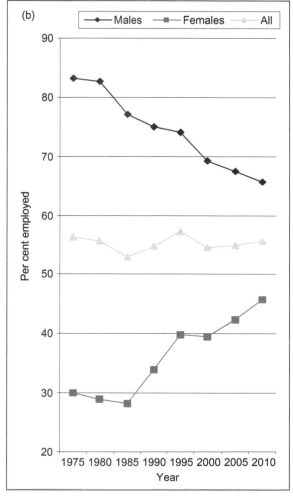

Figure 9.3   *Employment rate of people aged 55–59 by gender, Australia, 1975–2010 (actual and predicted): (a) flattened scale, (b) expanded scale* (de Vaus and Wolcott, 1997)

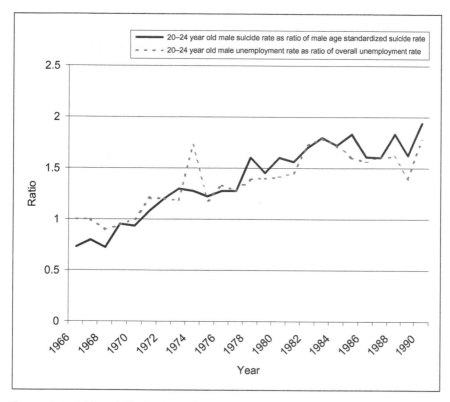

Figure 9.4   *Male suicide deaths and unemployment rate ratios, 20–24 year olds, Australia, 1966–90* (DHSH, 1995)

axis has been contracted and the Y-axis stretched which has the effect of exaggerating the trend rate of change.

Trends for multiple variables can be plotted on the same graph as illustrated in Figure 9.4. The figure plots two variables: suicide rate and unemployment rate of young people. In this figure the trend line for suicide of 20–24 year olds has been plotted alongside the unemployment rates for the same age groups. Plotting trend lines from different variables on the same graph can highlight the way in which trends on different variables co-vary. However, one must take care not to assume that this co-variation of trends demonstrates a causal relationship.

In Figure 9.4 each of the variables is measured on the same scale, so each variable can be plotted against the same Y-axis. Sometimes we may wish to compare trends on two different variables, each of which is measured in different units of measurement. In such a case we can use two Y-axes – each with a different scale of measurement. In Figure 9.5 the left hand Y-axis (primary Y-axis) is the serious crime rate per 500,000 population, while the right hand Y-axis (secondary Y-axis) represents the percentage of ex-nuptial births (births to unmarried mothers). Again,

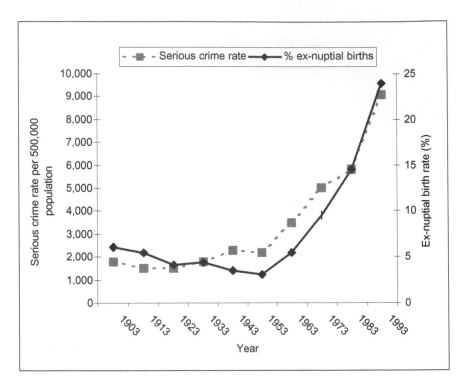

Figure 9.5   *Ex-nuptial births and serious crime rate, Australia, 1903–93*
(Sullivan et al., 1997)

great care must be taken not to confuse similar trends with causal connections.

Where a longitudinal study provides data for just two time points rather than long term trend data it will normally be more appropriate to use bar graphs to represent the two time points (Figure 9.6). To simply have two time points and join them together with a line to form a trend graph could be highly misleading since this could hide the variations in the intervening years (see Figure 9.1 for these variations).

Summary

Since a basic aspect of longitudinal designs is to describe and explain change, the focus of this chapter has been on analysis issues that arise with the measurement of change. One important problem is the problem of missing information which is caused by incomplete data collection at some point in the multiple data collection waves of longitudinal studies. The different types of missing data were described and strategies for dealing with missing data during data analysis were evaluated.

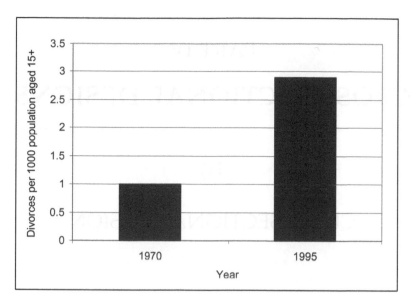

Figure 9.6   *Crude divorce rate, Australia, 1970 and 1995* (de Vaus and Wolcott, 1997)

When measuring change it is important to distinguish between change at the aggregate level and change at the individual level. This distinction has been discussed and its implications for analysis strategies have been considered. Problems of reliably detecting change have been identified and some ways of reducing these problems have been outlined. Finally, the chapter has discussed the need to standardize some measures over time so that real change can be identified. Different standardization strategies were described.

Note

1 It can also occur in experimental designs but can be avoided by adopting a randomized design without a pre-test measure.

PART IV

CROSS-SECTIONAL DESIGNS

10

CROSS-SECTIONAL DESIGN

Cross-sectional designs have three distinctive features: no time dimension; reliance on existing differences rather than change following intervention; and groups based on existing differences rather than random allocation.

No time dimension

In the standard cross-sectional design data are collected at one point of time. In this respect this design differs from standard panel designs and pre-test and post-test experimental designs where data are collected at a number of different points of time. As such the cross-sectional design can only measure *differences* between groups rather than change.

The distinction between measuring difference and measuring change is important and may be clarified with an example (Figure 10.1). Suppose we want to learn about the impact of children on marital happiness. A panel design would track people over time. It would begin with a group of childless married couples and measure their marital happiness. Five years after the initial wave of the study we might revisit the sample and remeasure their level of marital happiness. By this time some couples will have had children and some will have remained childless. Some couples will have had their first child recently (say within the last year) while others will have had their first child earlier (between 1 and 5 years ago). We could then think in terms of three groups: the childless, the new parents (first child within last year) and the established parents (first child between one and five years of age). The analysis could consist of looking at the degree of *change in marital happiness* of the three groups

Groups	Time 1 (T_1) Initial test	'Intervention' (X)	Time 2 (T_2) Five years later
1	Level of marital happiness	No children	Level of marital happiness (Y)
2	Level of marital happiness	Have first child within last 12 months	Level of marital happiness (Y)
3	Level of marital happiness	Have first child between 12 and 60 months previously	Level of marital happiness (Y)

Figure 10.1   *Cross-sectional design: marital happiness by parenthood status*

between wave 1 and wave 2. Different amounts of change in marital happiness of the three groups *could* reflect the effect of parenthood.

A cross-sectional design for the same research question would involve a one-off study in which we measured the levels of marital happiness of couples, whether they had any children, and, if so, the age of their eldest child. Using this information we could create three groups: those without children, those whose eldest child was less than 12 months old, and those whose eldest child was between one and five years old. We could then compare the level of marital happiness of the three groups to see if there is any difference. If there was any *difference* we might be tempted to attribute this to the effect on marital happiness of having children.

Essentially the difference between the two designs is that the panel design enables us to compare groups in terms of *different amounts of change* on the dependent variable while the cross-sectional design involves comparing the groups simply in terms of *difference* on the dependent variable.

Reliance on existing differences

Because the cross-sectional design entails collecting data *at* and *concerning* one point of time, all analysis relies on differences in the sample at that point of time. Unlike the panel design the cross-sectional design does not allow for differences to emerge over time. Unlike the experimental design where there is an active intervention by the researcher to produce change or to create differences, the cross-sectional design relies on existing differences rather than examining the impact of experimental interventions.

Cross-sectional designs employ a relatively *passive* approach to making causal inferences (Marsh, 1982: 6) and can be distinguished from experiments in this regard. Like cross-sectional designs, experiments explain variation in the dependent variable by seeing if this variation is systematically linked to variation in the independent variable. Is variation in marital happiness matched by variations in parenthood status? However, experiments actively create variation in the independent variable whereas cross-sectional designs rely on existing differences.

The nature of 'groups' in the cross-sectional design

The experimental design relies on comparing groups. Individuals are randomly allocated to groups so that prior to any experimental intervention the two groups should be identical. The researcher actively produces differences between the groups by a deliberate and controlled intervention. This intervention is the independent variable in the experimental design. Ideally, this differential treatment is the only difference between groups and therefore any group differences in regard to the outcome variable should be attributable to this differential intervention.

In the cross-sectional design the 'groups' are constructed on the basis of existing differences in the sample. The sample is divided up into groups according to the category of the independent variable to which they happen to belong. In the earlier example the comparison groups would be those without any children, those whose eldest child was less than 12 months old, and those whose eldest child was between one and five years old. The critical point, however, is that because we must rely on existing differences there can be no random allocation to groups. The groups may very well be different in other respects apart from the category of the independent variable to which they belong. This, in turn, can make it difficult to work out whether any group differences on the outcome variable are due to the independent variable or to other related differences between the groups.

Using the framework of the classic experimental design as a frame of reference the cross-sectional design can be represented diagramatically as in Figure 10.2. In this case the 'intervention' is simply being in a different category of the independent variable. The information about this and the outcome measure is collected at the same point of time.

Cross-sectional designs are not limited to comparisons between just two or three groups. The number of categories of the independent

Method of allocation to 'groups'	'Pre-test'	'Intervention' (X)	'Post-test'
Non-random	None	Existing characteristic (X_a)	Measure on outcome variable (Y)
Non-random	None	Different existing characteristic (X_b)	Measure on outcome variable (Y)

Figure 10.2 *Groups in cross-sectional designs*

variable determines the number of 'groups'. Often we will look at the correlation between continuous variables such as, say, age and income level. When looking at such a correlation, we are asking whether income varies according to age. That is, we compare all the age levels (or groups) and see whether income varies systematically across age levels.

In summary, cross-sectional designs differ from experimental and panel designs in that they do not have a time dimension. Consequently, they face difficulties in unambiguously identifying the time sequence of events. Because of this they face the problem of identifying causal direction. Furthermore, because cross-sectional designs rely on existing differences rather than random allocation, any apparent effect of the independent variable may in fact be due to other, uncontrolled differences between the groups. The problems created by this will be discussed more fully in the methodological problems section of Chapter 11.

Obtaining a time dimension: repeated cross-sectional studies

Cross-sectional designs are frequently criticized for lacking a time dimension. Because of this shortcoming they are unable to unambiguously establish the time sequence in which events occur. This is particularly a problem with one-off cross-sectional studies. However, the repeated cross-sectional design addresses this problem to a limited extent.

This design involves collecting information at a number of different time points *but from a different sample at each time point*. Rather than tracking a group of individuals over time and seeing how those individuals change, the repeated cross-sectional design obtains comparable samples at each time point. So long as the same questions are asked in

T_1	T_2	T_3	T_4	T_5	T_6
Sample 1	Sample 2	Sample 3	Sample 4	Sample 5	Sample 6
Question *a*	Question *a*	Question *a*	Question *a*	Question *a*	Question *a*
Question *b*	Question *b*	Question *b*	Question *b*	Question *b*	Question *b*
Question *c*	Question *c*	Question *c*	Question *c*	Question *c*	Question *c*
Question *d*	Question *d*	Question *d*	Question *d*	Question *d*	Question *d*

Figure 10.3 *Repeated cross-sectional design*

each of these independent cross-sectional samples we can build up a picture over time of whatever variables we have.

The national census in each country is an obvious example of this type of 'design'. To the extent that the same questions are asked in each census, changes can be tracked over long periods. Many countries have regular national social surveys that track a far wider range of matters than any national census. In the United States the General Social Survey has been conducted annually since 1972 and provides an excellent way of looking at changes in behaviour, beliefs, values and attitudes over the last quarter century. In Britain the British Social Attitudes Survey is used to achieve a similar end. The General Household Survey provides data for two decades and the Family Expenditure Survey yields time series data for over 30 years. The International Social Science Survey involves asking a similar core of questions each year to new samples in each of the countries that are members of the International Social Science Programme (35 countries in 2000). Repeated cross-sectional surveys provide an excellent snapshot of values at different points in a period of rapid change.

Diagrammatically the repeated cross-sectional design can be represented as a series of independent samples (Figure 10.3). Each time point draws on a new sample. Typically, each sample will provide a wide cross-section of cases so that useful cross-sectional analysis can be conducted within each sample. We can track changes by comparing patterns in each sample with those in previous or subsequent samples (e.g. rather than just one age group they include a wide range of ages so that at any given point of time the age differences can be examined).

While this design does not permit the tracking of individual change over time it enables longitudinal analysis at the aggregate level (see Chapter 9). Furthermore, these repeated cross-sectional studies can be used for cohort analysis. They allow the investigator to both track change and get some understanding of the nature of change. Cohort analysis will be discussed in Chapter 12.

Repeated measures designs can take two forms: prospective and retrospective. A prospective design is one where we begin now and repeat the study at various points in the future. The retrospective repeated measures design is one that draws on existing data sets to examine patterns of change up to the present point. Right now we could use the General Social Surveys of the last 25 years to examine patterns of change. Census data collected over the past years can be analysed in a similar manner to many other sets of data that are routinely collected (e.g. annual divorce statistics, marriage data, fertility statistics).

11

ISSUES IN CROSS-SECTIONAL DESIGN

Cross-sectional designs are probably the most widely used designs in social research. One reason for this popularity is that they enable the researcher to obtain results relatively quickly. Since data are collected at one point of time there is no need to wait for various follow-up stages or interventions before analysing the data. It is also true that, other things being equal (e.g. sample size, population, sample type), cross-sectional designs are more cost effective than comparable experimental and longitudinal designs. This is because cross-sectional designs do not entail the cost of repeated data collections, tracking respondents or of experimental interventions.

Cross-sectional designs can be ideal for descriptive analysis. If we simply want to describe the characteristics of a population, their attitudes, their voting intention or their buying patterns then the cross-sectional survey is a most satisfactory way of obtaining this descriptive information. But cross-sectional designs are not restricted to descriptive analysis. As will be argued below, proper analysis that uses statistical controls enables cross-sectional data to provide valuable information about causal processes and for testing causal models.

There are, however, a number of methodological and practical issues of which we need to be aware when using cross-sectional designs. An awareness of these issues should help minimize the shortcomings of this design.

Methodological issues

Internal validity

We encounter problems with internal validity when the *logic* and *structure* of the design does not enable us to choose unambiguously one explanation of our results over another explanation. Campbell and Stanley (1963) have identified a number of factors that threaten internal validity and these have been discussed in detail in Chapters 5 and 8 in relation to longitudinal and experimental designs.

However, most of these threats (history, maturation, instrument decay, statistical regression, mortality and testing effects) arise because of the over-time element of these designs. They are not problems with cross-sectional designs. The main threats to the internal validity of cross-sectional designs stem from two sources: problems in establishing cause without a time dimension; and problems at the level of meaning (Marsh, 1982). Problems at the level of cause are, of course, an issue with any design but cross-sectional designs are particularly prone to problems at this level. Problems at the level of meaning are also common to all designs and arise with equal force for experimental, longitudinal and cross-sectional designs.

Marsh (1982) has written clearly and forcefully about these two problems. She takes issue with those who dismiss cross-sectional survey designs because of their alleged problems with causality and meaning. She argues that this design is not nearly as flawed as it is frequently portrayed to be. The following discussion draws on Marsh's argument.

ESTABLISHING CAUSALITY AND CONTROLLING CONFOUNDING VARIABLES

There is no denying that cross-sectional studies face problems identifying causal variables. Even though two time-ordered variables might be correlated or groups might differ on an outcome variable we cannot be sure that these differences are due to a *causal link* between the variables (Blalock, 1964). In Chapter 10 I introduced an example of the effect of parenthood status (have no children; eldest child under one year old and eldest child between 1 and 5 years old) and marital happiness. Even if the three groups differed in terms of marital happiness we would have difficulty working out whether this difference was due to their different parental status. The three groups were likely to differ in ways other than just their parenthood status – how long they have been together, their age profile, level of workforce participation and so forth. *These* differences, rather than parenthood status, could account for differences in marital happiness.

STATISTICAL CONTROLS

This problem of confounding variables is tackled in cross-sectional designs at the *data analysis stage* rather than at the data collection stage as it is in experimental designs. The solution is achieved by making the groups as similar as possible by *statistically* removing differences between groups *after data have been collected*. When we compare groups we need to know how much difference X makes to Y *other things being equal*. Since other things may not be equal we need to remove as many of the differences as possible and compare like with like.

An outline of how this is done will be discussed in Chapter 12. However, the basic logic can be introduced now. For the children and marital happiness example we would compare the marital happiness of three groups: those without any children, those whose eldest child is under one year of age and those whose eldest child is between 1 and 5 years old. Someone might say that any differences in marital happiness are not due to children but due to the different age profiles of the three groups of parents. They argue that those who have been parents longer are, on average, older than those without children. They argue that it is the age of partners, not the presence of children, which influences marital happiness.

We can test this possibility by removing the age differences from our comparisons. We can make a number of restricted comparisons. First we might look at people aged between 20 and 24 and see whether *within* this particular age group the marital happiness of the three groups differed. That is, we restrict our comparison across the three groups to those who are much the same age. We could repeat this comparison separately within each age group (e.g. 25–29, 30–34, 35–39). Suppose we find that, *within* each age grouping, there are still differences in marital happiness between the groups (i.e between the childless, the new parents and those with a child aged 1 to 5 years) despite their comparable age profiles. We can then at least say that this relationship between marital happiness and parenthood status is *not* due to the different age profiles of the three groups. The logic of this is similar to the logic of *matching* groups that is sometimes used in experimental designs.

The more variables that are controlled for statistically, the more we can be confident that the final relationship we find between X and Y is reflecting a causal relationship between X and Y.

The problem with this, however, is that we can only control for variables that we have thought of and about which we have information. Random allocation in an experimental design effectively controls for all variables – known and unknown. When we control for variables statistically at the data analysis stage we can never be sure that we have controlled for all relevant variables. There is always the possibility that any relationship we have found between X and Y could be due to some uncontrolled variable.

But this is not to condemn cross-sectional designs as being of no use in exploring causal relationships. Indeed, since in social science research our capacity to intervene either practically or ethically and to manipulate situations as required by experimental designs is limited there is often few, if any, alternatives to cross-sectional designs.

Rather than rejecting cross-sectional designs as being useless for causal analysis we must proceed systematically and carefully with the analysis, and control statistically for factors that might plausibly explain the correlations we observe. Furthermore we must constantly remind ourselves of the tentative nature of any conclusions we draw in any scientific endeavour.

Although finding that two variables are correlated does not establish cause it does mean that a causal explanation is possible. As Marsh

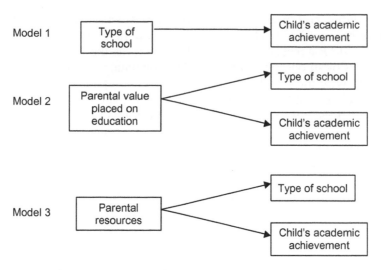

Figure 11.1   *Three causal models of child's academic achievement*

argues, 'finding a correlation between smoking and lung cancer in no way proves that smoking causes lung cancer, but it *does* mean that the hypothesis cannot be ruled out.' (1982: 73).

ELIMINATING VARIABLES AS CAUSES

Cross-sectional data can help establish that causal relationships do *not* exist. While it is true that a correlation between two variables does not establish causation it is a pre-requisite for establishing a causal relationship. If there is no correlation we can be confident that there is *not* a causal relationship.[1] *Eliminating* variables as causes can be of just as much scientific importance as locating causes. Certainly the tobacco manufacturers would consider a finding of *no* correlation between smoking and lung cancer to be an important finding.

MODELS: *A PRIORI* REASONING AND *AD HOC* REASONING

The most useful way to go about the causal analysis of cross-sectional data is to draw models or flow-charts or path diagrams of the type illustrated in Figure 11.1 and elsewhere in this book. The task of the data analyst is then to evaluate how well these models fit the data.

The use of theories and models as a guide to analysis is an important tool for the person analysing cross-sectional data. 'It is the model that stands between the researcher and unbridled empiricism in the attempt to draw causal inferences' (Marsh 1982: 72). It is important to develop the model *before* using cross-sectional data to draw causal conclusions.

There is a difference between *a priori* reasoning and *ad hoc* reasoning. *A priori* reasoning involves proposing, on the basis of theoretical considerations and previous research, that X will cause Y and will therefore be correlated. This reasoning is independent of the data we may have. *Ad hoc* reasoning, on the other hand, is the process whereby, on the basis of an observed correlation in our data, we make up a causal story as to why the correlation exists.

The problem with *ad hoc* reasoning is that we can always make up a story regardless of the correlation that we find. It is not hard to think up a story that is consistent with a correlation – it is quite a different matter to anticipate, on the basis of reasoning and theory, that a correlation should exist and then find that it does.

In summary, cross-sectional data can be quite effective in demonstrating where a causal relationship probably does *not* exist. Furthermore, it can help evaluate which, of various competing theoretically derived *a priori* models fit the data best. Finally, we can use cross-sectional data to evaluate and modify a given *a priori* model.

> Properly designed, anticipating rival causal explanations as far as possible and building in ways to test them, [cross-sectional] surveys can provide evidence for and against different causal models. The evidence is not proof, however; it is only as good as the model is. (Marsh, 1982: 97)

ESTABLISHING CAUSAL DIRECTION

Another problem with cross-sectional data is that even if we establish that two variables are correlated this does not establish their causal *direction*. In order to illustrate this point let us use the parental status and marital happiness example again. Suppose that the cross-sectional study showed that the childless couples are less happy than those with babies and that couples with the older children are the happiest. The problem is that even if we assume that this reflects a causal relationship between the two variables we know nothing about the *direction* of the relationship. What comes first – children or marital happiness? Do children increase marital happiness or are happily married people more likely than the unhappily married to have children?

A panel survey could resolve this question. We would know the level of marital happiness *before* children and again afterwards and see if there was any *change*. We could also check whether the initial level of happiness was linked with the likelihood of subsequently having children. However, there is no simple way of doing this when all data are collected at and about the one point of time.

One way of approaching this dilemma is to develop *a priori* models to test. While support for an *a priori* model does not prove causal direction it at least provides a theoretical basis for arguing a case and provides empirical data that at least are consistent with this. Having found data consistent with the thesis of a particular causal direction the next step would be to adopt a design that can establish for causal direction.

Even in those circumstances in which we cannot develop a new study to establish causal direction we can shed some light on the direction by collecting retrospective information and by asking people directly about any effect children may have had on their marital happiness. This approach does not yield unambiguous data but, bit by bit, it builds a picture regarding which causal direction is the more likely.

Establishing causal *direction*, however, is not always problematic. Some independent variables are fixed (e.g. gender, race), others are not readily subject to our manipulation (e.g. age, religious denomination) and for others the time orderings are straightforward (e.g. parent's education precedes respondent's education, education level usually precedes the type of job we get).

ADEQUACY AT THE LEVEL OF MEANING

By establishing causal explanations on the basis of correlations, cross-sectional designs are often accused of treating human action as determined by external forces and of neglecting the role of human agency. Marsh puts this view most clearly:

> The aim of explanation is not just to show high correlations between variables; sociological explanations would almost always turn out to be a flop anyway on these grounds. It must also show how the actions of the people involved were the actions of conscious human beings, reacting to an environment, trying to make sense of it and pursuing various goals and actions with more or less success. Only explanations that take cognizance of the meaningful aspect of social action will satisfy us as human observers. (1982: 98)

Herbert Blumer (1956) coined the term 'variable analysis' to describe the type of analysis and understanding provided by cross-sectional survey designs (he would also apply it to longitudinal and experimental designs of the type already considered). He argues that analysis using discrete, quantifiable variables is inadequate for at least three reasons. First,

> It leaves out the actual complexities of activity and the actual processes of interaction in which human life has its being. (1956: 101)

Second, it ignores the actor's interpretation of the situation and behaviour and the way in which these interpretations impact on their actions:

> The independent variable is put at the beginning of the process of interpretation and the dependent variable at the terminal part of the process. The intervening process is ignored . . . as something that need not be considered. (1956: 97)

By ignoring the intervening process one cannot understand *why* the independent and dependent variables are or are not related. Where human behaviour is intentional and based on understandings of a situation then these intentions and understandings should be part of the explanation of the behaviour. Blumer argues that variable analysis usually fails to do this.

Third, Blumer argues that variable analysis wrenches people and their behaviour out of their contexts. By trying to work with discrete, quantifiable variables one loses touch with the 'whole'. By dealing only with artificially isolated bits of behaviour the full meaning of the behaviour will be missed. By looking at particular aspects of people's beliefs and actions without looking at the context in which they take place it is probable that we will misunderstand the meaning of the behaviour.

In the end the question should be not whether the meaningful and intentional dimension of behaviour should constitute part of social explanations, but whether this aspect of behaviour can be captured using the data collection methods usually associated with cross-sectional designs.

There have been a variety of ways in which those using cross-sectional surveys have gone about providing 'meaningful' explanations. As Marsh observes, these

> approaches differ in whom they believe the meaning should be supplied by and how much and what type of evidence is required before one can validly attribute meaning to action. (1982: 101)

She identifies a number of approaches. The first, and least satisfactory, is that which she calls 'facesheet sociology'. This consists of correlating a set of socio-demographic characteristics (e.g. sex, class, age, religion and ethnicity) with the phenomenon one wants to explain. The more one can detect correlations the more we have 'explained' variance in that phenomenon. However, this approach does not provide sociologically meaningful explanations. To find that gender is correlated with religiousness is not to understand *why* gender is linked to religiousness. We need to understand what it is about gender and religion that explains why women are more religious than men. Typically, as Marsh points out, this approach to supplying meaning is brought from outside the data where, in an *ad hoc* way, the researcher supplies the explanation from their stock of plausible sociological ideas. While these explanations may be consistent with the data they are rarely compelling since many 'explanations' that are equally consistent with the data can be developed.

A second approach is to ask individuals to supply the meaning. We can ask them why they acted as they did. This approach is criticized by those who argue that often people do not know why they acted as they did. The response to this objection is that if people do not know why they acted as they did then there is not a problem since we cannot say that that behaviour is in any sense meaningful. A second objection to asking people to give their own explanations is that they misunderstand their behaviour. Experimental evidence shows that in certain experimental situations we can demonstrate empirically what causal factor led to given behaviour but the individuals themselves are unaware of what this factor is. This objection has some merit for some behaviour in some situations but it does not mean that individuals, in many situations, cannot supply at least some reasons why they have behaved as they did. To say that they do not have access to the full range of factors that affected their actions is not to say that they have no understanding of their behaviour. If we were to ask a mother with young children why she wanted to work part time she would no doubt be able to identify a number of the reasons behind her decision. That she might not be aware of or be able to articulate all the influences is not to invalidate the importance of those she has identified. A third objection is that individuals may indeed be aware of the reasons for their actions but, because the reasons may not be all that noble, social desirability factors will prevent them from reporting these reasons.

While these objections have some merit, it can still be useful to ask people for the reasons for their behaviour. Marsh argues that 'actors . . . do have privileged access to their own experience but not to all the determinants of their own behaviour' (1982: 107). However, Marsh says, we should not exaggerate what we will discover and we must treat the explanations provided by people themselves with circumspection.

A final approach to including a meaningful dimension to explanations is for the researcher to supply the meanings (1982: 111). There will be many situations where we simply cannot reliably ask individuals for their reasons. Often we can only identify reasons by looking at a number of people in similar situations and reading off commonalties between the cases. The individual actor will normally not have access to the additional insights available to the researcher who can observe from a *range* of cases.

Durkheim's (1970) study of suicide provides such an example. By studying the statistical regularities he identified the social groups that were most 'suigenic' – the groups with the highest suicide rates. By asking what these suigenic groups had in common he sought to provide the reasons for suicide. He did so by proposing that in these groups people were most likely to experience anomie – the feeling of normlessness and a sense of not belonging. He argues that this subjective feeling is distressing to the extent that people commit suicide. Durkheim supplies this meaning rather than it coming from the data. It is Durkheim who *argues* rather than *empirically demonstrates* that the suigenic groups suffer more anomie. However, he nevertheless attempts to make sense of the empirical correlations by supplying a subjectively meaningful account of the links between membership of certain social categories and suicide.

Marsh (1982) discusses at length a study of the social basis of depression by Brown and Harris (1978) where it was believed that those suffering from depression will not be fully aware of all the factors contributing to their depression. Brown and Harris adopt an approach not unlike that utilized by Durkheim in his study of suicide – but with one difference. They collected information about what *they* thought would be the social precipitating factors behind depression (life events which acted as provoking agents, such as family problems; poor housing; employment stressors; severity of stressors; access to support networks). They collected information about these factors because they thought it would help make sense, at a subjective level, of why some people were depressed and why others were not. By planning ahead and anticipating the possible reasons that might lie behind depression they were able to develop an account of depression that tried to build in the experiences of the actors. It is not a foolproof way of tapping the subjectively meaningful aspect of behaviour but it demonstrates an attempt in a cross-sectional survey design to include this form of explanation.

In summary, there is nothing inherent in cross-sectional designs that precludes trying to access the meaningful dimensions of human behaviour and building these into explanations. It makes sense to employ a range of strategies since no single approach is without its shortcomings.

External validity

Representativeness

Representative samples are necessary if we are to generalize from results obtained in a sample to the wider population that the sample is meant to represent. The surest way of achieving representative samples is to employ probability sampling methods. These are methods where each person in the population to which we want to generalize has an equal or known chance of being selected in the sample.

Cross-sectional designs can have more success than other designs in achieving representativeness.

Experiments encounter problems with representativeness for two main reasons. They often ask more of people than do one-off cross-sectional studies. They also involve active interventions and therefore have to rely on volunteers and availability samples. They consequently lack representativeness. Even where representative samples are obtained initially this can be lost as people drop out over the course of the experiment.

A similar problem of dropout can compromise panel studies. The more waves a panel study has the greater the cumulative dropout. To the extent that this dropout introduces important sample biases, representativeness can be progressively undermined.

Since cross-sectional designs do not have a time dimension they avoid the problem of bias being introduced by sample attrition. So long as the initial sample is well selected the cross-sectional survey should yield data that are reflective of the population they were designed to represent. For this reason cross-sectional surveys have become the design of choice for studies where accurate description is required (e.g. political polls, household expenditure surveys). While cross-sectional designs have potential weaknesses in unambiguously identifying causes (a matter of internal validity) they are strong at description.

Practical issues

Many of the practical issues discussed in this section are not peculiar to cross-sectional designs but are important issues for all research regardless of the design.

Method of collecting data

There is nothing about the logic of cross-sectional designs that requires a particular method of collecting the data. The essential thing in cross-sectional designs is to obtain a structured set of data that enable systematic comparisons between cases, or groups of cases.

The analysis of cross-sectional data requires data from multiple cases using the same variables. Analysis relies on comparing cases and accounting for variation between cases on one variable in terms of variation on another variable. For example, we will observe that there is variation in terms of income: some people earn more than others. We will then see if these variations correspond with variations in something else: for example, do people with higher income also tend to have higher education than those with low income? Do the high income earners tend to be male while the low income earners tend to be female?

This sort of correlational analysis requires what is sometimes called a variable by case matrix – a grid in which we have the same information for each case. In the example in Figure 11.2, case 1 is a 44 year old, middle class male with an annual income of $45,000. He votes Conservative and agrees with attitude A but has no opinion on attitude B.

The data in a variable by case matrix can be collected using any method: questionnaires, face-to-face interviews, observations, archival records, telephone interviews and so on. There is no reason why a mixture of methods cannot be used to complete the matrix. It is, nevertheless, important that the same mix of methods be used for each case. For example we should avoid collecting information on income from some people using an anonymous self-completion questionnaire while relying on a face-to-face interview for other people, and relying on personnel records for others, or taxation returns for a further set of people. Since the method by which data are collected can influence the way people answer questions we at least must ensure consistency.

Variables

		Sex	Class	Income	Age	Attitude to A	Attitude to B	Vote
Case	1	Male	Middle	$45K	44	Agree	No opinion	Conservative
	2	Female	Working	$25K	56	Disagree	Disagree	Non-Conservative
	3	Female	Upper middle	$70K	34	Strongly agree	Strongly agree	Conservative
	4	Male	Working	$34K	45	No opinion	No opinion	Non-Conservative
	5	Male	Middle	$52K	33	Strongly disagree	Disagree	Conservative
	6	Female	Lower middle	$40K	60	Agree	Strongly agree	Non-Conservative
	7	Female	Middle	$55K	41	Agree	Agree	Non-Conservative
	8	Male	Upper	$250K	32	Disagree	Strongly agree	Conservative
	9	Male	Working	$25K	64	Strongly agree	Agree	Non-Conservative
	n	Female	Middle	$43K	43	Strongly agree	Disagree	Conservative

Figure 11.2 *A variable by case matrix*

The choice of any particular data collection method will depend on many factors. These include size of the sample, the extent to which they are clustered in the one place or are widely scattered, the time and resources available, the degree of sensitivity of the material being collected, and the complexity of the material.

While a variety of methods can be used to collect information to form a structured data set it remains the case that structured questionnaires are the most widely used method. Structured questionnaires can be administered in a number of different ways, the most common of which are: (1) face-to-face by trained interviewers, (2) over the telephone with trained interviewers, (3) self-administered by the respondent where the questionnaire is normally received and returned through the mail.

Each method of administering questionnaires has its advocates and detractors and the methods have their strengths and weaknesses (Dillman, 1978; Rogers, 1976; Groves, 1979; Groves and Kahn, 1979). In selecting a particular method of administration you need to be aware of these relative strengths and weaknesses and how they might apply to the particular survey in which you are engaged. These strengths and weaknesses can be grouped into five broad categories. Table 11.1 provides a summary evaluation of how each of the three methods of administration rates on each of the criteria. A fuller discussion is available in Dillman (1978) and de Vaus (1996).

Sample sizes

The sample size depends on funds, time, access to potential participants, planned methods of analysis, and the degree of precision and accuracy required. In general, the larger the sample the better, but beyond a certain point increasing the sample size has smaller and more marginal benefits.

SUBGROUP ANALYSIS

The larger the sample size the more it can be subdivided so that meaningful subgroup comparisons can be made. If, in a general survey of households, we wanted to compare the wellbeing of children in couple households with that of children in sole parent households, we would need to ensure that the sample would be large enough to yield sufficient numbers of sole parent households. If we wanted to compare father headed and mother headed sole parent households we would need to recruit a very large initial sample simply to find enough father headed sole parent households.

Adopting the strategy of increasing the overall sample size to obtain sufficient hard to find groups can be inefficient: we can end up with more of the 'typical' respondents than we actually need. An alternative approach is to oversample the hard to find groups to ensure sufficient

Table 11.1   *Advantages and disadvantages of three methods of questionnaire administration*

	Face-to-face	Telephone	Mail
Response rates			
General samples	Good	Good	Good
Specialized samples	Good	Good	Good
Representative samples			
Avoidance of refusal bias	Good	Good	Poor
Control over who completes the questionnaire	Good	Good	Satisfactory
Gaining access to the selected person	Satisfactory	Good	Good
Locating the selected person	Satisfactory	Good	Good
Effects on questionnaire design			
Ability to handle:			
Long questionnaires	Good	Satisfactory	Satisfactory
Complex questions	Good	Poor	Satisfactory
Boring questions	Good	Satisfactory	Poor
Item non-response	Good	Good	Satisfactory
Filter questions	Good	Good	Satisfactory
Question sequence control	Good	Good	Poor
Open ended questions	Good	Good	Poor
Quality of answers			
Minimize socially desirable responses	Poor	Satisfactory	Good
Ability to avoid distortion due to:			
Interviewer characteristics	Poor	Satisfactory	Good
Interviewer opinions	Satisfactory	Satisfactory	Good
Influence of other people	Satisfactory	Good	Poor
Allows opportunities to consult	Satisfactory	Poor	Good
Avoids subversion	Poor	Satisfactory	Good
Implementing the survey			
Ease of finding suitable staff	Poor	Good	Good
Speed	Poor	Good	Satisfactory
Cost	Poor	Satisfactory	Good

Source: adapted from Dillman, 1978

numbers. This can affect the representativeness of the sample, but this can be adjusted for by reweighting the sample to take account of under- and oversampling (Chapter 9).

PRECISION AND ACCURACY OF ESTIMATES

When using samples there is always the likelihood of sampling error: the sample does not accurately reflect the population from which it is drawn. When we use random samples we can estimate, within a specified level of probability, how close the (real but unknown) figures in the *population* are likely to be to the figures we get from the sample. Thus we might find that 60 per cent of a sample say they support capital punishment. Given

Table 11.2   *Sample sizes required for various sampling errors at 95 per cent confidence level (simple random sampling)*

Sampling error[1] (%)	Sample size[2]	Sampling error[1] (%)	Sample size[2]
1.0	9,200	5.5	330
1.5	4,500	6.0	277
2.0	2,400	6.5	237
2.5	1,600	7.0	204
3.0	1,100	7.5	178
3.5	816	8.0	156
4.0	625	8.5	138
4.5	494	9.0	123
5.0	400	9.5	110
		10.0	100

[1] This is in fact two standard errors.
[2] This assumes a 50/50 split on the variable. These sample sizes would be smaller for more homogeneous samples.

that we have a sample we will want to know how close the real population figure is likely to be to this sample estimate. Using probability theory we can estimate with a high level of confidence that the real population figure will lie within, say ±2.0 per cent of the sample estimate (i.e. in this example, somewhere within the range of 58 per cent to 62 per cent).

One of the key factors that affects how precisely we can specify the population figures is the size of the sample. The larger the sample the narrower the band (called the confidence interval) within which we can estimate the population figure will lie. In the above example we might have had a sample of about 2400 people. With a sample this size we can say that the population will lie within a relatively narrow band of ±2.0 per cent around the sample estimate. If we wanted to narrow the band we would have to increase the sample size. The general rule is that to halve the confidence interval we need to quadruple the sample size. Thus to reduce the sample error from ±2.0 per cent to ±1.0 per cent we would need to increase the sample size to 9200 cases. Obviously there is a point at which the extra level of precision is not worth the extra cost. Where that point is will depend on the funds available and the degree of precision required.

Table 11.2 provides estimates of the sample sizes you would require depending on how much sampling error you would be prepared to tolerate. The table indicates what the confidence interval would be at what is referred to as the 95 per cent confidence level. Thus we can be 95 per cent confident that if we had a random sample of 100 cases the population estimate would be within ±10 per cent of the percentages we find in the sample. If 50 per cent of the sample supported a particular politician then we could be almost certain that the real level of support in the population would be somewhere between 40 and 60 per cent. If the sample was increased to 400 then the band of reasonable certainty would be 45–55 per cent (50 ±5 per cent).[2]

Sufficient variation in the sample on key variables

Since the analysis of cross-sectional data requires that we analyse variation in one variable in terms of variation in another variable, our measurements must be sufficiently sensitive to tap the variation that exists. For example, if we were trying to explain variations in income and simply collected income data using just two broad categories, $0 to $100,000 and $100,000+, we would mask most of the variation that exists and have little variation to 'explain'. By including most people within the one category (under $100,000) we would be treating them as though they are the same. Consequently, we would be unable to explain the variation *within* this category. Similarly, if we wanted to measure marital satis-faction and this was done in such a way that everyone appeared highly satisfied we would be unable to 'explain' variations in marital satis-faction. If our instrument is too blunt to pick up variations then we cannot explain variation since we have not measured it in the first place.

The same applies with the key explanatory variables: we must ensure variation. For example, if we thought that variations in income might be due to gender it is extremely unlikely that, in a sample consisting mainly of males, much of the variation in income will be due to gender differences. If we thought that income differences are partly due to age differences but then tested this using a sample that was fairly age homogeneous, we would find that age was not very important in explaining income variations in *this* sample.

Information for statistical controls

Because of the nature of cross-sectional designs we must be able to introduce statistical controls into our analysis (Chapter 12). This is essential if we are to get any clarity regarding causal processes using cross-sectional data. If we are to introduce statistical controls at the analysis stage these must be anticipated *before* collecting data since we can only control for factors about which we have information. This can only be achieved by first reading the relevant literature and thinking through the theoretical models we are planning to evaluate and antici-pating what variables will require controlling for statistically.

Length

When data are collected directly from respondents we need to be mind-ful of the burden placed on respondents. This burden can take many forms including inconvenience, invasion of privacy and time. How long should interviews last and how long can a questionnaire be?

It is impossible to be definitive. The optimal length of an interview or questionnaire will vary widely among different types of people. Some people will be busier and unable to spend time. Others will encounter language difficulties and find the interview/questionnaire more demanding. It will depend on how easy the questionnaire is to follow and how skilled the interviewer is. Even more important is how interesting people find the topic. Undoubtedly, the length of a market research questionnaire about something of little interest to people will need to be shorter than one dealing with matters of direct concern and about which they have first-hand experience.

Types of data

There is nothing about the logic of cross-sectional designs that requires the use of quantitative or qualitative data. The key thing is that data are systematic – that we have information on the same matters for each case. Whether these data are in the form of quantitative, numerical or coded data, or whether they are quotes from interviews, extracts from diaries or observations, is not important for the logic of the design.

Analysis is simpler (but not necessarily better) if data are collected using predefined variables and categories. This is why questionnaires are so widely used in cross-sectional designs. But even in structured questionnaires we must make choices between open ended and forced choice questions (see Foddy, 1993: 126–52 for a full discussion of the purported advantages and disadvantages of open and closed questions).

Structured questionnaires are one of the simplest ways of obtaining a structured data set. However, we might use less structured data collection techniques and from this construct a structured data set. Using in-depth interviews, for example, we might identify from the interviews a set of variables of interest to us. For each of these variables we would then construct a set of categories and then classify each case. For example, I conducted a set of in-depth interviews with adults that examined the nature of relationships with their wider family. As part of the interview we talked about relationships with parents. After completing the interviews I constructed a set of variables, a number of which were about adult–parent relationships. From my interviews I had identified what I thought were a number of different types of relationships. I used a range of pieces of information to identify the type of relationship I thought applied in a particular case. I then classified each case on the basis of a whole set of clues scattered through the interview. I repeated the same process for many other aspects of the interview (e.g. relationship with siblings, nature of marriage, degree of involvement in local community, centrality of work in life). In other words, I was able to use a range of qualitative information to produce variables and to classify individual cases. I was then able to systematically analyse patterns in the data (de Vaus, 1994).

Ethical issues

As with any research design the researcher using a cross-sectional design will need to attend to matters of confidentiality, privacy, avoidance of harm to participants, and informed consent.

In some respects cross-sectional designs can minimize some of the ethical problems that can arise with experimental and longitudinal designs. Since no tracking of participants is required it is much easier to ensure anonymity. There is no need to keep lists of names or to match names at all to responses. Furthermore, since the data collection is a 'one-off', cross-sectional studies can be less intrusive and, in this respect, can be less of an imposition on a person's privacy.

In some surveys confidentiality issues can arise even when information is provided anonymously. In a survey of an organization or a specific region or in a national census it is conceivable that individuals could be identified by examining a set of characteristics. For individuals with relatively unusual characteristics it may be possible to identify individual people. For example, in a national census data will be collected for each person that lists their geographic location (down to relatively small geographical areas called collector's districts), their age, gender, occupation, income, education, household characteristics, marital status and so forth. With detailed information of this type it would be possible for someone with access to the data to identify some individuals such as the doctor in a particular small town, the school teacher, the clergyman etc. Since some survey data and census data are made publicly available to researchers for further analysis it is important that no individual is identifiable by means of cross-classifying detailed information in individual cases.

To guard against this problem, data from census collections and surveys will be 'anonymized' before they are released to other people for further analysis. This is achieved in various ways. One way is to omit certain key information, such as any geographic identifiers, from any public release of the data. Another way is to reduce the precision of the data by collapsing categories. For example, instead of providing data with specific ages or birth dates, only age groups (e.g. in five-year age groups) will be released. Another strategy is to omit any linking information between cases. For example where information is collected from each member of a household the publicly released data may make it impossible to identify which individual cases belong to the same household. By controlling the detail and amount of publicly released information in these ways it is possible to prevent the identification of particular individuals from an anonymous data set.

Because cross-sectional designs rely on existing variations rather than introducing interventions they avoid many of the potential ethical concerns about harm to participants occurring as a result of the intervention. It is also an advantage that they avoid random allocation to experimental and control groups. Random allocation can give rise to serious ethical problems (see Chapter 6).

Summary

Since cross-sectional designs lack a time dimension and randomized control groups they encounter potential shortcomings for causal analysis. These shortcomings represent threats to the internal validity of cross-sectional studies. This chapter has outlined these shortcomings and identified some ways of minimizing their impact. While cross-sectional designs present some peculiar weaknesses in relation to internal validity it has been pointed out that they also have some particular strengths. Because they do not have a time dimension, they do not suffer from many of the other threats to internal validity that we have encountered with experimental and longitudinal designs. Cross-sectional designs are a simple and cost effective design and consequently are often able to employ excellent samples and avoid the problems caused by sample attrition. As such cross-sectional designs can have strong external validity.

The absence of randomized control groups means that the analysis of data from cross-sectional designs relies on considerable sample variance and on the creation of *post hoc* comparison groups. This has implications for sample size, sample type and the practical strategies of implementing cross-sectional studies. The chapter has outlined these practical and ethical considerations.

Notes

1 This needs to be qualified to the extent that *suppressor* variables may mask a causal relationship. Strictly speaking we would need to be able to eliminate the influence of all suppressor variables before we could be certain that the absence of a correlation between two variables really reflects the absence of a causal relationship. For a fuller discussion of suppressor variables see Rosenberg (1968: Chapter 4).

2 These estimates assume that we are dealing with variables where there is a 50/50 split. The estimated sample sizes will be different in more homogeneous populations.

12

CROSS-SECTIONAL ANALYSIS

Cross-sectional designs are well suited to descriptive analysis – at least for descriptions of things as they are at a given point of time. However, cross-sectional designs have been criticized for their weakness at the level of explanatory, causal analysis. Some researchers argue that, for several reasons, cross-sectional designs are worthless at the explanatory stage of a study. To support their judgement they cite the difficulties cross-sectional data present for establishing the causal order of events, for controlling for all the variables that might be influencing correlations, and for establishing, unambiguously, causal order. Although the judgement based on the criticisms is too harsh they are valuable because they draw attention to inherent weaknesses of the cross-sectional design that must be addressed.

Descriptive analysis

Cross-sectional designs are ideally suited to descriptive analysis and are widely used for these purposes. Their widespread use in market research and political polling bear this out. These are contexts in which researchers want simply to describe such things as: who uses or likes particular products; aspects of consumer behaviour; voting intention; level of interest in politics; feelings towards particular politicians; and attitudes towards a range of issues. Typically, this type of research focuses on questions of 'how many' and 'which types' of people do or think in particular ways.

The census is another example of a descriptive cross-sectional design. Its primary function is to provide an accurate description of the population of a country: how many people there are in the population, and how many people possess particular characteristics (e.g. gender, age, education, living in particular locations etc.). Household expenditure surveys provide a further example of cross-sectional data being used for descriptive purposes. In these surveys governments seek to map the expenditure patterns of individuals and households. Such surveys enable fine-grained descriptions of the expenditure patterns of different types of families and households and for people with different income levels in particular locations and at a particular stage of the family life cycle.

Since these surveys are not primarily designed to develop explanations of behaviour, problems of causation, of causal order or the influence of uncontrolled variables do not matter. The key thing is to ensure that samples are large enough so that we can get sufficient numbers in the various subgroups to provide reliable descriptions. The other key thing is to obtain samples in such a way that we can generalize beyond the sample to the population from which the sample was drawn.

The analysis issue then becomes a matter of the appropriate ways to describe the data. It is beyond the scope of this book to go through all the ways in which data can be described.

How many?

Counting is a basic aspect of descriptive analysis. The aim is to establish how many people have particular characteristics, have a particular opinion, behave in a given way and so forth. Market surveys will find out how many people like a particular product, a political poll will count how many people intend to vote for a specific party or candidate, a census will count the number of people in the population, whilst a household expenditure survey will describe how many people have particular patterns of expenditure.

As a result we count how many people give particular answers because we are interested in the *distribution* of cases. What is the typical response to the question? How typical is the typical response? Are people spread over a large number of categories? Are they clustered in just a few categories? How similar or dissimilar are people in the sample? Are they clustered towards one end of a distribution (e.g. low income end).

In other words in addition to simple counting we will look at the *shape* of any distribution and try to summarize in meaningful ways what the distribution looks like. These goals may be achieved with various summary statistics. To summarize what is *typical* in a distribution we would use an appropriate measure of central tendency (mean, median or mode). To summarize the spread and *variability* in a distribution we would use an appropriate measure of dispersion (e.g. range, interquartile range, variance and standard deviation). Other aspects of the shape of a distribution can be summarized with statistics such as skewness and kurtosis.

Graphical representations of distributions can often convey more and be more intuitively understandable than summary statistical measures. Pie charts, bar charts, line graphs, histograms, box and whisker plots, stem and leaf plots are just some of the graphical means of representing distributions. Most computer based statistical packages and spreadsheets produce a range of such graphs. Alternatively, we may choose to present the data in tabular form. Frequency distributions are the normal way of doing this.

Level of detail

When describing distributions we have to decide how much detail to provide. Continuous variables such as age (in years), income (in dollars) and hours worked each week can be analysed as continuous variables, or collapsed into groups. Alternatively, age might be collapsed into categories such as under 20, 20–29, 30–39, 40–49, 50–59, 60–69, 70–79 and 80+; income might be collapsed into income groups (less than $5000, $5000–10,000, $10,001–15,000, $15,001–20,000) and analysed in these groupings. Many ordinal variables might be collapsed into fewer categories. For example, respondents in a survey are asked how strongly they agree or disagree with a particular attitude statement (strongly agree, agree, can't decide, disagree or strongly disagree). We would need to make decisions about whether to collapse down to the categories 'agree', 'can't decide' and 'disagree' or, alternatively, if we are only interested in agreement we could simply use the categories of 'agree' and 'other'. Nominal variables, such as country of birth, may have a large number of categories – many of which can be combined for the purpose of simple and clear presentation. We might group countries into regions (e.g. Western Europe, Central and Eastern Europe, North America, Other America, South Asia, South East Asia, Oceania) or according to levels of development, or whether or not they are English-speaking (Chapter 6).

The degree of detail we retain will depend on factors such as sample size, the number of people in particular categories, and the way in which data are to be analysed and presented, and on the main points that need to be highlighted.

The way in which variables are collapsed can have important implications for patterns of results and care must be taken to not to simply recode to either create or mask a pattern. For example, Table 12.1 illustrates the way in which coding can mask a relationship.

There are two broad ways in which collapsing of categories of a variable will be done.

SUBSTANTIVELY

Using this approach, categories are combined because of the similarity of the categories. Thus combining the categories 'agree' and 'strongly agree' would be done because they both reflected agreement. Alternatively, depending on the purpose of the analysis we might combine 'strongly agree' and 'strongly disagree' as they both indicate people who feel strongly about the issue. With a variable such as income, substantive recoding would combine categories on the basis of the actual income values. Thus we might collapse income into categories such as below $10,000, $10,000–19,999, $20,000–29,999, $30,000–39,999, $40,000–49,999, $50,000–59,999, $60,000–69,999, $70,000–79,999, $80,000–89,999, $90,000–99,999, $100,000 and over.

Table 12.1 *An illustration of recoding masking a relationship*

	Unrecoded version			Recoded version	
	Male	Female		Male	Female
Strongly agree	50%	15%	⎫ → Agree	60%	60%
Agree	10	45	⎭		
Disagree	30	5	⎫ → Disagree	40	40
Strongly disagree	10	35	⎭		
N	500	500		500	500

DISTRIBUTIONAL

Using this approach we focus on the distribution of a variable as a basis for recoding and let the distribution rather than the substantive meaning of the categories determine how we combine categories. For example, rather than collapsing income in the way described above we might simply have two categories: people below the median income and those above the median income. If the median income was $35,000 then the two income categories would be below $35,000 and above $35,000. Or we might divide the sample into deciles: the bottom 10 per cent of income earners, the second bottom 10 per cent of income earners, through to the top 10 per cent of income earners. The specific dividing lines would be determined by looking at the actual distribution. Using this approach, definitions of low and high income are not imposed arbitrarily by the researcher but are defined *relatively* on the basis of the distribution.

Table 12.2 illustrates how the same variable might be collapsed differently depending on whether substantive or distributional methods of recoding were used.

Form of data

As well as deciding on how to present and summarize distributions and how to group values, there may be a need to attend to the *form* in which the data are analysed. Sometimes it is desirable to change the way in which our measurements are expressed.

We may need to convert variables so that they are all measured on a uniform base. This can be necessary when analysing data in repeated cross-sectional surveys where the value of, say, income needs to be adjusted for inflation. In cross-national studies some variables, such as income, may need to be converted into a common currency (say US dollars). This was discussed in Chapter 9.

Data may also be represented by expressing individual scores, not in terms of the units of the original variable (e.g. years for age or dollars for income), but in terms of how the score of an individual (or group) compares with the typical value for that variable. This might be done by

Table 12.2   *Illustration of dividing a variable into three groups using substantive and distributional recoding methods*

Question	How would you rate your marriage on a scale of 0 to 10, where 0 is terrible and 10 is excellent?				
	Substantive recoding	Score	%	Cumulative %	Distributional recoding
Terrible	Bottom 1/3 of codes	0	3	3	Bottom 1/3 of cases: relatively most unhappy
		1	5	8	
		2	3	11	
		3	4	15	
	Middle 1/3 of codes	4	7	22	
		5	10	32	
		6	9	41	Relatively 'in between' 1/3 of cases
	Top 1/3 of codes	7	10	51	
		8	15	66	
		9	15	81	Top 1/3 of cases:
Excellent		10	19	100	relatively most happy

re-expressing each person's income (for example) in terms of how much lower or higher it is than the average value. One way in which this is done is by expressing a person's individual score in terms of the number of standard deviations it lies above or below the mean.

We can go one step further and *standardize* variables. Standardization has the effect of expressing each person's score *relative* to that of others in the distribution. It has the effect of eliminating differences in the units of measurement across countries, across time and across different variables. It enables us to compare apples with oranges. By standardizing income, for example, we could then examine changes in the income position of men and women over time in different countries. If we could express each man's and each woman's in standardized form, then for any year or country we could calculate the average standard score of men and of women. We could do this over a large number of years and not be worried about the overall effect of inflation.

We would see that, on average, women would be receiving incomes below the average and males above the average. By standardizing variables we can readily see whether the gap between men and women is narrowing or widening over time. In the unstandardized form it would be more difficult to establish any increase or decline because the 'value' of incomes changes. The average dollar gap between the incomes of men and women may have increased in absolute dollar terms but in relative terms the gap may have narrowed.

Standardizing income also allows us to compare the differences between countries. By standardizing we could compare the relative position of men and women in Britain, America, Germany, Japan and France without being troubled by the differences between pounds, dollars, Deutschmarks, yen and francs. Instead we would be dealing in the common 'currency' of deviations from the mean.

A variable is standardized simply by subtracting the typical value (mean or median) from each person's actual score on that variable. The resulting value for each person is then divided by a measure of variation (standard deviation if mean was used and interquartile range – or whatever – if the median was used).

Who?

Describing distributions across a whole study is typically only the first part of a descriptive analysis. More often than not we want to see how distributions differ among different subsets of the people comprising the study. For example, do the income patterns of men and women differ? By how much? In what direction? Are there differences among the young, middle aged and the elderly? Do they differ according to region?

Comparing subgroups on a given variable (income, conservatism, religiousness, happiness) is essentially a descriptive exercise that entails establishing which types of people have particular characteristics, attitudes or behaviours. It stops short of attempting to explain why some groups are different from others (although that would be the obvious next step). We are simply describing patterns, which may, in turn, lead to accounts of why groups differ. The exercise of describing is, however, the first indispensable step prior to developing explanations. For example, before seeking to explain gender differences in income we must first establish the extent and nature of the differences.

Descriptions across subgroups can be examined using a wide variety of data analysis techniques but the researcher will always employ bivariate or multivariate methods of one sort or another. The techniques will vary from simple cross-tabulations and comparison of means to more complex multivariate techniques such as multiple regression and discriminant analysis. The analysis might rely on summary statistics (e.g. comparison of means, correlation coefficients, analysis of variance), use graphical representations (e.g. scattergrams, complex line graphs, clustered bar charts) or rely on tabular presentation (two-way cross-tabulations to multiway cross-tabulations).

The choice between these various approaches will depend on the characteristics of the data (e.g. level of measurement) and the type of audience to which the analysis is directed. Chapter 6 provides an outline of a range of analysis techniques and the data considerations that will affect one's choice between the alternatives.

Factor structures and scale structures

Another form of descriptive analysis delineates which sets of variables 'go together'. Factor analysis is often used to look for patterns in the way people respond to sets of questions. It is an approach to analysis that is frequently used in studies of attitudes and values and personality characteristics. Essentially it involves looking for patterns in sets of attitudes people hold. It seeks to discover whether there is an underlying structure to the pattern of responses to questions. For example, we might ask people to tell us what they consider to be the more important attributes for children to possess (e.g. good manners, obedience, neatness, imagination, independence and self-control). By observing the pattern of answers, we might find that some people emphasize good manners, obedience and self-control and place little emphasis on imagination and independence or vice versa. In other words certain variables cluster together. Some people will select characteristics that reflect the underlying factor of *conformity* while others select characteristics that reflects an *autonomy* dimension.

Similarly, we might be interested in the types of things people look for in a job. We might ask about the importance of the following things in a job:

1 good pay
2 opportunities to use initiative
3 having responsibility
4 the feeling of achieving something
5 absence of too much pressure
6 generous holidays
7 good hours.

We might analyse answers to see if there is a structure or a pattern in the way individuals respond to each of these job characteristics. We might find that there is a structure: some people tend to list the intrinsic job characteristics (opportunities to use initiative, responsibility and feelings of achieving something) while others list the extrinsic characteristics (pay, holidays, hours and no pressure).

By looking for a pattern in the way people respond to sets of questions we are able to develop a more sophisticated understanding of the structure of attitudes and behaviour.

How general? How close?

As well as describing patterns in a sample we will frequently want to generalize to the wider population from which the sample is drawn. We will want to know if the patterns we have described in the sample are likely to hold in the wider population and, if so, how close the population figures are likely to be to those we have found in the sample.

When we use a probability sample (Chapter 6) we can use inferential statistical techniques to answer these sorts of questions. Two main types of inferential statistics are commonly used in descriptive analysis: interval estimates and tests of significance.

Interval estimates allow us to estimate within what range of the sample figures the population figures are likely to lie. For example, in a sample we might find that 60 per cent say they intend to vote for a particular political party. We can use interval estimates to estimate within what range of the 60 per cent the population figure is likely to lie. Using a statistic called the standard error we would be able to say, for example, that we can be 95 per cent confident that the real population figure will be within a certain range of the sample estimate of 60 per cent (e.g. ±2 per cent or within the range of 58 per cent to 62 per cent).

Another way of using inferential statistics is to use tests of significance. These are frequently used in conjunction with correlation coefficients. They provide an estimate of the likelihood that a correlation at least as strong as that observed in the sample will also be found in the population. For example, a correlation in a sample could reflect a real correlation in the population or it could simply be the result of sampling error. Tests of significance provide an estimate of the likelihood that the sample correlation could be due simply to sampling error. If there were a reasonable chance that it could be due to sampling error we would not feel confident in predicting that the sample correlation would be found in the wider population.

Explanatory analysis

When trying to make statements about causal relationships, cross-sectional designs must rely on static comparisons between groups or on correlations between variables where measurements are made at the same point of time. The problems with this have already been discussed at length (Chapters 3 and 11). The basic strategy by which these problems are handled is by introducing statistical controls into the analysis.

The logic of statistical controls

The logic of statistical controls is best understood within the context of the logic of experimental designs. The experimental design relies on comparing change over time in two or more groups, which were initially identical in all relevant respects. Different groups are exposed to experimental treatments and a control group is exposed to no treatment. Following the treatment, any differences between the groups on the outcome variable is taken to be due to the effect of the treatment. However, if the groups were different to begin with we would not know whether any post-treatment differences between groups were due to the treatment or to the initial differences.

In cross-sectional designs the logic is to compare groups which are formed on the basis of existing differences (the independent variable). We then compare outcomes (the dependent variable) in these groups. Any differences may be interpreted as being due to the influence of different group membership. Thus differences in the income (dependent variable) of males and females (independent variable) might be due to the effect of gender on income. However, the male–female differences might be due not to gender *per se* but to other differences between the groups. The male group might be older, be better educated, include more full time workers, be drawn from different occupations than the female group. To work out whether the male–female differences in income are due to gender we need to compare comparable males and females.

The experimental design normally achieves comparability between groups by random assignment to groups. Cross-sectional designs seek to achieve comparability by *matching* (Chapter 3) but, since they rely on existing differences and all data are collected at a single time point, the matching is done at the data analysis stage – after data are collected rather than before.

This matching will always be a limited and a less adequate means than random allocation of achieving group comparability. We can only match in relation to variables about which information has been collected. This means we must anticipate relevant variables on which groups should be matched. Our anticipation will always be less than perfect.

If we were examining the impact of gender on income we would need to compare men and women who worked a similar number of hours per week. It would be inappropriate to compare a group of women where many worked part time with a group of men who were mainly full time workers. It makes most sense to compare men who worked full time with women who worked full time and observe income differences between these two groups. We could then compare men and women who worked say 25–35 hours a week, and then those that work 15–24 hours, and so forth. Sensible analysts will seek to *compare like with like*.

If income differences persist between men and women when we match for (control) hours of work then we know that the initial income differences are *not* due to different hours of work of men and women.

Although there may be other factors that may affect income differences between men and women, our analysis will at least have eliminated hours of work as the explanation for the income differences. We might want to compare income differences among men and women from similar occupations. We could control for (match) occupation and compare professional men with professional women, clerical men with clerical women, and so on. If men and women in the same type of job have different incomes then we would have to say that income differences between men and women are *not* due to the different types of jobs held by men and women.

Multiple statistical controls

The strongest analysis occurs when it is feasible to match on a whole set of variables *simultaneously*. The more variables we control at once, the more similar the groups we compare will be. For example, we might think that income differences between men and women are due to the cumulative effects of gender differences in hours of work, types of jobs, amount of workforce experience and educational background. We would try to remove all these factors from our comparisons of men and women. We might divide our sample into many groups so that one group might be women working full time in professional jobs who have tertiary qualifications and have at least 14 years workforce experience. These could be compared with a comparable group of men. Another pair of groups might be similar to the above in all respects, except that the men and women have trade jobs. Many other pairs of groups could be compared. By controlling for or removing male–female differences we can answer the question, '*When other things are equal*, does gender make any difference to income?' If, when all other things are equal, men and women still have different incomes, then we have evidence of gender discrimination. This means that gender itself is responsible for the income differences. If, when we control for a set of variables, gender differences in income disappear, we would say that the initial income differences were *due to* the variables we have controlled. Put differently, we would say that the controlled variables *explain* the initial differences.

Of course, it is not possible to control for every possible variable, so the possibility always remains that any gender related income differences could be due to these uncontrolled variables.

There are a variety of ways in which statistical controls are made and there are a variety of ways of interpreting the various patterns of results that can be obtained. One common method of controlling for variables is the elaboration technique.

The elaboration technique

There is insufficient space here to explore all the details of this technique. An excellent book that fully describes the method is that by Rosenberg, *The Logic of Survey Analysis* (1968).

Basic approach

However, the basic strategy and logic of elaboration analysis can be described. There are five basic steps?

1 *Conduct the bivariate analysis* This will examine the relationship between the independent and dependent variable (e.g. gender and income). This analysis might be in the form of correlations, tables or

comparison of means (Chapter 6). The relationship between these two variables is called the *zero-order* relationship.

2 *Identify a relevant control variable (the third variable)* This is the variable on which you are trying to match the groups (as defined by the categories of the independent variable). It is often called the test variable or the Z variable. Your selection of the third variable will be on the basis of theoretical models and what you expect could be responsible for the zero-order relationships. This will depend on whether you are proposing that the zero-order relationship is spurious (see below) or are proposing an indirect causal relationship (see below).

3 *Draw a model* of the relationship you are proposing between the three variables (see discussion below).

4 *Undertake the analysis* This may be in the form of tables, and/or correlations, or comparison of means. Essentially the analysis involves looking at the relationship between the initial two variables (X and Y) separately for each category of the control variable (Z). These relationships are called conditional relationships.

5 *Interpret the results* Ways of interpreting different results are discussed below.

Interpretation

There are four main ways of thinking about and interpreting the results of elaboration analysis, as follows.

SPECIFICATION

In this approach we begin with a zero-order relationship and then specify the particular subgroups to which it applies and does not apply. For example, there is a general relationship between gender and income as illustrated in the zero-order cross-tabulation in Table 12.3: there is a greater percentage of males than females who are high income earners. However, when we control for occupation (blue collar and white collar), and look at both occupational groupings separately, we find that the zero-order relationship does not hold consistently within each occupational group. The separate tables for blue collar and white collar are called *conditional tables*: they show the relationship between gender and income under different conditions (blue collar condition and white collar condition). The initial pattern of women doing worse persists within the blue collar workers but not among the white collar workers. The zero-order relationship seems to be specific to particular occupational groups rather than general to all groups.

Where the initial relationship holds for some categories of the control variable (occupation in this case) but not others, the independent variable and the control variable are said to *interact*: that is, the *combination* of the two variables can create a particular effect (i.e. being female *and* blue

Table 12.3 *Zero-order and conditional tables indicating specification*

(a) Zero-order table: zero-order relationship of gender and income

All		Gender	
		Male	Female
Income	Low	40%	70%
	High	60%	30%

(b) Conditional tables: relationship of gender and income controlling for occupation

Blue collar		Gender	
		Male	Female
Income	Low	50%	70%
	High	50%	30%

White collar		Gender	
		Male	Female
Income	Low	20%	20%
	High	80%	80%

collar) that neither on its own creates. The concept of interaction has been discussed earlier in this book (Chapter 4).

REPLICATION

Replication occurs where the zero-order relationship persists in *each* category of the control variable. Where this occurs then the control variable is not responsible for the initial zero-order relationship. In the example in Table 12.4 location (rural and urban) has been controlled. When comparing males and females in general (the zero-order table) there is a 30 per cent gap between males and females (60 per cent males versus 30 per cent females have a high income). The same pattern persists among rural men and women and also among urban men and women. In other words the zero-order relationship is replicated within each category of the control variable.

When this pattern occurs the zero-order relationship is said *not* to be due to the control variable.

Table 12.4   *Zero-order and conditional tables illustrating replication*

Zero order relationship

(a) Zero-order table: zero-order relationship of gender and income

All		Gender	
		Male	Female
Income	Low	40%	70%
	High	60%	30%

(b) Conditional tables: relationship of gender and income controlling for location

Rural		Gender	
		Male	Female
Income	Low	50%	80%
	High	50%	20%

Urban		Gender	
		Male	Female
Income	Low	30%	70%
	High	70%	30%

INDIRECT CAUSAL RELATIONSHIPS

Elaboration analysis can also be used to clarify the nature of the zero-order relationship. In this case we might be asserting that gender casually affects income. But we might want to know by what mechanisms it has this effect. Does gender affect income because gender affects hours of work, which, in turn, affects income (Figure 12.1)? Here we are controlling for hours of work in order to see if the relationship between hours of work and gender is *due to* the relationship between gender and hours of work *and* the relationship between hours of work and income. If the relationship between gender and income disappears among those with comparable hours of work then we would say that the

Controlling for hours

Figure 12.1 *Causal model of indirect causal relationship between gender and income*

initial relationship was due to the hours of work variable as represented in the figure.

This is also illustrated in the cross-tabulations in Table 12.5. In this case the zero-order relationship shows that a greater percentage of men than women are high income earners (55 per cent versus 40 per cent). The cross-tabulation for part timers shows that virtually the same percentage of men as women are high income earners (31 per cent versus 33 per cent). Similarly, among the full timers, the same percentage of men and of women are high income earners (65 per cent versus 65 per cent). In other words, in this hypothetical example, when men and women have comparable hours of work the income differences between men and women disappear. The zero-order relationship is due to the relationship between gender and hours of work and the relationship between hours of work and income. The fact that there were far more part time women than part time men in the sample generated the correlation between gender and income. Had the sample had the same number of part time men and women then the initial relationship between gender and income would not have appeared.

Spuriousness

A spurious relationship is one where the correlation between two variables is *not* because of any causal relationship between them but because both the variables are related to, or outcomes of, some third variable (Chapter 3). For example, let us suppose that people who attend religious schools are more religious than those who attend secular schools. If this relationship because religious schools make people more religious or is it because both factors are produced by some third factor?

In this example the model is proposing that the reason for the relationship between type of school and religiousness is *not* because one causes the other but because religious parents are more likely than non-religious parents to send their children to religious schools (Figure 12.2). Religious parents are also more likely to raise religious children. Thus the reason why young people in religious schools are more religious than those in secular schools is because religious parents sent their children to such schools *and* raise religious children.

Results such as those in Table 12.6 would be consistent with this interpretation. The initial relationship disappears when controlling for

Table 12.5 *Zero-order and conditional tables illustrating an indirect causal relationship*

(a) Zero-order table: zero-order relationship of gender and income

All		Gender	
		Male	Female
Income	Low	45%	60%
	High	55%	40%
	N	1000	1000

(b) Conditional tables: relationship of gender and income controlling for hours of work

Part time		Gender	
		Male	Female
Income	Low	69%	67%
	High	31%	33%
	N	300	800

Full time		Gender	
		Male	Female
Income	Low	35%	35%
	High	65%	65%
	N	700	200

Controlling for parental religiousness

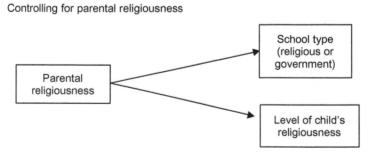

Figure 12.2 *Model indicating indirect relationship between school type and student religiousness*

Table 12.6 *Zero-order and conditional tables illustrating a spurious relationship*

(a) Zero-order table: zero-order relationship of school type and religiousness

All		Type of school	
		Religious	Secular
Child's religiousness	Low	48%	71%
	High	52%	29%
	N	800	800

(a) Conditional tables: relationship of school type and religiousness controlling for parental religiousness

Religious parents		Type of school	
		Religious	Secular
Child's religiousness	Low	35%	37%
	High	65%	63%
	N	600	200

Non-religious parents		Type of school	
		Religious	Secular
Child's religiousness	Low	85%	82%
	High	15%	18%
	N	200	600

parental religiousness. Among those with religious parents we see the same level of religiousness among children regardless of the type of school attended: 65 per cent of those children in religious schools were highly religious compared to 63 per cent of those in secular schools. The same pattern is repeated among those with non-religious parents: 15 per cent of children attending religious schools were religious compared to 18 per cent of those in secular schools.

SUMMARY OF INTERPRETATION OF DIFFERENT PATTERNS

The strategy in elaboration analysis is to compare the pattern in the zero-order relationship with that in the conditional relationships. The

Table 12.7 *Interpretation of conditional relationships compared to zero-order relationships*

Conditional relationship compared to zero order	Interpretation		Illustration
1 Same as zero order	Replication	Zero-order relationship is not due to test variable	Z_1 $X \rightarrow Y$ Z_2 $X \rightarrow Y$
2 Split	Specification	Interaction between independent variable and test variable; X only affects Y under specific conditions	Z_1 $X \rightarrow Y$ Z_2 X Y
3 Less than zero order and test variable precedes both X and Y in time	Spuriousness	Zero-order relationship is non-causal	$Z \begin{smallmatrix} \nearrow X \\ \searrow Y \end{smallmatrix}$
4 Less than zero order and test variable comes between X and Y timewise	Intervening causal relationship	Zero-order relationship is causal but mediated by the intervening variable (test variable)	$X \rightarrow Z \rightarrow Y$

comparison provides the key to interpreting the way in which the control variable affects the original relationship. Table 12.7 provides a simple summary of ways to interpret the comparison between zero-order relationships and conditional relationships.

Problems with the elaboration model

The elaboration model has a number of problems that can limit its usefulness as a way of controlling for variables in cross-sectional analysis.

A major problem is that this sort of matching requires very large samples. Because it involves subdividing the sample into separate groups for each category of the test variable we can quickly end up with quite small groups for analysis. If the test variable has, say five categories, each subgroup can be small. If we want to match for two variables at once this problem is compounded. The difficulties created by running out of cases are so serious that this form of analysis is limited frequently to matching on just one variable at a time.

As well as running out of cases the results obtained from elaboration analyses can become very complex and difficult to interpret. When we have many different conditional tables the logic involved in interpreting the varying patterns can become very complex. It can become extremely difficult to explain and present the results of anything but the quite simple elaboration analyses.

Multivariable analysis

Elaboration analysis is a simple form of multivariate analysis. It usually focuses on the role of a third variable in understanding an initial bivariate relationship. Other forms of multivariate analysis such as partial correlation, multiple regression, discriminant analysis, path analysis and log-linear analysis allow us to control for a number of other variables simultaneously. Various forms of multivariate analysis can enable powerful and informative explanatory analysis of cross-sectional data.

1 We can remove the confounding effects of a set of variables at once and focus on the 'pure' effect of an independent variable. The more variables we can control for at once the more valid our comparison of groups becomes, and the more confident we can be that any observed effect of an independent variable is due to that variable and not the confounding effects of other variables.
2 These multivariate analysis techniques can tell us about the *joint* effect of a set of independent variables.
3 By controlling for a set of variables simultaneously these multivariate techniques enable us to examine the discrete effect of each variable within a set of independent variables. While gender, education and hours of work may each have some effect on income, multivariate analysis enables us to explore how much each one has independently of the others. This strategy enables us to identify the *relative importance* of each of a set of independent variables.
4 Multivariate techniques enable the testing of causal *models* as well as the impact of single variables. By testing models these techniques can be effective in helping identify causal *processes* or at least in evaluating how well a model fits a set of cross-sectional data.

There is insufficient space here to describe the various multivariate techniques. Many simple yet sophisticated introductions are available (Kerlinger and Pedhazur, 1973; Tabachnick and Fidell, 1983; Grimm and Yarnold, 1995).

Cohort analysis

Cross-sectional designs are limited in the extent to which they can provide information about change over time. However, repeated cross-sectional studies can provide valuable insights about change. Cohort analysis can use a series of repeated cross-sectional studies to describe *aggregate* change over time and to identify the extent to which this change is attributable to period effects, ageing and cohort effects (Chapter 7).

For example we might want to study changes in church attendance. This can be achieved by constructing what Glenn (1977) calls a *standard cohort table*.

Constructing and reading cohort tables

When a series of equally spaced surveys (e.g. a population census every 10 years) has been conducted, a standard cohort table can be constructed. In order to construct the table we would establish an *age cohort span* that is the same as the interval between each survey. Thus if data were collected every 10 years we might establish age cohorts of 20–29, 30–39, 40–49 etc.

The table would consist of age cohorts down the side and data collection years across the top. In each cell of the table we would insert the relevant information that applied to the particular age cohort in the particular year. If the dependent variable was church attendance, each cell would contain some measure of church attendance (e.g. percentage attending church at least monthly, the average number of times people in that age group attend church each year, a measure of variance regarding church attendance or some other way of summarizing church attendance) for the relevant age cohort for the particular study year (see Tables 12.8 to 12.10).

We can then read the standard cohort table in three different ways to detect different patterns of change.

AGEING EFFECTS

Ageing effects or developmental effects are those where change is attributable to people growing older. These can be detected by reading the standard cohort table *diagonally from top left to bottom right* to identify *intracohort trends*. Reading down the diagonals of the table enables us to see how a particular age cohort changes as it ages (Table 2.8). How have people who were in their 20s in 1970 changed as an age group as they have moved into their 30s in 1980, into the 40s by 1990, and into their 50s by the turn of the century?

Table 12.8 shows perfect ageing effects. Ten per cent of the cohort of 20 year olds in 1970 was attending church at least monthly. Ten years later, when this cohort would have been 30 or so years of age, the church attendance of this cohort increased to 15 per cent. Another 10 years later (1990) this cohort – now in its 40s – displays a further increase in church attendance. The same ageing pattern can be seen in any left to right downward diagonal.

The conclusion one would draw is that as people get older they increase their church attendance. This is consistent regardless of the years one examines, or the age group examined.

Table 12.8 *Cohort table of percentage attending church at least monthly by age cohort and year, 1970–2000: ageing effects*

Age group	Year of data collection			
	1970	1980	1990	2000
20–29	10	10	10	10
30–39	15	15	15	15
40–49	20	20	20	20
50–59	25	25	25	25
60–69	30	30	30	30
70–79	35	35	35	35

PERIOD EFFECTS

Clear period effects are evident if, within any particular year, there are no differences between the age groups (i.e. within a column) but there are differences between each column. In Table 12.9 we see that in 1970 all age groups had the same proportion of regular church attenders. Age groups were indistinguishable. This irrelevance of age persists in every decade. Period effects are evident by looking at the trend across columns. In each decade the proportion of regular attenders changes, and it changes in an identical way for each age group.

An examination of these period effects enables us to see how people within the same age group differ at different periods. Thus in Table 12.9 we can see that people in their 20s in 1970 are quite different from those in their 20s at the turn of the century. The age group is constant: the period in which this age group is living is different.

COHORT EFFECTS

Cohort effects are evident in Table 12.10. That is, *within any given year* the age groups have different proportions of regular attenders: the age group makes a difference to the level of frequent attenders.

CROSS-SECTIONAL DESIGNS

Table 12.9   *Cohort table of percentage attending church at least monthly by age cohort and year, 1970–2000: period effects*

	Year of data collection			
Age group	1970	1980	1990	2000
20–29	25	20	15	10
30–39	25	20	15	10
40–49	25	20	15	10
50–59	25	20	15	10
60–69	25	20	15	10
70–79	25	20	15	10

Table 12.10   *Cohort table of percentage attending church at least monthly by age cohort and year, 1970–2000: cohort effects*

	Year of data collection			
Age group	1970	1980	1990	2000
20–29	25	20	15	10
30–39	30	25	20	15
40–49	35	30	25	20
50–59	40	35	30	25
60–69	45	40	35	30
70–79	50	45	40	35

Cohort effects are evident where there is change within a column and within the rows, and the direction of change in a column (e.g. from low to high per cent) is opposite to the direction of change within the rows (e.g. from high to low per cent).

While a cohort table can be very helpful in identifying ageing, period and cohort effects there is an important difficulty with this approach. It is impossible to completely isolate a 'pure' ageing, period or cohort effect (Glenn, 1977: 130). Any table that demonstrates one type of effect invariably displays one other type of effect. For example, Table 12.8, which was designed to illustrate ageing effects (change in the diagonal), also displays cohort effects (change in column). Table 12.9, designed to display period effects (change across columns), also displays ageing effects. Table 12.10 was designed to display cohort effects but also displays period effects. While it is not possible to disaggregate these effects we can, nevertheless, see the *absence* of particular effects and the *possibility* of other effects.

UNEVENLY SPACED SURVEYS

Unfortunately, we do not always have the luxury of studies being conducted at evenly spaced or convenient time intervals. When these conditions do not prevail we need to modify the way in which the cohort table and the age cohorts are constructed. This is illustrated in Table 12.11.

To construct this table we first establish our cohort widths for the first year, 1979 (in this case 10-year age bands). For the year of the next data collection (1984) we will construct age cohorts of the same age space (i.e. 10 years) but the lower and upper limits of the cohort will be adjusted for the interval between the data collections. The same procedure would be used to adjust cohorts between each data collection phase.

For example, cohort 1 in 1979 comprised the 20–29 age group (10-year span). The next data collection was 1985 (five years later). To track the initial 20–29 year old cohort five years later we identify the 25–34 age group in 1984. The comparable cohort two years later in 1986 will be 27–36. Three years later, in 1989, the comparable cohort will be 30–39 years. The basic strategy entails establishing a fixed age span for the cohort and then adjusting the lower and upper ages for the cohort equivalent to the gap between the data collections.

This cohort table has to be read a little differently from the standard cohort table:

1   To identify ageing effects we read *across* rows rather than down a cohort diagonal. In this case we can see an ageing effect as the percentage of regular attenders increases as we track the age cohort across successive surveys.

Table 12.11   *Cohort table for irregularly spaced surveys: ageing and cohort effects for percentage regular church attendance (at least monthly)*

		Year					
		1979	1984	1986	1989	1996	2000
Cohort 1 Age	20–29	25–34	27–36	30–39	37–46	40–49
		15%	17%	18%	20%	23%	24%
Cohort 2 Age	30–39	35–44	37–46	40–49	47–56	50–59
		17%	19%	20%	22%	25%	26%
Cohort 3 Age	40–49	45–54	47–56	50–59	57–66	60–69
		21%	23%	24%	26%	29%	30%
Cohort 4 Age	50–59	55–64	57–66	60–69	67–76	70–79
		25%	27%	28%	30%	33%	34%
Cohort 5 Age	60–69	65–74	67–76	70–79	77–86	80–89
		26%	28%	29%	31%	34%	35%

Source: adapted from Glenn, 1977: 47

2   To identify cohort (age level) effects we would continue to look down a column within a given year. In this case we can see a cohort effect as the percentage of regular attenders within any survey increases the older the age cohort.

3   To identify any period effects (changes within an age level over time) we need to construct a second table in which age level data from each data collection are provided (Table 12.12). In this table to identify period effects we would simply compare across each row. The columns would be the same as in the first table and could also be used to detect age level effects. In this table, because the age spans are not the same as the gaps between data collection years, we cannot use the diagonal to track ageing effects.

Table 12.12 *Cohort table for irregularly spaced surveys: period effects for percentage regular church attendance (at least monthly)*

Age group	Year					
	1979	1984	1986	1989	1996	2000
20–29	15%	14%	14%	12%	10%	9%
30–39	17%	16%	16%	14%	12%	11%
40–49	21%	20%	20%	18%	16%	15%
50–59	25%	24%	24%	22%	20%	19%
60–69	26%	25%	25%	23%	21%	20%

Problems with cohort analysis

While cohort analysis can be an excellent way of identifying some of the aggregate level patterns of change over time without the expense and difficulties of collecting panel data, it faces important problems.

One problem is the limited explanatory power of cohort analysis. It is limited to testing three different explanations of change – that any change is due to people getting older, to the period in which people were raised, or to cohort effects (differences between age groups at a specific time). While cohort analysis can be an effective means of identifying the type and direction of change (ageing, period or cohort) it does not help us identify *why* that type of change takes place.

Second, there are problems of comparability – of working out whether measured change reflects real change or changes in methodology. In panel studies considerable attention is given to ensuring comparability over time of questions, samples and data collection method. However, since the data collection used in cohort analyses are stand-alone collections there may be changes in question wording, coding, sampling, data collection methods and the like between studies that make it difficult to compare response patterns over time. Census collections, which can provide excellent cohort data analysis, are often guilty of changing questions, definitions and coding categories over time. This can create difficulties for cohort analysis.

Summary

This chapter has provided guidelines for the descriptive and explanatory analysis of data generated by cross-sectional designs. It has not considered the specific techniques, but many of the statistical guidelines provided in Chapter 6 apply to cross-sectional analysis.

The chapter considered the particular problems of using cross-sectional data for causal analysis – problems created by the absence of a time dimension to the design and the lack of randomized control groups. The general way of dealing with these problems is at the analysis stage rather than at the research design stage. The chapter outlined the logic of using statistical controls and multivariate analysis so that cross-sectional data can be useful for causal analysis. It then described one particular form of multivariate analysis – elaboration analysis – to provide an understanding of the ways in which the problems of causal analysis can be tackled. Finally, the chapter discussed a method of analysing data from repeated cross-sectional studies. In particular it focused on cohort analysis – how to construct and interpret cohort tables and to be aware of the limits of this type of analysis.

PART V

CASE STUDY DESIGNS

13

CASE STUDY DESIGN

For many years the case study has been the ugly duckling of research design. Most research methods texts either ignore case studies or confuse them with other types of social research. When case study designs have been discussed they have generally been seen – from a methodological point of view – as 'soft' options. Some commentators believe case studies should be used only for exploratory research: to generate hypotheses for future testing with more rigorous research designs.

The methodology of case study design has not been neglected because case studies have been unimportant in social sciences. Indeed they have been fundamental to the substantive and methodological development of the social sciences. In social anthropology studies of tribes have been case studies *par excellence*. Community studies such as the Lynds' *Middletown* (1929) and small group studies like Whyte's *Street Corner Society* (1943) have made major contributions to the development of sociology as a discipline. Psychoanalysis has thrived on a case study approach (Freud, 1955). Educational research, evaluation research and organizational research have all made extensive use of case studies to foster their development.

The lack of a systematic discussion of case study designs has begun to be addressed in recent times. Yin (1989; 1993) has provided a particularly useful treatment of case study designs and a powerful defence of their value.

This chapter examines a range of ways of developing case study designs. This is a different task to that undertaken for experimental, longitudinal and cross-sectional designs because, as Yin points out, 'unlike other research strategies, the potential "catalog" of research designs has not yet been developed' (1989: 27).

What is a case?

Units of analysis

A case is the 'object' of study. It is the unit of analysis (see Chapter 2) about which we collect information. In case study designs it is the unit that we seek to understand as a whole. The unit of analysis may be a person about whom we try to build up an understanding that is informed by the *context* in which the whole case exists.

But case studies are not restricted to *individuals*. We can select many other types of cases – units of analysis. A marriage, a family or a household may serve as a case. *Places* such as a block of houses, a residential community, a region or a country can all serve as cases; as can *organizations* such as a business, a school, a government department or a union. A case might be an *event* such as a divorce rather than the person who divorces. Alternatively, a *decision* (e.g. decisions about downsizing an organization) might be the unit of analysis for the case study. The case study could involve understanding the decision as a whole, examining the process by which it was made, the participants, the consequences etc. *Time periods* might be the unit of analysis. We might study the 1960s or the 1990s: each of these can be the 'thing' about which we collect information.

Holistic and embedded units of analysis

It is helpful to distinguish between cases as a whole and cases that consist of various levels or components. Yin (1989) uses the terms 'holistic' and 'embedded' designs to refer to this distinction.

Some cases consist of multiple levels or components. For example, a school as a case includes teaching staff, administrative staff, staff at different levels of seniority and experience, students, students at different year levels, parents, government and community members and so forth. A school can be conceived of at the 'holistic' level where we focus on characteristics of the school that apply to that level. The school exists as an entity and has school level characteristics (e.g. size, type of school, location, culture of school, a set of rules, a structure, a system of management, a school philosophy, strengths and weaknesses). But there are also many sublevels of elements to the school. A full picture of the school in all its complexity would only be obtained if we collected information from a wide range of the constituent elements (embedded units) of the larger unit.

A marriage provides another example. At the holistic level we would treat the marriage as a whole in terms of things such as its length, stage, type, level of conflict and intimacy, equality, modes of interaction etc. We could also treat the husband and the wife as embedded units and build up a much fuller and different picture of the marriage by incorporating the experiences and perspectives of the husband and the wife (subunits).

A well-designed case study will avoid examining just some of the constituent elements. It will build up a picture of the case by taking into account information gained from many levels. The final case study will tell us more than, and something qualitatively different from, that which any constituent element of the case could tell us. In the case of a school, the insights gained from students, teachers, parents, administrators and community members will probably differ and, when taken together, provide a much fuller, more complex understanding of the whole than would the perspective provided by any particular element of the case. The whole is greater than the sum of its parts.

Since many cases will consist of different elements, different methods of data collection may be required for the different elements. A survey of students might be appropriate; observation of classrooms and staff meetings might also be worthwhile; while interviews might be a good way of gaining information from teachers. An analysis of school records and archives could provide useful information about the historical context within which the school operates.

Case studies and theory

Although some case study researchers conduct case studies as though they only have to collect the facts about the case and write about these in an engaging way, the task of the case study researcher is fundamentally theoretical. Collecting and analysing information from case studies must be guided by theory.

Explanatory case studies

Case study designs differ from the designs discussed earlier in this book in that they seek to achieve both more complex and fuller explanations of phenomena. They seek to achieve idiographic as well as nomothetic explanations (see Chapter 14). They also differ in the way in which they go about trying to achieve causal explanations (see Chapters 14 and 15).

Case study research in social sciences must have a theoretical dimension. Without a theoretical dimension a case study will be of little value for wider generalization – one of the goals of social science research. This section considers three ways in which theory is used in designing case studies.

THEORY TESTING

This approach, which is seen by Yin (1989) as being at the heart of case studies, begins with a theory, or a set of rival theories, regarding a particular phenomenon. On the basis of a theory we predict that a case with a particular set of characteristics will have a particular outcome. The theory may be simple or complex.

For example, the case study might begin with the following question: 'What is the effect of devolved, school based control of staffing on the quality of education in a school?' Devolved or school based staffing control involves each school appointing, dismissing and promoting staff as well as setting pay levels and teaching conditions. Devolved staffing systems can be contrasted with centralized systems where public service bureaucrats manage these staffing matters at head office level. We might begin with the proposition that devolved control will yield much better educational outcomes than centralized control. The reasoning would be that local control makes people far more accountable, enables a school to build a staff profile appropriate to its needs, and makes it much easier to reward staff who are achieving the outcomes desired by the school. The implicit theory here is that educational quality is fundamentally a result of teacher quality (as opposed to the nature of students, school resources, organizational structure, parental involvement) and that teacher quality is a function of teacher accountability and teacher 'fit' with the school.

The selection of a case to test this theory would lead us to find a school that has introduced a devolved staffing system. By thoroughly investigating the school (including the 'embedded elements' such as teachers, management, parents, past and present students) we would build up a picture of the quality of education in the school (however defined) and map out any links that exist between the educational quality and the staffing system. If possible we would collect historical data relating to the time before the devolved system was introduced to see if there was evidence of improvement after its introduction. We would also seek to identify what else was happening in the school that might have led to improvements in the quality of education or factors that might have prevented improvements despite the introduction of the devolved system.

The point of the case study would be to see if the theory actually worked in a real life situation. If it did work then the theory is supported (not proven). If it did not work then we would seek to understand, from a careful analysis of the case, why the predicted outcome (better education) did not eventuate. Is it because the theory is completely wrong? Does the theory require some refinement? Is the theory applicable only under specific circumstances?

Instead of this simple proposition we might develop a more complex model that specified what would happen with the introduction of a devolved staffing system. The model might anticipate positive effects in particular aspects of educational outcomes and negative effects in others. It might specify positive effects only after a given period of time, and only when the devolved system is implemented in a particular way (e.g. with full teacher and community consultation, with appropriate checks and balances). In other words, the theory we specify might anticipate that when conditions $A + B + C + D$ are met then the devolved system will achieve improvements in aspects X and Y after a period of N years.

Regardless of the complexity of the theory, this approach to case studies begins with a set of expectations derived from previous research and/or theories. We approach the case study with the purpose of testing our theory in a real life situation. Clearly the selection of the real life situation (the case) would need to match the conditions under which the theory proposes particular outcomes (Chapter 14).

THEORY BUILDING CASE STUDIES

Using a theory building approach to case studies we select cases to help develop and refine the propositions and develop a theory that fits the cases we study. For example, we might start with the simple proposition that the introduction of devolved systems will improve educational outcomes. We might select a school where such a system has been introduced and find that educational outcomes did, in fact, improve. We might then find a school in which the introduction of the devolved staffing system did *not* produce better educational outcomes. Why did it produce good outcomes in some cases and not others?

Our analysis of each case would aim to highlight differences between cases where it did and did not work. Our analysis would also identify commonalities among cases where devolved staffing was successful and commonalities among cases where it was unsuccessful (e.g. the way in which the system was implemented). These case studies could then be used to develop a set of propositions about the conditions and context under which devolved staffing systems lead to improvements (Chapter 15).

The difference between the theory testing and theory building approaches is that in the former we *begin* with a set of quite specific propositions and then see if these work in real world situations. In the theory building model we begin with only a question and perhaps a basic proposition, look at real cases and *end* up with a more specific theory or set of propositions *as a result* of examining actual cases.

CLINICAL CASE STUDIES

While the two above case study approaches are *theory centred* in that the goal is to use the case to test, refine and develop theoretical generalizations, the clinical case study uses theories very differently. Clinical case studies are *case centred*. They use theories to understand a case.

The way in which a clinician deals with a client illustrates this style of case study. A child may visit a psychologist because he is performing poorly at school and has become disruptive. The task of the clinical psychologist is to work out what is going on in this case and why it is happening. A good clinician will start with symptoms: what is happening at school? In what areas of school is the child performing poorly? The clinician will undoubtedly have a range of possible explanations for poor school performance and disruptive behaviour at school. She will gather information to build up a picture of what is going on. She will develop hunches and collect further information to test these hunches. The psychologist may give the child various tests to establish his intelligence quotient, and any specific learning disabilities. The psychologist does this to see if a cognitive explanation of the learning difficulties fits. She may have the child's eyesight or hearing tested to see if sight or auditory problems are contributing to his learning disabilities. The psychologist may evaluate the child's relationship skills to establish if problems in this sphere contribute to the learning difficulties. Alternatively she might probe into the child's family relationships to see if something that is going on at home is creating problems at school. Perhaps the child and the teacher do not get on and the problems spring from their relationship difficulties. It is also possible that the child is suffering from anxiety, depression or some other clinical syndrome.

The point is that the clinician will have a battery of potential explanations for the child's problems. Her task is to build up a full picture of the case so that she can evaluate which explanation best fits the facts of the case. Having correctly diagnosed the nature or cause of the child's problems the clinician can begin treatment.

In this example the goal is to understand the case and solve a problem for this case. The purpose is not to test or *develop* theories but to *use* existing theories. The clinician works with plausible rival hypotheses and progressively collects information to help sort out which fits best.

The same logic can apply in consultancy case studies. An organization might be suffering a great deal of conflict and poor morale. A consultant may have a range of possible explanations for this and should go about the task of collecting information about the organization that can help establish which of the explanations fits this particular organization. The goal is not to develop a theory of organizational conflict and morale loss but to identify which of several alternative theories makes most sense in this particular case.

Descriptive case studies

Although this chapter and the following two chapters focus on explanatory case studies it is important to discuss descriptive case study designs. It is important to consider descriptive case studies for two reasons. The first is that unless we can do good descriptions of cases we will be in no position to achieve good explanations using those cases. The second reason is that a discussion of descriptive case studies further highlights the importance of theory in case study research.

DESCRIPTION AND THEORY

The problem in any description is where to begin and where to end. This is especially so with case studies. A case study deals with the *whole* case

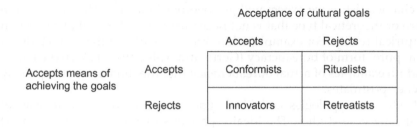

Figure 13.1 *Theoretically derived typology of deviants*

but this cannot possibly mean that the case study consists of *everything* about the case. To describe everything is impossible: there must be a focus.

Description must not, indeed cannot, be atheoretical. We always select and organize that which we describe. Descriptions will highlight aspects of the case. It will be more like a painting of a landscape than a photograph; it will be an interpretation rather than a mirror image. We might do this using explicit theories or pre-existing conceptual categories, or using implicit theories of what is relevant and what categories are important. For example, when describing a person I might, as a sociologist, highlight their personality, ethnicity, age, gender and the like because I see these as the critical elements that constitute a social person. Another person, a biologist, might focus much more on physical, genetic attributes. Each of the descriptions reflects a different focus of interest and a different assessment of what is relevant in describing a person.

TYPOLOGIES AND IDEAL TYPES

Descriptive case studies may consist of single or multiple cases. One way of reporting multiple case studies is to use typologies and ideal types.

Typologies may be theoretically derived or empirically derived. A theoretically derived typology is one that is logically or theoretically possible. For example, Merton (1968) developed a typology of types of deviants based on the notions of cultural *goals* and institutionalized *means* of achieving those goals (Figure 13.1). Thus the *conformist* is a theoretical construct defined as someone who accepts the *goals* of culture and the *means* by which the culture prescribes the achievement of these goals. The *innovator* accepts the goals but not the prescribed means for achieving them. The *ritualist* rejects cultural goals but nevertheless goes along with the prescribed cultural behaviour. The *retreatist* rejects both the goals and the means of achieving those goals.

Typologies constructed in this deductive way represent a set of ideal types (Coser, 1977: 223–4). Ideal types are a theoretical description of sets of characteristics we expect will go together in a case. They represent a pure or theoretical type that is not necessarily found in that pure form in empirical reality. For example, while Weber identified the characteristics of a 'pure' form of bureaucracy (Gerth and Mills, 1946: 196–204) we may find no examples of actual bureaucracies that function in exactly the way Weber postulates.

Deductive typologies and ideal types can provide a useful way of analysing case studies. The ideal type can serve as a yardstick against which to compare actual cases (Chapter 15). The template provided by the ideal type can guide the way in which we investigate the case; it can guide what we look for.

INDUCTIVE TYPOLOGIES

An inductively derived typology is one in which we start with a question and then examine cases in the light of the question. A comparison of cases can then highlight *clusters* of similar cases. For example, I commenced a set of case studies with the question, 'How do adults get on with their elderly parents?' I studied a range of cases and found that cases differed along a range of dimensions (e.g. level of conflict, tension, dependence, balance, enjoyment, intimacy and intrusiveness). I then noticed that cases tended to exhibit distinct clusters of characteristics. On the basis of these common elements I characterized particular cases as being of a particular type. Working from a question and actual cases I then developed a fourfold case based typology of adult–parent relationships that I called parent centred, child centred, remote, interdependent (de Vaus, 1994).

The particular characteristics of each type need not concern us here. The point is that typologies can be developed in different ways – either deductively or inductively. Regardless of the way in which they are developed they can provide a helpful template for conducting, analysing and reporting (Chapters 14 and 15) descriptive case studies.

Other elements of case study designs

When designing case studies there are a number of elements, apart from those discussed above, that can be built into the design.

Single or multiple cases?

A case study design can be based on single or multiple cases. A single case design will normally be less compelling than multiple case designs. Using the logic of replication (Chapter 14) a single case represents only one replication and does not necessarily provide a tough test of a theory. However, we may have little choice. Limited access to cases or the extreme nature of the case may mean that we can only study a single example. In other situations we may rely on a single *critical* case. This can be appropriate when we have a clear theory with well-formulated propositions and we have a single case that meets all the requirements of the theory. Such a case can provide a moderately convincing test of a complex theory (Yin, 1989).

Multiple cases, strategically selected, can provide a much tougher test of a theory and can help specify the different conditions under which a theory may or may not hold. Furthermore, multiple cases are essential if the case studies are being used for inductive purposes (see Chapter 15 on analytic induction). Given sufficient resources and access to cases, multiple case designs will normally be more powerful and convincing and provide more insights than single case designs.

However, when using a multiple case design we should endeavour to treat each case as a single case so that we are able to establish a full account of that case before engaging in cross-case comparisons. The unity of the single case should be respected (Stake, 1994; Yin, 1989: 56–7).

Parallel or sequential?

A parallel design is one where all the case studies are done at once (e.g. different investigators each doing a case). Only at the completion of the investigation of each case study are comparisons made between the cases. This strategy can be appropriate when the project adopts a simple theory testing approach.

A sequential design is one where case studies follow one another. Using this approach one investigator could, in principle, conduct each case study. An advantage of the sequential approach is that the selection of each case and some of the issues examined can be informed by puzzles identified in earlier cases. One case can throw up ideas that can influence the selection of subsequent cases and that can be followed up in these later cases (Chapters 14 and 15). When adopting a more inductive, theory building approach a sequential design is more appropriate than a parallel approach.

Retrospective or prospective?

Most case studies, and all explanatory case studies, will incorporate a time dimension. Without this dimension any adequate causal explanation is not possible. Case studies can provide a good way of carefully mapping the sequence of events, which is the basis of causal explanations. It has to be decided whether this time dimension is obtained retrospectively or prospectively.

A *retrospective* design involves collecting, on the one occasion, information relating to an extended period. This requires the reconstruction of the history of the case. This might be done through the use of archival records and documents, or interviews with people who participated in or observed past events.

This design has the obvious problems associated with loss of evidence, reconstruction of the past in the light of the present, and mistaking the sequence in which events occurred. However, in many situations there is little choice but to draw on people's ability to recall the past. With case studies the use of multiple sources of evidence can reduce the problems that go with this approach.

A *prospective* design involves tracking changes forward over time. It has the obvious advantage of enabling the investigator to look at events as they occur rather than relying on partial and reconstructed accounts. Depending on the issues under consideration and the types of cases, prospective case studies might last for years. The obvious disadvantage can be the time and resources required. These constraints can severely limit the number and range of cases that can be studied. This, in turn, can result in very limited tests of a theory.

Regardless of whether a retrospective or prospective approach is adopted, the goal is to build up a clear and reasonably detailed picture of the sequence in which events took place and of the context in which they occurred. To build meaningful causal explanations we must get the sequence and the context right. A convincing causal explanation will be able to track the 'story' by which one (or a set of) event(s) ended up producing a particular outcome.

Types of case study designs

Unlike other types of research design there is, as yet, no inventory of types of case study design (Yin, 1989). However, the discussion of elements of case study designs discussed in this chapter provides a way of thinking about the different ways in which case studies can be structured. These elements are:

- descriptive or explanatory
- theory testing or theory building
- single case or multiple case
- holistic or embedded units of analysis
- parallel or sequential case studies
- retrospective or prospective.

A cross-classification of these elements results in the logical possibility of 64 different variations of case study designs (Figure 13.2). This figure is presented not to overwhelm with the range of possibilities, nor to develop 64 different names for different case study designs, but to provide a way of thinking about different alternatives for shaping a case study design. The decisions made in relation to these six elements will result in different ways of conducting the case study, and of analysing the data collected in the study.

Explanatory?			Descriptive				Explanatory			
		Time	Retrospective		Prospective		Retrospective		Prospective	
		Case order								
Cases	Units	Theory	Parallel	Sequential	Parallel	Sequential	Parallel	Sequential	Parallel	Sequential
Single case	Embedded units	Testing								
		Building								
	Holistic	Testing								
		Building								
Multiple cases	Embedded units	Testing								
		Building								
	Holistic	Testing								
		Building								

Figure 13.2 *Variations of case study designs*

What a case study is not

Before ending this chapter it is worth saying what case study designs are *not*.

Not the one-shot case study

The taxonomy of research designs outlined by Campbell and Stanley (1963) and by Cook and Campbell (1979) has led to misunderstandings of what a case study design can be. Using the template of the classic experimental design they identify a design which they refer to as the *one-shot case study*. This is represented diagramatically in Figure 13.3.

As a simple example of this type of design we could consider a group of children whose parents divorced within the last year and for whom we obtained a measure of emotional adjustment. In effect this design consists of members of an 'experimental' group only and relies only on 'post-intervention' information.

The earlier discussions of the logic of experimental, longitudinal and cross-sectional designs indicate how this design tells us nothing of value about the impact of parental divorce on the emotional adjustment of children. We cannot tell from this design whether children with divorced parents are in any way *distinctive* from other children, and whether there is any *change* in emotional adjustment following divorce.

Representing this type of design as an example of case study design is unfortunate and provides a misleading picture of the potential of a well-conceived case study design. Indeed Cook and Campbell (1979) have acknowledged this and have renamed the design as a *one-group post-test only* design, and now stress that it should not be confused with true case study design.

Not a data collection method

Case studies have frequently been equated with qualitative methods, especially participant observation and unstructured, in-depth interviews. This identification is no doubt partly because some of the early, influential case studies used participant observation methods (e.g. *Street Corner Society* and *Middletown*). Similarly, most ethnographic case studies used in social anthropology employ participant observation, and ethnographies and case studies have sometimes been taken to be the same thing.[1] In other contexts case studies are equated with unstructured in-depth interviews that enable the researcher to build up a much fuller picture of a case than is possible with more quantitative based methods of data collection. In general there is a tendency to equate 'thick description' (Geertz, 1973) with case studies.

If we equate case studies with a particular data collection method we misunderstand case study design. Yin argues that case study *design* is

Method of allocation to groups	Time 1 (T_1) Pre-test	Intervention (X)	Time 2 (T_2) Post-test
'Experimental' group	None	Group is uniform in terms of the proposed causal variable	Measure on outcome variable (Y)
'Control' group	None	No 'treatment'	None

Figure 13.3 *One-shot case study design (one group, post-test only design)*

the logic whereby initial hypotheses or research questions can be subjected to empirical testing. Deciding between single and multiple case studies [see later], selecting specific cases to be studied, developing a case study protocol and defining relevant data collection strategies [e.g. the period to be covered – retrospective, prospective] are all part of case study design. (1993: 33)

Any method of data collection can be used within a case study design so long as it is practical and ethical. Indeed, one of the distinguishing features of the case study method is that multiple methods of data collection will often be employed (see Chapter 14). Case studies seek to build up a full picture of a case, its subunits (see earlier discussion on units of analysis and embedded designs in this chapter) and its context.

Summary

Case study designs constitute a major design for social research. They offer a flexible approach, which can result in an extensive variety of particular designs. They make use of a wide variety of data collection methods and they are particularly suited to using a diverse range of units of analysis. Case studies in social science research should be fundamentally theoretical.

Case study designs are particularly suited to situations involving a small number of cases with a large number of variables. The approach is appropriate for the investigation of cases when it is necessary to understand parts of a case within the context of the whole. Case studies are designed to study wholes rather than parts. They are also particularly appropriate when we need to investigate phenomena where it is not possible to introduce interventions. While experimentally based designs allow us to exclude the influence of many variables, case study designs are particularly useful when we do not wish or are unable to screen out the influence of 'external' variables but when we wish to examine their effect on the phenomenon we are investigating.

Note

1 Yin (1993: 60ff) carefully distinguishes ethnographies from case studies. One reason Yin provides for this distinction is that ethnographies are not suited to theory testing whereas case studies are. A further basis for the distinction is that ethnographies do not assume a single objective reality that can be investigated following the traditional rules of scientific inquiry.

14

ISSUES IN CASE STUDY DESIGN

All research designs should be internally valid and externally valid, should produce reliable results and should be amenable to replication. Case study designs are often seen to be deficient in all these areas. However, careful attention to these matters at the design stage can deal with many of these criticisms.

Methodological issues

Internal validity

The internal validity of many of the research designs examined in Parts II to IV of this book depends on having groups that are comparable except in relation to specific key variables. Internal validity in these earlier designs relies on screening out the influence of variables other than the key causal variables. They involve focusing on a small number of variables and removing the influence of other variables by controls of one sort or another. Threats to internal validity stem from the danger that factors other than our key variable are producing any changes we observe.

IDIOGRAPHIC AND NOMOTHETIC EXPLANATIONS

By focusing on a very restricted range of variables the earlier designs achieve a narrow or *nomothetic* explanation. That is, they achieve partial explanations of a class of cases rather than a 'full' explanation of a particular case. They involve an examination of fewer causal factors and a larger number of cases. For example, a nomothetic explanation might examine divorces as a class of cases and identify key factors that contribute to divorce overall (e.g. age of marriage, external family stressors etc.). The nomothetic approach contrasts with *idiographic* explanation. Idiographic explanation focuses on particular events, or cases, and seeks to develop a complete explanation of each case. For example, an idiographic explanation of a divorce would examine a particular divorce and develop a *full* picture of why *that* divorce occurred.

Case studies can be utilized for both types of explanation. A case study adopts an idiographic approach when a full and contextualized understanding of a case is achieved. But case study designs can adopt a nomothetic approach. This occurs when particular cases are used to achieve a more generalized understanding of broader theoretical propositions (see discussion of case studies and theory in Chapter 13).

By developing a full, well-rounded causal account, case studies can achieve high internal validity. By seeing particular causal factors in combination with other causal factors we can assess both the relative importance of particular causes and the way in which various causes interrelate. As such, case studies can achieve a sophisticated and balanced account of causal processes and, in so doing, avoid mistaking cause with correlation.

WHOLES, NOT JUST PARTS

The designs discussed in earlier parts of this book focus on *variables* rather than *cases*. They examine how different traits of cases are associated with one another (Mitchell, 1983: 192). Typically, however, these traits are not considered within the context of the case of which they are part. By wrenching traits out of the context in which they occur we strip them of much of their meaning and consequently risk misreading their meaning and significance and thus misunderstanding their causes.

Blumer (1956) uses the term 'variable analysis' to describe analysis that focuses on variables rather than cases. He argues that although such analysis can establish statistical relationships between variables they do not provide much insight into causal processes. He argues that:

> The independent variable is put at the beginning part of the process of interpretation and the dependent variable is put at the terminal part of the process. The intervening process is ignored . . . as something that need not be considered. (1956: 97)

Although this is a somewhat simplistic version of the statistical analysis of relationships between variables, it contains some truth. While many of the designs covered earlier in this book can isolate variables that produce particular outcomes, they are not so good at telling us *why* they produce these outcomes.

Case studies, on the other hand, emphasize an understanding of the whole case and seeing the case within its wider context. Goode and Hatt (1952) describe case studies as

> a way of organizing social data . . . to preserve the *unitary character of the social object being studied* . . . it is an approach which views any social unit as a whole. (1952: 331, their italics)

They stress the importance of looking at parts within the context of the whole.[1] The case also must be seen within the context in which it exists. By examining this context fully the researcher can gain a fuller and more rounded picture of the causal processes surrounding a particular phenomenon. Yin argues that

> a major rationale for using [case studies] is when your investigation must cover both a particular *phenomenon* and the *context* within which the phenomenon is occurring either because (a) the context is hypothesized to contain important explanatory information about the phenomenon or (b) the boundaries between phenomenon and context are not clearly evident. (1993: 31)

The study of context is important because behaviour takes place within a context and its meaning stems largely from that context. The same behaviour can mean very different things depending on its context. Furthermore, actions have meanings to people performing those actions and this must form part of our understanding of the causes and meaning of any behaviour. To simply look at behaviour and *give* it a meaning rather than *take* the meaning of the actors is to miss out on an important source of understanding of human behaviour.

An example can illustrate this point. The research literature on extended families assumes that exchange of help and care between the generations (e.g. adults and older parents) reflects the quality and strength of intergenerational ties. However, if we examine the meaning of intergenerational help within its context we might interpret its meaning differently. Within a particular family there may be a great deal of intergenerational help: the adults in the family are attentive to the elderly parents, visiting often and helping out where they can. But is this a sign of family solidarity, closeness and caring, or is it a sign of control, dependence, manipulation and blackmail (adults help out of guilt, concern about inheritance, worry that siblings will be favoured unless they help)? Is the help reciprocal? What were the patterns of help in the past? What is the history of parent–child relationships in this family? What particular forms of help are given? What type of help is withheld? Why do people give the help? How happily is it accepted? What happens if help is not offered? What are the norms regarding family loyalty and help within the community, class and ethnic group in which this family is situated? What are the rules of inheritance in this society? What are the legal obligations, if any, of children to care for elderly parents? We would need to address these and other questions before we could build up a picture of the meaning of intergenerational help and the possible causes of help in a particular case. To isolate the behaviour from this broader context and to strip it of the meaning given to it by actors is to invite misunderstanding, and thus threaten the internal validity of the study.

To take a further example: our research goal may be to gain an understanding of drug addiction. To make sense of addiction in a particular case we would need to understand its social and institutional context. Was addiction the outcome of medical treatment to control pain (addiction from treatment)? Did it originate with emotional distress following relationship breakdown (addiction as escape)? Was drug use a taken for granted part of the immediate social context in which the person lived (addiction as conformity)? Did the person come from a very anti-drug background (addiction as rebellion)? The context is all-important for understanding the phenomenon (addiction) and presumably is crucial in shaping appropriate ways of managing or treating the addiction.

In summary, explanations based on case studies involve much more than explaining variation in one variable in terms of variation in another variable. Case study designs are devised to yield a sensible, plausible account of events and in this way achieve internal validity. They achieve explanations by building a full picture of the sequence of events, the context in which they occur, and the meaning of actions and events as interpreted by participants and their meaning as given by a context. In the end an adequate causal explanation is one that makes sense. It involves telling a plausible, convincing, and logically acceptable story of how events unfold and how they are linked to one another.

HISTORY AND MATURATION

The way in which 'history' and maturation can threaten the validity of causal explanations has been discussed in previous chapters. Experimental designs seek to deal with the problems of history and maturation by using randomized control groups and focusing on *differences* in change between these groups rather than on absolute change (Chapters 4 and 5).

Case study designs try to deal with the 'problem of history' and maturation by looking closely at the wider context and exploring the extent to which these sorts of concurrent events contribute to observed outcomes. That is, rather than *eliminating* historical/contextual and maturational factors from the analysis (by controlling them out) the case study designs *include* them in order to enhance our understanding. In this way we can arrive at a fuller and richer understanding while, at the same time, avoiding the threats that history and maturation present to the internal validity of our case study conclusions. The quality of the case study will largely rest on how well it identifies these historical/contextual and maturational factors and includes them in any explanation.

REACTIVE EFFECTS

Simply *doing* a case study can produce changes in the case and we can confuse the effects of doing the study with the effects of other variables. Whether or not this will be a problem in a particular case study will depend, in part, on the type of case, the data collection methods, and the nature of the outcome variables.

A life history of a dead person, which relies on documentary evidence, is unlikely to suffer from reactive effects. Retrospective designs will be less prone to reactive effects than prospective studies. But a study of a tightly knit group in which the researcher uses participant observation and interviews will inevitably affect the way in which the group operates.

We can try to reduce the threats of reactivity by using unobtrusive data collection methods (Kellehear, 1993). For some types of cases this can work well. In others it may not be possible to use unobtrusive methods for either practical or ethical reasons. If data can only be obtained by interviews or observation it is very difficult to avoid the reactivity of being a 'foreign object' (Denzin, 1978: 200).

External validity

While case studies may achieve excellent internal validity by providing a profound understanding of a case, they have been widely criticized as lacking external validity. A profound understanding of a case, it is argued, provides no basis for generalizing to a wider population beyond that case. A case is just that – a case – and cannot be representative of a larger universe of cases.

THEORETICAL AND STATISTICAL GENERALIZATION

It is correct to say that case study designs cannot provide a basis for making statistically valid generalizations beyond that particular case (see Chapter 15 on statistical analysis). A case study may consist of just one case (one community, one organization, one person) and we cannot be confident, in any statistical sense, that the case represents a wider class of cases. Even if we conduct multiple case studies, say 10, our n remains too small for credible statistical generalization.

However, case studies do not strive for this type of external validity. There are two types of generalization: statistical and theoretical. *Statistical generalization* is achieved by using representative random samples. On the basis of statistical probability we generalize our findings to a wider population that our sample is designed to represent.

Theoretical generalization involves generalizing from a study to a *theory*. Rather than asking what a study tells us about the wider population (statistical generalization) we ask, 'What does this case tell us about a specific theory (or theoretical proposition)?' In Chapter 13 I argued that case study designs are fundamentally theoretical. They are designed to help develop, refine and test theories. They do this using the logic of replication.

REPLICATION

To understand the concept of theoretical generalization it is necessary to understand the logic of *replication* in research design (Yin, 1989). This is the logic that lies at the heart of generalizing from experiments. Since experiments typically do not use representative probability samples they provide no basis for statistical generalization to a wider population. An experiment might employ an excellent design that ensures a high degree of internal validity but unless it is based on a probability sample we do not know if those findings will occur in the wider population. There may be something about the particular sample that means that the findings will apply only to the people who participated in the experiment.

Experiments using non-probability samples argue for external validity on the basis of *replication logic*. That is, if the experiment can be repeated again and again under the same conditions and produce the same results we can be confident that the experimental results will hold up more generally. If the experimental results hold up under different conditions and with different types of experimental participants our confidence in the generalizability of the results grows. If the experimental results cannot be replicated under particular conditions then we will need to specify conditions to which the experiment cannot be generalized. We gain confidence in the value of and robustness of experimental findings by repeating the experiment. Where the experiment is repeated with different samples and under different conditions we get more of a sense of the limits of generalizability. Repeated experiments provide some idea of the range of generalization. If an experiment only works once with a particular group of people and the results cannot be reproduced we would have little confidence in its findings or its applicability more generally.

Experimental science is based on the logic of replication. No finding is accepted on the basis of a single experiment. The same logic applies to case studies. Indeed a single case study can be thought of in much the same way as a single experiment. In Chapter 13 I argued that the findings of a case study are tested by repeating case studies (more of this later). We can examine different types of cases under different conditions and maybe even using different methods. The more the cases behave in a way that is consistent with the way we would expect on the basis of our theory, the more confident we are about our theory. If we find that some cases do not behave in the way we would have predicted we need to modify our theory to accommodate that case in the same way that theories will be modified to account for the experiment that does not give the expected results.

STRATEGIC SELECTION OF CASES

The external validity of case studies is enhanced by the *strategic* selection of cases rather than by the statistical selection of cases. The strategic selection of cases contributes to *literal* and *theoretical* replication (Yin, 1989).

Case study designs involve selecting cases for theoretical and targeted purposes. We select a case because it tests whether a theory works in particular, real world situations. Alternatively, we select a case because we think it might disprove a proposition, or because we want to see if the theoretical proposition works under particular conditions (like repeating an experiment under different conditions).

The strategic selection of cases means that we know something of the characteristics of a case before the case study proper begins. Since cases are selected because they meet particular requirements (as opposed to being randomly selected) we must first know something about each case. This may require extensive case screening before actual cases are finally selected (see later in this chapter).

How cases are selected strategically can be illustrated by using the earlier example of devolved staffing systems. If we begin with the proposition that 'the introduction of devolved staffing systems in schools improves the quality of education' our first case study will target a school in which such a system had been introduced. We would predict that in this school there would be evidence of educational improvement. Furthermore, we would predict that an intensive study of the school would show the following:

1   The improvement in education could be traced back to the new system.
2   The reasons the new system was effective were those that were anticipated in the theory (better fit of teachers with school, greater feelings of accountability and greater belief that effort was rewarded).

If we found that the case matched what the theory predicted, a *literal replication* of the theory would have been achieved (Yin, 1989: 54). Since this outcome may be due to chance we could seek out some other schools in which the devolved system was introduced and examine its impact on the quality of education in those schools. If the same patterns occur we have further literal replications.

We could then attempt to test the theory in a different way. Since we had concluded that the improvement in education was due to the introduction of the devolved system we would expect, on the basis of our theory, that where a centralized system was retained there would be no improvement in education. We would deliberately seek out instances of schools still functioning with a centralized system to see whether our theoretical predictions were supported.

As a tougher test we might look for cases that run counter to the basic proposition: that is, cases of a failed devolved system. Alternatively, we might look for cases of centralized systems that, over the same period, also delivered improvements in educational quality. However, our theory may be such that it can account for these 'deviant' cases. It might specify that the basic relationship will only work under particular conditions. If we find that the basic propositions do not hold up and this is predictable on the basis of the theory we have added further support to our theory. This is called *theoretical replication* (Yin 1989: 54).

Practical issues

Sampling

METHOD OF CASE SELECTION

Since cases are used for theoretical rather than statistical generalization there is little point in selecting cases because they are in some sense representative of some wider population.

Nor do we need to look for 'typical' cases.[2] We have no sure way of knowing whether a case is truly typical and no way of estimating its typicality. The desire by some people to find typical cases reflects confusion about what Mitchell (1983) calls enumerative and analytic modes of induction or what Yin (1989) calls statistical generalization and theoretical generalization. Since the purpose of case studies is *not* to generalize to a wider sample of cases (enumerative induction or statistical generalization) there is little point in trying to find a typical case for a case study. The need is to find cases that will provide valid and challenging tests of a theory.

Glaser and Strauss (1967) have used the term *theoretical sampling* to describe the normal method of selecting cases in case study designs. Hakim (1986) uses the term *focused sampling* to describe the same process. These terms refer to the strategy of selecting cases that will provide illuminating examples of a type of case (as in descriptive case study designs) or that will provide appropriate tests of a theory.

NUMBER OF CASES

There is no correct number of cases to include in a case study design. Case study designs can consist of a single case or multiple cases (Chapter 13). With multiple case studies the number of cases is a matter of judgement (Yin, 1989: 57). A significant factor in determining the number of cases will be the rigour with which the propositions are to be tested. Using the logic of replication a single replication tells us something but repeated replications give us more confidence in findings. If we seek theoretical replications we will need to conduct additional case studies. Where we find cases that do not fit with our expectations this may produce the need to conduct additional case studies to enable us to follow up hypotheses that the 'deviant' case throws up. The search for cases designed to *disprove* our propositions will also add to the number of case studies we can conduct.

The complexity of our predictions may influence the confidence we have in our replications. The more complex our predictions the more confident we can be in the single case where our predictions are replicated. Where our predictions are simple (e.g. when A exists then Z will occur) a single case study may not represent a tough test and we may want multiple replications before we feel confident in the results. Where our predictions are more complex and demanding (e.g. when $A+B+C+D$ exists then $W+X+Y+Z$ will occur) it is relatively unlikely that this complex pattern will occur due to chance. Accordingly we may feel quite confident in the toughness of the test that the single case study provides.

How many case studies we conduct will also depend on our knowledge of external factors that might affect results. That is, if we expect that our results will hold up under a wide range of external conditions we may need fewer case studies. Where we are uncertain about the external conditions under which our predictions will hold we may need more case studies under these different conditions to see how consistently our findings hold (Yin, 1989: 58). For example, we may be unsure whether the link between devolved staffing systems and educational performance will hold regardless of region (e.g. inner city, suburban, rural and remote). Or, again, we may not know if the positive impact will hold at different levels (primary, secondary or tertiary), or in the different types of school systems (private, religious or state). In the face of uncertainties we may need to include case studies that accommodate some of these differences to see if the predictions can be replicated in these different conditions.

A further factor that may affect the number of cases is the conceptual framework with which we are working. For example, if social class was an important concept in the study it would be necessary to include cases from each of the different social classes. The number of cases would depend on how social class was conceptualized and on how many class categories this conceptualization included (e.g. just middle class and working class, or a more refined class classification that includes upper class and various classifications within the middle and working classes).

We could go on forever and check things out under any number of different conditions. In the end we must make judgements about likely variations and have good reasons for expecting that these different conditions might affect the patterns. We also must be guided by what is practical within the constraints of time, money and access to relevant cases. The critical thing is to select the most strategic cases to test our propositions rather than aiming for a large number of cases.

CASE SCREENING

The strategic selection of cases involves selecting cases because they have particular characteristics. If we want to know whether centralized or self-governing schools have better educational outcomes we need to know which schools have which system. We might also need to know, for selection purposes, how long a school has had a particular system. We might want to select schools that had good and poor educational outcomes. To do this we would need to have this information before the case selection process took place.

Strategic case selection can require considerable groundwork to identify the characteristics of a large number of cases in order to see which ones satisfy the criteria for selection. This process can be time consuming but is critical and must be built into time lines and budgets. Case screening may be done in any number of ways, depending on the type of case. A survey questionnaire, annual reports of an organization, archival records, databases or a wide range of other sources may yield the relevant screening information.

Even when screening is introduced we may still end up selecting inappropriate cases. Nevertheless, these cases may be useful for other purposes. Alternatively, we may decide to discontinue that particular case study since it does not help answer the original research questions.

COST AND ACCESS

The number of cases selected, and the particular cases selected, will be affected by the amount of time and money available. Well-executed case studies can be very time consuming. Consequently, only a limited number can be conducted. The cost factor highlights even more the importance of the strategic selection of cases: since only a few case studies can be completed, each one has to 'earn its keep'.

Access to cases is the other critical factor that affects both the number of cases studied and the particular cases selected. Certain cases may be identified as being strategically ideal for the design but practical matters may mean that such cases are not available for research purposes. Gaining access to cases that have been identified as strategically appropriate needs to be approached with considerable care and effort.

Number of investigators: getting consistency

Case studies may involve a number of different investigators. In 'parallel' designs it is almost inevitable that a number of investigators will be involved – perhaps with a different investigator conducting each study. In multiple case designs each case study should be conducted in a consistent way since inconsistency between cases can invalidate case comparisons. Yin (1989) urges the use of case study protocols to help achieve this consistency.

Planning to ensure consistency across case studies and across investigators is important for two reasons. First, it enhances the reliability of our information. Gaining reliable information is a prerequisite for good research. This means that the information must not simply be an artifact of the particular circumstances of its collection. We need to be confident that the same information would emerge if it were sought again in comparable circumstances. We certainly do not want comparisons between cases to be invalidated by sloppy collection or different approaches being applied in each case study because that makes cases incomparable. For example, it would be completely inappropriate to compare marriages where in one case marital satisfaction was ascertained by using a structured battery of questionnaire items while in another satisfaction was measured by investigator observation, or in a third satisfaction was determined on the basis of reports of other people (e.g. friends, children, parents). Although each case study would provide information about 'marital satisfaction', the way this concept is measured using the different techniques means that, in effect, it is being conceptualized very differently in each case.

Second, it is imperative that any study is capable of replication. Meeting this condition requires that if other investigators conducted a similar study they would find the same patterns. Successful replication is a safeguard against fraud. It also enables others to see if the pattern only occurs when a particular person conducts the observations or interviews. If findings are only capable of being found by one person they provide little basis for generalizing to theoretical propositions.

When to go into the field

The temptation is to 'get your hands dirty' early on – to get out there and learn from the cases in full confidence that the truth of the case will somehow emerge. Too often people commence case studies without knowing what their research question is or what propositions they are evaluating.

This is a recipe for disaster. It is essential that we have a clear research question before beginning a case study.[3] Indeed we cannot even begin to select cases until we have a clear statement of the research question. We need to go beyond having a question. We should be able to formulate some initial propositions – some initial answers to the question that the case studies will help us test.

There will be those who urge that fieldwork should be free of theories since these impose our preconceptions and pre-existing categories on the data. Some will urge that we should go into the field free from theoretical encumbrances as these simply blind us to what we might otherwise see and make us deaf to what people are trying to tell us. Our job, they will say, is to allow others to tell us their story rather than us imposing a theoretical interpretation on their story, or using their story for theoretical purposes.

In my view this is not the task of the social scientist. It might be the role of a biographer, a novelist or an activist. The role of a social scientist is to develop and evaluate theoretical generalizations that enable us to understand whole classes of cases – not, in the final analysis, individual cases.

We do not have to have a well-formulated theory to test. Our questions may be such that there are no obvious theories to test. But this does not release us from the need to be well read and well prepared theoretically before going into the field. Pasteur observed that, 'Where observation is concerned chance only favours the prepared mind' (quoted in Mitchell, 1983: 204). If we are unaware of relevant theories, concepts, debates and the like, we will probably miss the significance of much of what we might come across. Without having some idea of what we are looking for we will not know what we have found.

Presenting case studies

Case studies can involve the collection of a vast amount of information. This information must be carefully processed and distilled before it can be presented. We cannot simply describe the case and somehow let the facts speak for themselves. Any attempt to present all the facts will result in an indigestible mess that is unreadable and unread.

The facts do not speak for themselves and we should not pretend otherwise. Describing a case always involves selection and ordering and at least implied construction of causal sequences and interpretations.

There are many different ways in which case studies might be presented. We might describe each case as a whole so that the reader builds up a clear picture of the case. Alternatively, we might describe good examples of particular types of cases and then compare these different types of cases and draw general conclusions regarding our theories. Hochschild's *The Second Shift* (1989) provides a good example of this type of reporting. She describes a series of marriages and from each of her cases she extracts lessons about the domestic division of labour and the processes by which marital inequality in this sphere is maintained.

Alternatively, we might report the results of a series of case studies by extracting *themes* from the case studies and reporting the findings of the case studies thematically. For example, Vaughn (1986) conducted retrospective case studies of couples whose intimate relationships had ended. From these case studies she identified a set of underlying patterns and stages beneath each disintegrating relationship. Another approach is to focus on a series of *questions* and report the cases in terms of how they shed light on these questions. For example, Dempsey (1990) conducted a single case study of a small country town. The guiding questions in the case study were questions such as, 'How unequal are people in this community?', 'What are the key bases of social differentiation?', 'How, in the face of considerable social inequality, does the community maintain a strong sense of cohesion?' These questions guided the study and provided the framework around which the study was reported.

Regardless of which approach is adopted it is highly desirable that the logic of the research design remains clear. The reader should be clear about the proposition(s), and why a particular case was selected to test the proposition. The reader should be able to see that there is a structure and a logic to the selection of cases – that they have been selected for a purpose rather than simply because they happen to be available.

Any report that merely provides a number of stories is incomplete. In reporting case studies it is critical that we relate the cases to propositions and that we seek to draw comparisons between cases and arrive at generalizations or more refined propositions as a result of the case studies. We need to tell the story of the set of cases – the generalizations, the propositions and the questions they answer and the propositions we end up supporting.

Ethical issues

The same ethical principles apply to case study designs as to the designs discussed in previous chapters. The particular ethical issues confronted will vary, depending on the type of case study design adopted and the particular form of data collection used for that design.

For example, the ethical issues will be different if the case study involves an active intervention or a passive intervention, or requires that we obtain a retrospective account of an event, intervention or change. The ethical issues will also differ according to whether data are collected by interviewing individuals, using informants, analysing official records, passive observation, conducting a survey of case elements, or using participant observation. Since case studies frequently employ a range of different data collection techniques for the one study it is likely that a greater range of ethical issues will arise when using a case study design than with other designs

There is no point in repeating the ethical matters identified earlier in this book. You should read these earlier sections carefully and you should see how they apply to the specifics of the particular case study design you adopt. However, since case study designs frequently involve obtaining more in-depth information and frequently employ participant observation techniques, some ethical issues arise that are less of an issue with other designs.

I argued earlier that reactivity can be a significant threat to the internal validity of case study designs: the presence of a researcher can alter the dynamics of the cases being observed. This can be particularly so where participant observation techniques are used. One way in which some researchers might try to reduce the effects of reactivity is to disguise their identity as researchers to avoid their *researcher* identity intruding. For example, an investigator may want to examine sexual harassment in the workplace. If he went into a company revealing his identity and purpose it is likely that people in the organization would behave differently while the investigator is present and thus undermine the study. As an alternative the investigator might undertake the research by obtaining a job with the company and covertly observing what goes on.

The ethical issues of deception, and failure to obtain informed consent, obviously arise in this situation. The dilemma it highlights is the tradeoff that occurs between ethics and internal validity: keeping to ethical guidelines can threaten the internal validity of the study.

There can be little doubt that revealing one's identity and gaining informed consent can undermine a great deal of what Punch (1994) calls 'street style' ethnography. In some cases revealing one's identity can effectively kill the research project. In these situations careful consideration must be given to the merits of some form of deception in the light of the likely benefits of the research and the potential for harm to the participants. While it is easy for a researcher to rationalize that the benefits will outweigh any potential for harm, there is a lot of sense in obtaining advice or even in having decisions made by third parties such as institutional ethics committees.

Investigators will need to resolve competing ethical considerations. To what extent should the ethics of informed consent and voluntary participation take priority over the value of research exposing highly unethical behaviour?

Even if a researcher revealed his/her identity and gained permission to undertake the study, the question arises of how to get informed consent, and from whom to obtain that consent. If we were conducting a study of sexual harassment in a workplace, would we obtain permission from the gatekeepers in the organization, or from all people whom we might observe in the course of the study?

Do people need to be informed that their *public* behaviour is being observed for the purpose of research? Clearly in many cases this is simply impractical (e.g. observing the behaviour of people at a party, in a demonstration, shopping at sales). In my view observing public behaviour raises few ethical problems. So long as individuals are not identifiable there should be no danger of harm to participants. After all, if the behaviour is public there is hardly any invasion of privacy.

Another ethical problem that is more likely to arise when using observation in a case study is the problem of what to do when we observe illegal or harmful behaviour. Should the ethical issues of informed consent and voluntary participation take priority over exposing highly unethical behaviour? For example, what would be your ethical responsibility if your case studies of families revealed cases of domestic violence or child abuse? What should you do when conducting a case study of a school and you learn of the identity of a person selling dangerous drugs to students? What do you do if you discover, during your research, that a group participant is about to commit a crime? Is the betrayal of trust of those around you more unethical than one's responsibility to those in danger?

What is the responsibility of the researcher to other researchers? If one researcher betrays the trust of a community, even if for ethical reasons, does this then undermine the capacity of other researchers to study in that community? Once a group has learned to distrust social researchers it can be very difficult to conduct any further research with that group, and this may have further ethical consequences. The behaviour of some researchers with indigenous groups has led to profound mistrust by some indigenous communities of outside researchers.

How do you resolve the objective of feminist research to promote identification, trust, empathy and non-exploitative relationships between the investigator and those participating in the research on the one hand, and to expose unethical and harmful behaviour on the other?

We lack clear-cut answers to these dilemmas. They highlight the fact that ethical principles can often conflict with one another, and that ethical issues can certainly compete with methodological and practical principles.

Summary

This chapter has emphasized that the internal validity of case studies relies on a logic that sets this design apart from the other designs discussed in this book. Case studies focus on a large number of variables and the way in which they interrelate. In contrast, the other designs rely on controlling out the influence of other variables and on focusing on the influence of a very limited number of variables. One of the strengths of case studies is that they attempt to understand the significance of particular factors within the context of the whole case rather than by screening out this context. As such case studies have the potential for good internal validity based on a more thorough understanding of the meaning of particular behaviour and events than the other designs provide.

The external validity of case studies is based on the logic of replication rather than on sampling logic. Case studies are used to generalize to a theory rather than to a population. Cases in case study designs are selected strategically rather than statistically and are selected as critical tests of theoretical propositions. Issues in selecting cases, the selection of research methods to collect information about the case, and conducting case studies were discussed. Finally, particular ethical questions that can arise in case studies, particularly those employing participant observation and ethnographic methods, were raised.

Notes

1 The concept of a whole is, as Goode and Hatt (1952) point out, a construct itself. It is us who defines what the 'whole is'. The delineation between the case (the whole) and its context is indeed arbitrary.

2 'Typical' cases should not be confused with selecting 'ideal typical' cases – cases that may represent an ideal type (Chapter 13).

3 It may be appropriate to conduct case studies without clear research questions or propositions when we are doing exploratory case studies. If we are using the case study to clarify concepts, then to help identify questions we might enter the field before a research question has been finalized. But this type of case study, designed to help produce a research question, is very different from a case study design. A case study *design* is the structure of a study that will enable us to answer research questions. It refers to the logic and structure of the study.

15

CASE STUDY ANALYSIS

Methods for analysing case studies are less systematically developed than are the techniques for analysing data collected with other types of research designs. Analysis with these other designs typically uses statistical techniques that rely on having many cases and revolve around comparing groups of cases. Furthermore, attempts to generalize from these designs are based on probability theory which, in turn, relies on having sufficient cases from which to generalize with a given level of precision and certainty.

The research designs dealt with earlier all rely on comparisons *between* groups using a limited number of variables. Case studies, however, achieve explanations by intensive analysis of many variables *within* a case. Multiple cases are used to replicate results – not as a means of locating causal explanations. In addition multiple case studies are useful for making comparisons between cases and thus extrapolating to broader theories.

Statistical analysis

Although the logic of the earlier designs does not require statistical analysis, such analysis is widely used. Methods such as correlations, cross-tabulations, regression and comparison of means rely on *sets* of cases and on building a typical picture or describing trends across *multiple* cases rather than reflecting the characteristics of any particular case.

Because case study designs focus on individual cases they employ different methods of analysis. A number of such methods have been developed or are in the process of being developed. Case study analysis revolves around assessing the 'fit' between an individual case and the theory or theories being tested. The goal of case study analysis is theoretical generalization rather than statistical generalization (Chapter 14). This goal affects the way in which we go about our analysis.

Because the focus is on individual cases it is inappropriate, when analysing case data, to *count* the number of cases that had particular characteristics or behaved in a particular way. The small number of cases and the atypical nature of the cases selected make it meaningless to analyse case studies by counting.

This is not to say that case study analysis cannot have a quantitative or statistical element. A case can be *described* statistically. A particular region might be a case in a research project. It can be described in terms of its size, wealth, average age, unemployment rate, crime rate and the like. However, the focus of the analysis is to describe the region – to build up a picture of that case.

Furthermore, where cases include embedded units of analysis (see Chapter 13) the analysis of some levels may well include the sort of analysis typically associated with other designs. For example, a case study of a region might include a survey of residents in the region (the residents being an embedded unit within the case). The survey of residents would include the type of analysis typically used in a cross-sectional design. However, the focus of the overall analysis would be on the case as a whole – the region. The survey results would simply be one piece in the jigsaw to build up a picture of the whole case.

In Chapter 13 I emphasized that case studies are fundamentally theoretical. Their analysis is also fundamentally theoretical. The analysis needs to be built around the theoretical propositions being tested or developed.

Meaning and context

In Chapter 14 I stressed that case studies are particularly suited to research problems when the phenomenon in which we are interested either cannot be distinguished from its context or must be seen within its context. Many social scientists believe that adequate causal explanations need to take account of the meaning that participants in a social situation attribute to their behaviour. They argue that the meaning of behaviour helps us 'make sense' of why one event produces particular outcomes. Therefore when conducting case studies it is very useful to collect information about the subjective meaning of behaviour for participants and build this subjective data into our analysis of the case.

Analysis in descriptive case studies

Theoretical dimension of descriptive analysis

Case descriptions should be structured around theoretical ideas. There are scholars, however, who argue that case descriptions should simply describe the case and not seek to interpret it. This view argues that we should let the 'facts' speak for themselves and avoid imposing our own interpretation on 'the facts'. Such an approach is both undesirable and impossible. Any description of any case always involves a *selection* of facts. This selection will be based on what we see as relevant and important. The very act of selecting means that we are making decisions about what is relevant. This selection process will be heavily influenced by our implicit theories. Furthermore, any reporting of a case will involve *ordering* the selected facts. The inevitable selectivity and ordering will mean that all descriptions are *our* descriptions, rather than *the* description of the case.

The inevitable subjective element of case study analysis does not mean that such analysis is therefore not worthwhile. What it does mean is that we should be explicit about the basis on which we are constructing the description.

IDEAL TYPE ANALYSIS

One way of constructing description is to use ideal types (see Chapter 13). This involves constructing theoretically derived descriptions of types of cases. On the basis of theoretical considerations and our knowledge of the existing research literature we can list the elements of a type (e.g. an authoritarian person, a perfectly bureaucratic organization, a democratic electoral system, an egalitarian marriage).

The analytic strategy is to use this ideal type as a template to guide the analysis of an actual case. We can use the template to see how closely our actual case fits the template. We might have good reasons for expecting that particular cases will represent the characteristics of a particular type. For example, we might expect, for various reasons, that a government department in a Westminster form of government might be close to an ideal type of a bureaucracy as defined by Weber (Gerth and Mills, 1946). Using our template of an ideal type bureaucracy we can examine a selected department (case) to see how closely it approximates the ideal type. As well as identifying where the case fits the ideal we would also use the template to help highlight where the case diverges from the ideal. Repeated case studies (e.g. a range of government departments) might show us that empirical examples consistently diverge from the ideal in so far as ministerial interventions might override the ideal of rule-governed decision making which is a characteristic of the ideal type bureaucracy. It should be remembered, however, that the ideal type still stands as an ideal type regardless of the empirical findings from a set of cases. The ideal type remains a 'pure' idealized abstraction.

The use of the ideal type provides a way of looking at and organizing the analysis for the descriptions of actual cases. Using this approach we avoid description that simply describes whatever we happen to find out about the case or simply reports the features that catch our attention. Instead, the description is structured, planned and purposeful.

TYPOLOGIES

A typology consists of a set of types. Thus we might develop typologies of different sorts of personality, forms of government, types of organizational structure or types of marriage. This set of types may be based on a set of ideal types or be derived empirically (see Chapter 13). Typologies and ideal types provide excellent methods of analysis in which the 'wholeness' of a case is preserved. Rather than just concentrating on traits, a typology attempts to build up an overall picture of a case taking a wide range of characteristics into account.

Where we employ a theoretically derived typology the task of analysis is simply an extension of the ideal type analysis described above.

Where we use our case studies to derive empirically grounded typologies (i.e. those based on our actual cases) we need to adopt a different approach to analysis. These approaches are only possible if we have multiple cases.

Cluster analytic approaches   These approaches involve identifying a set of variables we want to use as the basis for our typology. For example, in a study of an organization we might have collected from our case studies information about the way decisions are made, the way in which rules and regulations are used, the degree of hierarchy, degree of rationality etc. In a set of case studies we could then group cases that had similar constellations of characteristics.

If we have a small number of cases that we know well we can do this manually. If we have a larger number of cases we can use a statistical technique called cluster analysis to achieve the same end. Essentially, this technique involves identifying the characteristics on which we want the typology to be based, coding each case in terms of each of those characteristics, and then feeding that information into a cluster analysis computer program. The program will then identify which cases are most similar to one another. It will cluster cases into groups that have relatively similar sets of characteristics.

TIME ORDERED DESCRIPTIONS

Rather than presenting cases in terms of types we can represent a case as a history of some sort or another. If we are dealing with individuals the case description might be presented as a biography – an account of a life. The biography will necessarily be selective and will represent the person in a particular light. It is likely that the biography will go beyond simple description and will include either implicit or explicit theories of why the person's life went in particular directions.

Histories of events, organizations, policies, or whatever the unit of analysis might be, represent a way of describing a case where the emphasis is on the sequence of events. The sequential account may seek to explain the course of events and may be designed to support a particular explanation. Alternatively, it may simply be designed to provide a record of events without an explicit attempt to explain or interpret those events.

Explanatory case studies

As in descriptive analysis, in explanatory analysis theory plays a key role. Theoretical propositions will either direct the analysis or be the goal of analysis.

When multiple case studies are being conducted the aim of the first step in the analysis is to understand each case *as a whole*. Only after a picture of each case has been constructed is it appropriate to *compare* the cases (Yin, 1989; Stake, 1994). The analysis of each case must be organized around questions and theoretical concepts. Each case should be used either to test or to build theoretical propositions. When each case is analysed around a common framework it is then possible to compare the cases to arrive at higher level generalizations, or to provide tougher tests of theories. If each case is examined in an idiosyncratic way then it will be very difficult to compare cases meaningfully.

The way in which we approach the analysis of explanatory case studies will vary somewhat depending on whether we are using them for theory testing or theory building.

Theory testing analysis

There are a number of ways of using case studies when testing theoretical propositions. Yin (1989) outlines two approaches: pattern matching and time series analysis. In my view time series analysis is simply a type of pattern matching but in the discussion below I will treat them separately.

PATTERN MATCHING

Pattern matching is a form of theory testing analysis that establishes a detailed set of predictions before the case study is conducted. These predictions stem from a theoretical model and therefore represent a clear theory testing approach. The analysis could proceed by establishing a set of alternative patterns we would predict on the basis of competing theories.

The form and complexity of pattern matching can vary considerably. The basic principle is that the more elaborate the predicted pattern (so long as it still follows logically from the theory) the tougher the test of a theory. Having predicted a particular pattern we would then conduct the case study to see if the case does, in fact, match the predicted pattern. If the case matches the predicted pattern then the case supports the theory

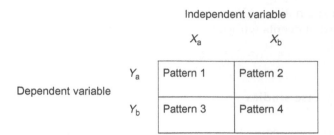

Figure 15.1 *Pattern matching for two variables each with two categories*

in the same way that a successful experiment supports a theory. If, however, the case does not match the predicted pattern the theory requires modification.

Yin (1989) describes pattern matching that varies in complexity according to the number of independent and dependent variables included in the predicted patterns.

Simple patterns   At its simplest level pattern matching involves one independent variable with two values (e.g. male and female) and one dependent variable with two possible values (behaves in one of two ways in a particular situation). In this case there are four possible different patterns (Figure 15.1). For a given case with a given characteristic we could predict one of two patterns. Which pattern we predicted would depend on theoretical considerations.

The pattern we might predict for a particular case that we know has value X_a on the independent variable is that the case will have value Y_b on the dependent (outcome) variable. The prediction takes the form: if X_a then Y_b.

For example, our theory of work performance in schools might lead us to expect that when staffing appointments, dismissals and promotions are managed at the local school level rather than by a highly bureaucratic, centralized and remote system (X variable), staff teaching commitment (Y) will be high. If devolved staffing systems are symbolized as X_a and high level of teacher commitment is symbolized as Y_b, our prediction is:

When X_a (local based staffing system) exists then Y_b (high levels of teacher commitment) will follow.

We would also expect that when X_b (centralized system) exists then Y_a (low levels of teacher commitment) will follow.

Our test, even in this very simple example of pattern matching, would be more interesting and more powerful if we were testing alternative theories that predicted different patterns. One theory might predict

Independent variable

	X_a	X_b	X_c
Y_a	Pattern 1	Pattern 2	Pattern 3
Y_b	Pattern 4	Pattern 5	Pattern 6
Y_c	Pattern 7	Pattern 8	Pattern 9

Dependent variable

Figure 15.2   *Patterns for two variables each with three categories*

pattern 1 while a competing theory might predict pattern 3. The case study would enable us to see which pattern emerged and therefore which of the rival theories was supported in this case.

For example we might propose the following two rival theories:

- *Theory A*   Local control will lead to higher commitment to work because effort and 'fit' is seen and rewarded (and lack of effort and not fitting in with school needs is punished).
- *Theory B*   Local control makes people feel more demoralized, and vulnerable to local politics and prejudices, and does not recognize wider professional development etc. This leads to a lack of commitment and a lack of professionalism and to playing politics to win favour rather than fostering performance.

A slightly more complex version of essentially the same situation would arise if either of the variables had more categories (e.g. medium levels of performance and a hybrid of local and centralized staffing models). The more values either variable or construct possessed, the greater the number of possible patterns we could predict. For example, if both variables had three possible values there are nine possible patterns we could find in any particular case (Figure 15.2). In this situation we would still predict a particular pattern for a given case: if they were X_a we might predict Y_c.

For example, we might have a theory about the impact of parenting styles on child behaviour. Each of these two factors might have three categories as illustrated in Figure 15.3. Using this example we might predict that authoritarian families will produce children who are rebellious (pattern 1) A case study of an authoritarian family will help address whether this proposition receives support. Repeated case studies of authoritarian families will provide a firmer test. A further proposition may be that permissive families will produce children who constantly engage in limit testing behaviour (pattern 9).

Parental style of authority

		Authoritarian	Authoritative	Permissive
	Rebellious	Pattern 1	Pattern 2	Pattern 3
Child behaviour	Compliant	Pattern 4	Pattern 5	Pattern 6
	Limit testing	Pattern 7	Pattern 8	Pattern 9

Figure 15.3   *Pattern matching for parental style and child behaviour*

The best test of the theory would be a series of case studies predicting particular types of child behaviour for each parenting style and for *each* of the mutually exclusive propositions to be confirmed by the relevant case studies.

More complex patterns: multiple independent variables   A more complex set of patterns can be predicted if two independent variables are used: a different outcome is predicted for each *combination* of independent variables (Figure 15.4).

Here we might make different predictions, depending on the combination of parental authority style combined with the child's level of anxiety. We might predict a different outcome pattern of permissive parenting depending on whether we are looking at a family where the child is anxious or secure/confident. We might predict that the anxious child with permissive parents will exhibit the 'tests parental limits' response (pattern 24) while the confident/secure child with permissive parents may set her own limits (pattern 17).

We could extend this example to include more independent variables and thus anticipate even more possible patterns.

Figure 15.4 illustrates the *logical* possibilities – the different patterns one could conceivably find. Of course, our theoretical reasoning will lead us to predict *particular* patterns in particular circumstances, that is, for particular types of cases as illustrated in the shaded cells in Figure 15.4.

Having established the possible patterns and the predicted patterns we would then seek out cases that enable us to test the propositions. For example, we would conduct a case study on a family in which authoritarian parenting and child anxiety occur. Our prediction would be that the child would be very compliant. If this proved to be true we would have achieved a *literal replication*. We might then look for a case of authoritarian parenting with a child who is not anxious. Our prediction here might be that the child will *not* be compliant. This would be a *theoretical replication*. That is, where the particular combination of factors

Dependent variables

Parental authority style		Authoritarian		Authoritative		Permissive	
	Child anxiety level	Low	High	Low	High	Low	High
Compliant		Pattern 1	Pattern 2	Pattern 3	Pattern 4	Pattern 5	Pattern 6
Rebellious		Pattern 7	Pattern 8	Pattern 9	Pattern 10	Pattern 11	Pattern 12
Child sets own limits		Pattern 13	Pattern 14	Pattern 15	Pattern 16	Pattern 17	Pattern 18
Tests parental limits		Pattern 19	Pattern 20	Pattern 21	Pattern 22	Pattern 23	Pattern 24

Independent variables (at left); *Child behaviour* (vertical label)

Figure 15.4   *Logical patterns with two independent variables and one dependent variable*

is not present we will not get a specific outcome (see later for fuller discussion).

Another approach to collecting and analysing case study data is to look for cases with particular outcomes (e.g. highly compliant children) and predict that these children will be anxious and have authoritarian parents. In terms of the predictions in Figure 15.4 we have predicted this, but if we find cases of highly compliant children who are neither anxious nor have authoritarian parents then our theory needs refining.

One way of testing a theoretical proposition is to demonstrate, through case studies, that when certain conditions apply (e.g. authoritarian parenting and child anxiety) there will also be a specific outcome (highly compliant child). The problem with this sort of matching is that it only specifies *sufficient conditions* for an outcome. It does not tell us whether these are the *only* conditions under which the outcome occurs. As such it does not represent a demanding test of a proposition. A more demanding test would involve looking for cases where the particular outcome is present and then asking whether this outcome *only* occurs under the theoretically predicted conditions.

Independent variables

		Condition 1			Condition 2		
		Values of dependent variables			Values of dependent variables		
		Low	Medium	High	Low	Medium	High
	A	1	2	*3*	*1*	2	3
	B	1	2	*3*	*1*	2	3
Dependent variables	C	*1*	2	3	1	2	*3*
	D	1	*2*	3	1	*2*	3
	E	1	2	*3*	*1*	2	3

Figure 15.5   *Logical patterns with one independent variable and five dependent variables*

A further test of a proposition is whether we find cases where all the conditions are met but the outcome does *not* occur. For example, do we find cases of authoritarian parenting and anxious children where children are not compliant? If we do then our proposition is not supported and our theory will need to be revised to accommodate this type of case.

More complex patterns: multiple dependent variables   The previous section focused on situations in which we predict a single outcome variable under a particular *set* of conditions (multiple independent variables). We can envisage situations where the opposite applies – where we have a specific condition (one independent variable) and predict that this condition will produce a particular *set* of outcomes. That is, we will predict a *pattern* of outcomes under a given condition (Figure 15.5). We will then match that predicted pattern with cases that meet the condition.

Here we predict a pattern of outcomes in cases that meet condition 1 and a different pattern for cases that meet condition 2. The pattern is a particular *combination* of outcomes. In this case we predict that for cases meeting condition 1 (on the independent variable) we will find the

Independent variables

Values of DV		High level of worker autonomy			High degree of direct control over worker		
		Low	Medium	High	Low	Medium	High
Morale		1	2	*3*	*1*	2	3
Work quality		1	2	*3*	*1*	2	3
Staff turnover		*1*	2	3	1	2	*3*
Efficiency		1	*2*	3	1	*2*	3
Innovation		1	2	*3*	*1*	2	3

Dependent variables

Figure 15.6 *Predicted patterns of outcomes on five dependent variables by level of worker autonomy*

following characteristics on the five outcome variables (A, B, C, D, E): A_3, B_3, C_1, D_2, E_3. For cases that meet condition 2 we predict a different pattern of outcomes: A_1, B_1, C_3, D_2 and E_1.

This can be illustrated with an example (Figure 15.6). The theory being used here is one that predicts that autonomy leads to better outcomes than high levels of supervision. While there may be no payoff in terms of efficiency, worker autonomy has positive benefits in terms of morale, work commitment, initiative and improved work quality.

In other words we predict that organizations (cases) that permit high levels of autonomy among members of their workforce will display a particular *pattern* of outcomes: high morale + high quality of work + low staff turnover + moderate levels of efficiency + high levels of innovation.

Organizations with high degrees of supervision and direction are predicted to behave differently. They are predicted to have a different *set* of outcome characteristics: low morale + low quality of work + high staff turnover + moderate levels of efficiency + low levels of innovation.

Highly complex pattern matching   The most complex version of pattern matching will occur when we have a *set* of independent variables and a *set* of dependent variables. In this situation we may be able to predict that when a case has a particular *set* of causal attributes they will be matched to a particular *set* of outcomes.

For example, we might predict that when an organization is fairly small, and possesses a 'flat' organizational structure, respected consultative mechanisms and worker reward plans, then there will be a valued set of outcomes. These might be high worker commitment, excellent quality output, strong ties between workers outside the workplace, ready acceptance of innovation, low levels of absenteeism and no industrial disputation.

Refining theories   Strictly speaking theory testing involves specifying a theoretical proposition, testing it and either accepting or rejecting the proposition. In reality, however, if a proposition is not supported by a case study then the next step is to refine the theory so that it can take account of the exception provided by the case. In this way the proposition covers a wider and wider set of cases and becomes more powerful. This process is called *analytic induction* and will be outlined more fully later in the section that deals with theory building.

TIME SERIES ANALYSIS

Although Yin (1989) treats this method of analysis as separate from the pattern matching described above, the logic is identical and it should therefore simply be treated as a form of pattern matching. Instead of predicting a particular pattern for a set of variables it predicts a particular trend or sequence of events. The analytic strategy involves predicting a particular pattern of change over time. This type of pattern analysis can take one of two forms: *trend* analysis and *chronological* (event sequence) analysis.

Trend analysis   Trend analysis is an examination of the direction of change in a particular variable or set of variables. We address the question of whether the trend is upward (steep or gradual), shows no change, variable (up and down) or downward (steep or gradual).

Predicted trends can range from the *simple* to the highly *complex*. The simplest forms predict a trend in one dependent variable. We might then predict a different pattern of change on this variable in different contexts. For example, we may anticipate that enrolments in a particular type of university course (the case) will increase in the short term but decline in the longer term. Another course might be predicted to maintain stable enrolment levels while another type of course is predicted to experience sharp increases in enrolment levels.

Trend analysis could be far more complex. Rather than simply predicting a different trend on the same variable for different cases, a complex version of trend analysis would predict trends for a set of variables in any given case. For example, we might predict that in a given course the enrolments will increase, the ratio of females to males will improve with the increased enrolment levels, there will be an increase in mature age students, and there will be no reduction in the quality of students. In another course we might predict a different combination of trends: a steady enrolment, a decline in standards, a decline in mature age students, and fewer female students.

Trend analyses can be either *interrupted* or *uninterrupted*. Interrupted time series analysis refers to a situation where a specific event takes place somewhere within the sequence of events. This enables us to examine the pattern of events before and after the interruption (or intervention). In this respect an interrupted time series analysis is similar to a before and after design. Although it does not involve a control group, we would conduct studies of cases where the interruption did and did not take place. While we cannot control for other differences between cases we can collect detailed information about all cases to enable us to consider whether these other differences (rather than the interruption) might be responsible for the apparent effect of the interruption.

Interrupted trend analysis would involve predicting a pre- and post-interruption pattern (e.g. decline pre and increase post, followed by longer term stability) and matching this predicted pattern with that for actual cases.

Not all trend studies will have an interruption. Some will simply predict a trend that will be anticipated in a particular context. For example, we might anticipate from what we know about the demographic and economic profile of a region (the case) that it is likely to experience long term population decline. Another region with a different mix of demographic and economic characteristics might be predicted to experience growth while yet another region with a different profile might be predicted to stagnate.

Chronological analysis Chronological analysis involves predicting a *sequence* of events (or even a sequence of trends) involving a number of different events or variables. That is, we would predict what would change, or what events would take place, and in what order. The sequence of events might be a *cause and effect* sequence or it might be a descriptive sequence that proposes particular *stages* in a process.

Examples of a staged version of chronological analysis might be models that propose predictable stages in becoming a marijuana user (Becker, 1966), stages in the disintegration of intimate relationships (Vaughn, 1986), stages in the process of adjustment to retirement (Atchley, 1976), or changes in the relationships between adults and their parents as parents age (Marsden and Abrams, 1987).

Regardless of whether the analysis involves a cause and effect sequence of events, or a set of predicted stages, the analytic question is whether the predicted *pattern of change* occurs in the cases where theory would expect it to occur. Or does the pattern occur when we would predict it should *not* occur?

The forms of the predicted patterns can vary. Yin (1989) indicates four types of ways in which events might be predicted to change in relation to each other. We can predict chronologies in which:

- some events must always occur before other events, with the reverse *sequence* being impossible;
- some events must always be followed by other events, on a *contingency* basis;
- some events can only follow other events after a specified *passage of time*; or
- certain *time periods* in a case study may be marked by classes of events that differ substantially from those of other time periods [stages]. (1989: 119)

Literal and theoretical replication

In Chapter 13 I argued that generalizing from case studies relies on the replication logic of experiments rather than the statistical logic of surveys. We gain confidence in experimental results not just from the elegance of the experiment but from our capacity to predictably replicate results and to predictably fail to replicate results (i.e. we anticipate that the intervention will have its effect under specific conditions but not under other conditions).

Similarly we gain confidence in case study findings when we can accurately predict which types of cases will display particular patterns and which cases will *not* display specific patterns.

Where we have a predicted *set* of outcomes and a single causal factor a similar logic holds. We would ask the following sorts of questions:

1   Does the full set of outcome characteristics occur when the presumed causal factor is present? If so we have confirmation of our theory.
2   We would then find another case where the presumed causal factor is present and see whether the full set of outcomes is also present in that case. If so we have a literal replication of the previous case and further confirmation of our theory.
3   Do we get cases where the presumed causal factor is present but only *some* of the predicted outcome characteristics are present? If we find such cases then we have failed to replicate the theory and we would either reject or modify the theory. If we could find *no* cases where the cause was present and the full set of outcomes was *not* present then we have a theoretical replication.
4   We would then seek to find a case in which the presumed causal factor is *not* present. We would expect that the full set of outcomes would not occur when the cause was not present. That is, we should

not find cases where we have the effects without our presumed cause.[1] If we *fail* to find any such cases we have achieved further theoretical replication.

Analysis for theory building: analytic induction

At its heart, analytic induction is 'a strategy of analysis that directs the investigator to formulate generalizations that apply to all instances of the problem' (Denzin, 1978: 191). It is a method that can be used to achieve descriptive generalizations or to arrive at causal explanations. It is a strategy that moves from individual cases and seeks to identify what the cases have in common. The common element provides the basis of theoretical generalization (see Figure 1.2).

Analytic induction is a strategy that seeks to arrive at generalizations that apply to *all* cases. In this respect it differs from the strategies of analysis discussed in previous sections of this book. In Chapter 3 I distinguished between deterministic and probabilistic notions of causation. The modes of analysis discussed in previous sections are based on probabilistic causation: we estimate whether one group is more likely than other groups to behave in a particular way. Analytic induction, however, seeks to achieve universal generalizations.

Denzin (1978: 192) summarizes six key steps in the process of analytic induction:

1 Specify what it is you are seeking to explain (the dependent variable).
2 Formulate an initial and provisional possible explanation of the phenomenon you are seeking to explain (your theory).
3 Conduct a study of a case selected to test your theory.
4 Review (and revise if necessary) your provisional theory in the light of the case or exclude the case as inappropriate.
5 Conduct further case studies to test the (revised) proposition and reformulate the proposition as required.
6 Continue with case studies (including looking for cases that might disprove the proposition) and revise the proposition until you achieve a causal proposition that accounts for all the cases.

The process might be illustrated using the hypothetical example in Chapter 13 about the impact on the quality of education of devolved versus centralized school staffing systems.

In this example the quality of education is the phenomenon we are seeking to explain (step 1). Our provisional (partial) explanation is that devolved staffing systems will produce greater improvements in the quality of education in a school than will centralized systems (step 2). We would therefore anticipate that cases (schools) with devolved systems would have better quality education than those with centralized systems (other things being equal). Alternatively, we might anticipate that schools that introduced a devolved staffing system would exhibit an improvement in the quality of education and that this improvement would be greater than in schools that did not introduce such a system.

We would then select a case to test our proposition (step 3). We might find a school that has recently introduced a locally based staffing system. Having developed a definition of what constitutes educational quality and worked out how to measure this, we could then conduct a case study to see if the introduction of the new staffing system had led to the predicted improvements. Let us suppose that the predicted improvements had in fact taken place. This lends support to our proposition but the support is hardly overwhelming and probably would not convince a sceptic (step 4). The sceptic could say that one case hardly proves the point, that there may have been a general improvement in educational quality in all schools over the same period, and that schools that had kept the old system might have also exhibited an improvement in educational quality. At the very least they might say that they could find a school with a central system that had improved their quality of education over the same period. They might also argue that they could find examples of schools where the local system was introduced with disastrous consequences for educational quality.

We would need to do more work – further case studies (step 5). Initially we might look for further cases of newly introduced local staffing systems to check that the initial case study was not just good luck.

Let us imagine that we then come across a school that our critics alluded to – one where the introduction of the new system had been a disaster. It had led to teacher, student and parent dissatisfaction, loss of morale and a clear decline in many aspects of educational quality. How do we make sense of this case? What is different about this case that should make it behave differently from that which we predicted provisionally, and so differently from the other cases we have already studied?

Since our study should produce a complete picture of each case and its social and cultural context we will probably pick up some initial clues. How is the 'deviant' school different from the others? We might notice some features about the *process* by which the devolved scheme was introduced in the school in which it was a failure. For example, teachers report that it was imposed on them. They were not consulted and there are no processes of appeal against the principal's decisions. Our hunch then is that the success of this type of scheme depends on the way in which it is implemented.

We then look back at our earlier cases to see if this explains the different outcomes. Do the successful cases stand out as having different implementation processes to the disastrous case? Let us suppose that the successful cases implemented the scheme only after a great deal of consultation and there was widespread consensus about the desirability of the scheme and the process by which it was to operate. We would then be in a position (step 6) to modify our initial, provisional proposition to read something like: 'When implemented in a climate of consultation and consensus, devolved staffing systems will produce improvements in educational quality.'

However, our next case causes problems. We have located another case where the locally based staffing system also has been a disaster. In this case, however, the system was implemented only after careful consultation and with the full agreement of staff and others. This is not what we expected. Why does this case not fit? Further examination of the case reveals that the school has had a new principal appointed since the system was introduced. This principal is not trusted and is believed to play favourites. He is also believed to victimize particular popular staff. Maybe these are the reasons why the system did not work. Checking back on earlier cases, the success stories all had principals who were widely liked and trusted.

Do the two failures have anything in common? Although the cases are different in certain ways, what they have in common is that teachers do not have any *confidence in the system*. In one case it was forced on them without consultation. In the other, the principal has undermined their confidence in the fairness of the system. We might then modify our revised proposition to something like: 'Where teachers have confidence in the fairness of a devolved staffing system it will lead to improvements in the quality of education.'

We could go on with additional case studies to check out how well this proposition holds. In addition to looking at cases where a local staffing system was introduced we should look at some cases where the centralized system was retained. We would expect that we would not see the same level of improvement in education in these schools. If this proved to be so it would strengthen our confidence in our initial theory about the impact of local staffing systems.

We might look for cases that could *disprove* our theory. For example, if we could find a school that had kept the centralized system and had shown an improvement in educational quality we might be able to further improve our theory. We might study a school where we have identified that there has been an improvement in education but the centralized staffing system had been retained. This would tell against our revised proposition. However, further investigation of the school might show that when we look at the school in its wider context there is a hostile relationship between the school and the local community. We learn that there had been a previous attempt by the school council (on which there were many local community representatives) to introduce a local staffing scheme. Teachers had successfully resisted this and felt that the centralized staffing system was protecting them.

When we learn these things about what at first sight looks like a 'deviant case' that disproves our proposition, in fact it further confirms our proposition that stresses the notion that teachers must have confidence in the system. Perhaps this case would cause us to further broaden our proposition to emphasize the importance of teachers having confidence in the system and to identify the factors that produce that confidence rather than stress the importance of a local or centralized system in itself.

Summary

This chapter has stressed the point that case study analysis should be fundamentally a theoretically informed undertaking. This applies equally to descriptive and explanatory case studies. The use of ideal types as a method of analysing descriptive case studies was discussed. Two broad methods of analysing case studies for explanatory purposes were outlined. Where case studies are used to test a theory, pattern matching provides an appropriate way of analysing and comparing cases. Pattern matching can range from matching very simple predicted patterns to highly complex patterns involving multiple independent and dependent variables. Where case studies are used to build a theory, analytic induction provides a useful way of analysing and using each case study.

Note

1 Of course this logic assumes that our causal variable is the only factor that can produce a given outcome. If we find cases where the effects occur but our favoured cause is absent then we have alternative explanations of the phenomenon. Our research design should be designed to eliminate such alternative explanations.

REFERENCES

Aronson, E. and Mills, J. (1959) 'The effect of severity of initiation on liking for a group', *Journal of Abnormal and Social Psychology*, 59: 177–81.

Atchley, R.C. (1976) *The Sociology of Retirement*. Cambridge, MA: Schenkman.

Baumrind, D. (1964) 'Some thoughts on ethics of research: after reading Milgram's "Behavioral study of obedience"', *American Psychologist*, 19: 421–3.

Becker, H.S. (1966) *Outsiders: Studies in the Sociology of Deviance*. New York: Free Press.

Blalock, H. (1964) *Causal Inferences in Non Experimental Research*. Chapel Hill, NC: University of North Carolina Press.

Blau, P. (1964) *Exchange and Power in Social Life*. New York: Wiley.

Blumer, H. (1956) 'Sociological analysis and the "variable"', *American Sociological Review*, 21: 683–90.

Brown, G.W. and Harris, T. (1978) *The Social Origins of Depression: a Study of Psychiatric Disorder in Women*. London: Tavistock.

Buck, N., Ermisch, J. and Jenkins, S. (1995) *Choosing a Longitudinal Survey Design: The Issues*. ESRC Research Centre on Micro-Social Change, University of Essex.

Campbell, D.T. (1989) 'Foreword', in R.K. Yin (ed.), *Case Study Research: Design and Methods*. Beverly Hills and London: Sage.

Campbell, D.T. and Stanley, J.C. (1963) *Experimental and Quasi-Experimental Designs for Research*. Boston: Houghton Mifflin.

Cohen, J. (1987) *Statistical Power Analysis for the Behavioural Sciences*. New York: Academic Press.

Cook, T.D. and Campbell, D.T. (1979) *Quasi-Experimentation: Design and Analysis Issues for Field Settings*. Boston: Houghton Mifflin.

Coser, L.A. (1977) *Masters of Sociological Thought: Ideas in Historical and Social Context*. New York: Harcourt, Brace, Jovanovich.

Davis, J.A. (1985) *The Logic of Causal Order*. Beverly Hills, CA: Sage.

Dempsey, K. (1990) *Smalltown: a Study of Social Inequality, Cohesion and Belonging*. Melbourne: Oxford University Press.

Denzin, N. (1978) *The Research Act: a Theoretical Introduction to Research Methods*. New York: McGraw-Hill.

Department of Human Services and Health (1995) *Youth Suicide in Australia: a Background Monograph*. Canberra: Australian Government Publishing Service.

de Vaus, D.A. (1994) *Letting Go: Relationships between Adults and their Parents*. Melbourne: Oxford University Press.

de Vaus, D.A. (2001) *Surveys in Social Research*. London: Routledge.

de Vaus, D.A. and Wolcott, I. (eds) (1997) *Australian Family Profiles: Social and Demographic Patterns*. Melbourne: Australian Institute of Family Studies.

Dillman, D. (1978) *Mail and Telephone Surveys: the Total Design Method*. New York: Wiley.

Durkheim, E. (1970) *Suicide*. London: Routledge and Kegan Paul.

Foddy, W. (1993) *Constructing Questions for Interviews and Questionnaires: Theory and Practice in Social Research*. Cambridge: Cambridge University Press.

Freeman, D. (1984) *Margaret Mead and Samoa: the Making and Unmaking of an Anthropological Myth*. Harmondsworth: Penguin.

Freud, S. (1955) *Two Case Histories (Little Hans and Rat Man)*. London: Hogarth Press and the Institute of Psycho-Analysis.

Geertz, C. (1973) 'Thick description: towards an interpretive theory of culture', in C. Geertz (ed.), *The Interpretation of Cultures: Selected Essays*. New York: Basic. pp. 3–32.

Gerth, H.H. and Wright Mills, C. (1946) *From Max Weber: Essays in Sociology*. Oxford: Oxford University Press.

Glaser, B.G. and Strauss, A.L. (1967) *The Discovery of Grounded Theory: Strategies for Qualitative Research*. Chicago: Aldine.

Glenn, N.V. (1977) *Cohort Analysis*. Beverly Hills, CA: Sage.

Goldenberg, S. (1992) *Thinking Methodologically*. New York: HarperCollins.

Goode, W.J. and Hatt, P.K. (1952) *Methods in Social Research*. London: McGraw-Hill.

Graetz, B. (1993) 'Health consequences of employment and unemployment: longitudinal evidence for young men and women', *Social Science and Medicine*, 36: 715–24.

Grimm, L.G. and Yarnold, R.R. (1995) *Reading and Understanding Multivariate Statistics*. Washington: American Psychological Association.

Groves, R.M. (1979) 'Actors and questions in telephone and personal interview surveys', *Public Opinion Quarterly*, 43: 190–205.

Groves, R.M. and Kahn, R.L. (1979) *Surveys by Telephone: a National Comparison with Personal Interviews*. New York: Academic Press.

Hage, J. and Meeker, B.F. (1988) *Social Causality*. London: George Allen and Unwin.

Hakim, C. (1986) *Research Design: Strategies and Choices in the Design of Social Research*. London: Allen and Unwin.

Henry, G.T. (1995) *Graphing Data: Techniques of Display and Analysis*. Thousand Oaks, CA: Sage.

Hertel, B. (1976) 'Minimizing error variance introduced by missing data analysis in survey analysis', *Sociological Methods and Research*, 4: 459–74.

Hochschild, A. (1989) *The Second Shift*. New York: Avon.

Homan, R. (1991) *The Ethics of Social Research*. London: Longman.

Homans, G. (1961) *Social Behaviour: its Elementary Forms*. New York: Harcourt, Brace, Jovanovich.

Johnson, A. (1977) *Social Statistics without Tears*. New York: McGraw-Hill.

Kalton, G. (1983a) 'Compensating for missing survey data', Research Report Series, Institute of Social Research, University of Michigan.

Kalton, G. (1983b) *Introduction to Survey Sampling*. Beverly Hills, CA: Sage.

Kalton, G. (1986) 'Handling wave non-response in panel surveys', *Journal of Official Statistics*, 2: 303–14.

Kellehear, A. (1993) *The Unobtrusive Researcher: a Guide to Methods*. St Leonards: Allen and Unwin.

Kerlinger, F.N. (1973) *Foundations of Behavioural Research*. New York: Holt, Rinehart and Winston.

Kerlinger, F.N. (1979) *Behavioural Research: a Conceptual Approach*. New York: Holt, Rinehart and Winston.

Kerlinger, F.N. and Pedhazur, E.J. (1973) *Multiple Regression in Behavioural Research*. New York: Holt, Rinehart and Winston.

Kimmel, A.J. (1988) *Ethics and Values in Applied Social Research*. Beverly Hills and London: Sage.

Lepkowski, J.M. (1989) 'Treatment of wave non-response in panel surveys', in D. Kasprzyk, G. Duncan, G. Kalton and M.P. Singh (eds), *Panel Surveys*. New York: Wiley.

Lewis, O. (1951) *Life in a Mexican Village: Tepoztlan Restudied*. Urbana, IL: University of Illinois Press.

Loether, H.J. and McTavish, D.G. (1974a) *Inferential Statistics for Sociologists: an Introduction*. Boston: Allyn and Bacon.

Loether, H.J. and McTavish, D.G. (1974b) *Descriptive Statistics for Sociologists: an Introduction*. Boston: Allyn and Bacon.

Lynd, R.S. and Merrell-Lynd, H. (1929) *Middletown: a Study in Modern American Culture*. New York: Harcourt, Brace and World.

Lynn, P., Purdon, S., Hedges, B. and Mcaleese, I. (1994) 'An assessment of alternative weighting strategies', Youth Cohort Survey Report, Education Department, Sheffield.

Marsden, D. and Abrams, S. (1987) 'Liberators, companions, intruders and cuckoos in the nest: a sociology of caring relationships over the life cycle', in P. Allatt, T. Keil, A. Bryman and B. Bytheway (eds), *Women and the Life Cycle: Transitions and Turning-Points*. London: Macmillan.

Marsh, C. (1982) *The Survey Method: the Contribution of Surveys to Sociological Explanation*. London: George Allen and Unwin.

Marsh, C. (1988) *Exploring Data: an Introduction to Data Analysis for Social Scientists*. Cambridge: Polity.

Mead, M. (1943) *Coming of Age in Samoa: a Study of Adolescence and Sex in Primitive Societies*. Harmondsworth: Penguin.

Menard, S. (1991) *Longitudinal Research*. Newbury Park, CA: Sage.

Merton, R.K. (1968) *Social Theory and Social Structure*. New York: Free Press.

Milgram, S. (1964) 'Issues in the study of obedience: a reply to Baumrind', *American Psychologist*, 19: 848–52.

Mills, C.W. (1959) *The Sociological Imagination*. New York: Oxford University Press.

Mitchell, J.C. (1983) 'Case and situation analysis', *Sociological Review*, 31: 187–211.

Moser, C.A. and Kalton, G. (1971) *Survey Methods in Social Investigation*. London: Heinemann.

Mueller, J.H., Schuessler K.F. and Costner, H.L. (1977) *Statistical Reasoning in Sociology*. Boston: Houghton Mifflin.

Punch, M. (1994) 'Politics and ethics in quantitative research', in N. Denzin and Y. Lincoln (eds), *Handbook of Qualitative Research*. Thousand Oaks, CA: Sage. pp. 83–97.

Redfield, R. (1930) *Tepoztlan, a Mexican Village: a Study of Folk Life*. Chicago: University of Chicago Press.

Roethlisberger F.J. and Dickson, W.J. (1939) *Management and the Worker*. Cambridge, MA: Harvard University Press.

Rogers, T.F. (1976) 'Interviews by telephone and in person: quality of responses and field performance', *Public Opinion Quarterly*, 40: 51–65.

Rose, D., Buck, N.A. and Corti, L. (1991) 'Design issues in the British Household Panel Study', Working Papers of the ESRC Research Centre on Micro-Social Change, Paper 2, University of Essex, Colchester.

Rosenberg, M. (1968) *The Logic of Survey Analysis*. New York: Basic.

Spector, P.E. (1981) *Research Designs*. Beverly Hills, CA: Sage.

Stake, R.E. (1994) 'Case studies', in N.K. Denzin and Y. Lincoln (eds), *Handbook of Qualitative Research*. Thousand Oaks, CA: Sage. pp. 236–47.

Sullivan, L., Maley, B. and Warby, M. (1997) *State of the Nation: Statistical Indicators of Australia's Well Being*. Melbourne: Centre for Independent Studies.

Suppes, P. (1970) *A Probabilistic Theory of Causality*. Amsterdam: North Holland.

Tabachnick, B.G. and Fidell, L.S. (1983) *Using Multivariate Statistics*. New York: Harper and Row.

Tajfel, H. (1984) *The Social Dimension: European Developments in Social Psychology*. Cambridge: Cambridge University Press.

Vaughn, D. (1986) *Uncoupling: Turning Points in Intimate Relationships*. New York: Oxford University Press.

Whyte, W.F. (1943) *Street Corner Society: the Social Structure of an Italian Slum*. Chicago: University of Chicago Press.

Yin, R.K. (1989) *Case Study Research: Design and Methods*. Beverly Hills and London: Sage.

Yin, R.K. (1993) *Applications of Case Study Research*. Beverly Hills and London: Sage.

INDEX